The St. Petersburg Imperial Theaters

The St. Petersburg Imperial Theaters

Stage and State in Revolutionary Russia, 1900-1920

Murray Frame

McFarland & Company, Inc., Publishers
Jefferson, North Carolina, and London

Library of Congress Cataloguing-in-Publication Data

Frame, Murray, 1969–
    The St. Petersburg imperial theaters : stage and state in
revolutionary Russia, 1900–1920 / by Murray Frame.
        p.   cm.
    Includes bibliographical references and index.
    ISBN 0-7864-0688-7 (library binding : 50# alkaline paper) ∞
    1. Theater—Russia (Federation)—Saint Petersburg—
History—20th century.   2. Theaters—Russia (Federation)—
Saint Petersburg—History—20th century.   I. Title: Saint
Petersburg imperial theaters.   II. Title.
PN2726.S25 F73   2000
792'.0947'21—dc21   99-53097

British Library Cataloguing-in-Publication data are available

Manufactured in the United States of America

McFarland & Company, Inc., Publishers
    Box 611, Jefferson, North Carolina 28640
        www.mcfarlandpub.com

To my grandmother, Elizabeth Lindsay Todd,
and to the memory of my other grandparents

Contents

Acknowledgments

I would like to express my gratitude to the Master and Fellows of St. John's College, Cambridge, the Scottish Office Education Department, and the Research Committee of the Department of History, University of Dundee, who supported research for this work at different stages.

I would also like to express my thanks to the staffs of the archives and libraries I worked in, especially those of the Russian State History Archive, St. Petersburg; the manuscripts department of the Central State Theater Museum, Moscow; the Cambridge University Library; the State Public Library, St. Petersburg; the Bodleian Library, Oxford; and the Sterling Memorial Library, Yale University. All were most helpful and accommodating. In particular, Ray Scrivens of Cambridge University Library provided invaluable assistance.

Three chapters of this book have appeared in slightly different versions as articles: Chapter 6 in *Revolutionary Russia* (vol. 7, no. 2, December 1994), reproduced by kind permission of Frank Cass & Company; Chapter 4 in *Proceedings of the Scottish Society for Russian and East European Studies* (1996), reproduced by kind permission of the editor; and Chapter 2 in *Australian Slavonic and East European Studies* (vol. 11, nos. 1/2, 1997), reproduced by kind permission of the editor.

During my work on this project, I received invaluable advice and encouragement from many people. Most of all, it is a pleasure to thank Dr. Jana Howlett (Jesus College, Cambridge) who supervised the doctoral dissertation of which this book is a modified version. Her kindness, counsel, and patience were highly valued and rendered my task all the more enjoyable.

Of the many other individuals who provided friendship, hospitality, and guidance at various stages, I would like to thank in particular Cathryn Brennan, Paul Dukes, Dmitry Fedosov, Jonathan Haxton, Eileen Hunt, Bob McKean, Victor Mauer, and Shoumi Mustafa.

Of course, responsibility for the contents of the book is mine alone.

Murray Frame
November 1999

A Note on the
Technical Apparatus

Throughout the text the titles of Russian books, journals, statutes, etc. are generally given in an English translation with the transliterated Russian original either in brackets or in the nearest note; in the notes, the transliterated Russian original is always given. Titles of all Russian plays, operas, and ballets have been translated into English throughout, but an Appendix of Titles giving the original Russian names has been included. Titles of non–Russian plays, operas and ballets are generally given in their original, but the Russian equivalents are included in the Appendix of Titles.

All Russian words and names have generally been transliterated according to the Library of Congress system, but the more familiar English-language equivalents have been used where appropriate (e.g., Peter Tchaikovsky, not Pëtr Chaikovskii). In the notes, however, I have used a dual system: Strictly Library of Congress system for Russian names and titles when part of an actual book or article reference (to aid identification); otherwise the familiar English-language equivalent.

On February 1, 1918, the Soviet government abolished the Old Style Julian calendar which had been in use in Russia for several centuries and which had rendered the Russian calendar thirteen days behind the Western Gregorian calendar. The Julian calendar was replaced by the New Style Gregorian calendar, bringing the Russian calendar into line with the rest of Europe. Thus, February 1, 1918 in Russia became February 14. All dates in this study are given according to the style which obtained at the time. In other words, all dates before February 1918 are given in the Old Style, while those during and after February 1918 are given in the New Style.

Preface

The central theme of this study is the institutional identity of the St. Petersburg Imperial Theaters and their relationship to the Russian state between 1900 and 1920. The St. Petersburg Imperial Theaters were subsidized and administered by the Russian imperial court from the mid-eighteenth century to the revolution of 1917. Given this close association between theatrical culture and state power, the question arises: How far did the Russian government use the Imperial Theaters, and for what purposes? Did the St. Petersburg Imperial Theaters, as state-controlled institutions, function as "pillars of the autocracy"; or was the connection between culture and power merely nominal and the history of the theaters shaped by factors other than their proximity to the Russian state?

This question is particularly apposite for the period under investigation because at a time when the Russian autocracy was under increasing pressure to modernize, its prominent critics included individuals and institutions from the cultural milieu—writers, artists, academics, and so on. The Imperial Theaters were central to the vibrant cultural world of St. Petersburg, a cultural world that was increasingly antagonistic to tsarism. Yet they were also an integral part of the administrative structure of the tsarist state. It is this "dual status" that makes their history so intriguing, and that raises the chief questions addressed by this study.

These questions fall into three main groups: (1) Did the Russian state seek to use the Imperial Theaters in any way, and was artistic freedom compromised by court supervision? (2) Was court association an important factor in the status and reputation of the Imperial Theaters in the cultural life of St. Petersburg? (3) How were the St. Petersburg Imperial Theaters affected by the pressures of war and revolution, and did they remain loyal to the state that subsidized them in its times of crisis?

The principal objective of the study, in other words, is to examine the ways in which the history of the St. Petersburg Imperial Theaters in the late tsarist period reflected, or was conditioned by, their court status.

1

The study begins in 1900, when a commission to clarify the status and regulations of the Imperial Theaters in the context of a flourishing Russian theater culture published its findings. It concludes in 1920, when the Bolsheviks effectively re-established full state control of the former Imperial Theaters. This important period in the history of Russian theater was also the period, broadly defined, of the Russian Revolution, that is, the *longue durée* transition from tsarist Russia to Soviet Russia. Historians no longer view the revolution narrowly as the events of 1905, February 1917, and October 1917, but as a broader period of transformation incorporating, for example, student unrest at the turn of the century and the years of civil war after the October Revolution,[1] and it is within that broad context that the present history is conceived.

The salient argument running through the study is that, despite the close administrative, financial, and symbolic associations between the St. Petersburg Imperial Theaters and the imperial court, the identity of the theaters remained equivocal in the late tsarist and early Soviet periods. That is to say, while functioning as loyal institutions which represented the opulence and grandeur of the state, they also exhibited characteristics that allied them closely to the social and political forces that were gradually challenging the legitimacy of the tsarist autocracy. Indeed, although the St. Petersburg Imperial Theaters were closely supervised by the court and were expected to function as its obedient instruments to promote court panoply, they were certainly not shielded from the wider social and political pressures from which the Russian court seemed to believe itself immune right down to 1917. Yet, ultimately, the St. Petersburg Imperial Theaters' flirtation with reform and revolution was lukewarm, and they remained dutifully loyal to state authority. This was underlined during the three years following the February Revolution of 1917. During that period, the new authorities—the Provisional Government, then the Bolsheviks—retained the former Imperial Theaters as State Theaters, for their own political purposes. In a sense, the state continued to need theater; but theater, in this case, also needed the state, a fact that was amply demonstrated by the relative ease and minimum fuss with which the Imperial Theaters adapted to the new governments. To a large degree this was a response to material need, such as the promise of state subsidies and privileges; but the issue was more complex. The point is that the St. Petersburg Imperial Theaters were not reluctantly connected to the Russian state during the period under examination. Consequently, the institutional history of the St. Petersburg Imperial Theaters between 1900 and 1920 is, to a surprising extent, a story of continuity.

The study is organized in the following manner. The Introduction surveys the historiography, origins, and development of the St. Petersburg Imperial Theaters, and outlines the social, political, and cultural contexts in which they functioned between 1900 and 1920. Chapter 1 explores the formal administrative structures which bound the Imperial Theaters to the state, specifically to the imperial court, and how they were expected to observe, exemplify, and symbolize certain values, rituals, and characteristics of the court. Chapter 2 investigates the relationship between the Directorate of Imperial Theaters and the theater troupes in order to ascertain the extent to which the administration shaped the artistic activity of the theaters. In particular, the conventional accusation that the Directorate impeded the artistic creativity of the theaters is critically assessed. Chapter 3 examines the audience in order to establish a profile of the Imperial Theater clientele: who frequented these court institutions, and why? Chapter 4 analyzes the drama repertoire of the Alexandrinsky Theater, and Chapter 5 the opera and ballet repertoire of the Mariinsky Theater, with a view to establishing whether they conveyed a conformist court/state identity for the St. Petersburg Imperial Theaters, or whether there was an oppositional dimension to the repertoires that associated them more with the broader concerns of the cultural intelligentsia. Chapter 6 examines the extent to which the St. Petersburg Imperial Theaters were associated with wider social and political activities that their court status officially prohibited; particular attention is paid to their experience during the 1905 Revolution. Chapter 7 examines the experience of the theaters during the First World War, the February Revolution of 1917, and the period of the Provisional Government. Taken together, Chapters 6 and 7 are concerned to establish how far the St. Petersburg Imperial Theaters remained loyal to tsarism, or were compelled by officialdom to support it during revolutionary crises, and how far, if at all, they were associated with the radical and revolutionary movements. Finally, Chapter 8 analyzes the relationship between the St. Petersburg Imperial Theaters—after February 1917 called State Theaters—and the Bolshevik regime down to 1920, when the State Theater autonomy that had obtained after the February Revolution was emasculated.

While each chapter in its own way pursues the unifying theme of institutional identity in the context of the Imperial Theaters' court status, the study is essentially empirical. As the only history of its subject in any language to date, its main purpose is to provide a general introduction to the various dimensions of the St. Petersburg Imperial Theaters as institutions in the era the Russian Revolution.

I am conscious of the fact that many issues could be explored in greater depth. Acknowledging that the themes of all chapters could easily be expanded into books of their own, the study does not claim to be definitive. Nevertheless, it does fill an important gap in the literature on Russian theater history. While historians are familiar with many of the prominent artists who were employed by the Imperial Theaters such as Vaslav Nijinsky, Anna Pavlova, and Fyodor Chaliapin, until now a study of the St. Petersburg Imperial Theater as a distinct institution, the milieu in which such artists worked, has not been undertaken.

Finally, in order to emphasize the specific aims and scope of this study, two points should be clarified from the outset. First of all, as an institutional history that is concerned primarily with the political dimension of the St. Petersburg Imperial Theaters, this work does not consider in any detail the art of the Imperial Theaters, or what might be termed the "repertoire in performance." That is to say, it does not reconstruct performances or analyze the artistic styles and stories of particular artists or theatrical genres. Similarly, it does not offer literary criticism of plays or libretti. This is certainly not to deny the centrality of the repertoire to theater history. Indeed, this book contains two chapters on the repertoire; but they are conceived from the point of view of institutional, not literary history. Of course, however discrete the two disciplines are, there is bound to be a certain amount of overlap. Secondly, I have focused most of the detailed analysis on the two pre-eminent Imperial Theaters of St. Petersburg, the Alexandrinsky and the Mariinsky. The other Imperial Theaters, the Mikhailovsky French drama theater in St. Petersburg and the court theaters at the various imperial residences in the environs of the capital, were much less important in the cultural life of the city, though they are not entirely neglected. The Moscow Imperial Theaters functioned on much the same lines as those in St. Petersburg, though points of comparison will be made where appropriate. Some comparison will also be made with non-Imperial Theaters in Russia and Europe in order to illustrate ways in which the St. Petersburg Imperial Theaters were similar and dissimilar to theater of the modern period in general. Where the Imperial Theaters were unique, I have tried to underline this without becoming overly concerned with the comparative dimension at the expense of providing a history of the St. Petersburg Imperial Theaters.

Introduction

In 1900 there were three Imperial Theaters in St. Petersburg: the Alexandrinsky, where performances of Russian drama were staged; the Mariinsky, for performances of opera and ballet; and the Mikhailovsky, where French drama was presented by a resident troupe of French artists. The status of the Imperial Theaters amid St. Petersburg's rich theatrical culture of the Silver Age was unique. In administrative, financial and symbolic terms, they were closely connected to the Russian court and government, arguably the most important feature that distinguished them from other theaters in the capital.* They were venerated as models of *fin-de-siècle* theater art, as guardians of the exemplary traditions of Russia's theater culture, and as institutions whose reputation was increasingly international. The Mariinsky Theater in particular was justly described by a contemporary guidebook to the imperial capital as occupying "a prominent place not only among Russian theaters, but among European theaters."[1] Many of the ballets choreographed by its eminent *maître de ballet*, Marius Petipa, are still performed throughout the world today, and it was there that the flamboyant impresario Sergei Diaghilev recruited the superlative talents—many of whose names are still legendary— that forged his renowned Ballets Russes, which enthralled West European audiences.[2] The Alexandrinsky Theater, although attacked from some quarters for its increasingly outmoded production techniques, remained a popular drama theater due to the efforts of its talented stars, some of whom, such as Maria Savina, broadened their reputations and heightened their profiles by touring the theaters of Europe. The contemporary profile of the Mikhailovsky Theater was less marked, perhaps because its French-language productions restricted its accessibility and precluded easy comparison with other thespian fare available to Petersburgers. Nevertheless, it was diligently

*By Russian court I mean the Ministry of the Imperial Court established in 1826, which was responsible for running the imperial family's household and services; and by Russian government I mean the other Ministries—such as Interior and Finance—that contributed to the supervision and maintenance of the Imperial Theaters. Their specific responsibilities are delineated in Chapter 1.

patronized by "high society" whenever tickets to the opera or ballet were unobtainable.

The primary function of the St. Petersburg Imperial Theaters was to stage exemplary theater art for the entertainment of audiences, and therefore much of their story belongs to the history of drama, opera, and ballet, that is, to the realm of traditional theater studies. But an important aspect of Imperial Theater history that merits consideration was their status as court/government institutions. It is the purpose of this study to explore aspects of their history from that perspective, in particular the administration, the audience, the repertoire, and the impact of revolution. Like the Russian Orthodox Church since the early eighteenth century, the Imperial Theaters were cultural institutions that had effectively become departments of state. This study focuses on the significance of that status for their identity in the late tsarist period.

Historiography

The corpus of historical writing that deals with the Imperial Theaters collectively, as a distinct institutional category, is small. The earliest works appeared in the 1880s: S. V. Taneev's *From the Past of the Imperial Theaters* (1885), and his *The Decline of Theater. Materials for the History of the Imperial Theaters* (1887). The majority of full-length works on the subject were published by the Directorate of Imperial Theaters, beginning with the four-part *Archive of the Directorate of Imperial Theaters, 1746–1801* (1892), edited by V. P. Pogozhev, A. E. Molchanov, and K. A. Petrov.[3] In the same year, the Directorate began to publish the *Yearbook of the Imperial Theaters* to provide an "illustrated account of the work of the Imperial Theaters."[4] The chief value of the *Yearbooks*, which were published until 1915, lies in their encyclopedic information about the repertoire, the officials, and artists of the theaters. As the editorial to the first volume explained: "Readers will not find reviews [*kritiki*] in the 'Yearbook,' as that does not correspond to the objective character of our purely informational publication."[5] However, subsequent volumes contained historical articles, for example on Ivan Elagin, writer and first Director of the Imperial Theaters (*Yearbook* number 4); on Fyodor Volkov and the founding of the Russian state theater in the eighteenth century (number 10); on the architecture of the Alexandrinsky (number 10); on the history of the Moscow Bolshoi (number 10); on the Imperial Theater administration during the reign of Alexander I (number 12); and on the Alexandrinsky, to mark the occasion of its seventy-fifth anniversary (number 16). Under the editorship of Baron Nicholas Drizen (1909–15) the *Yearbook* became essentially a theater journal appearing as seven or eight separate issues a year, containing critical articles which reflected lively contemporary debates about the function and future of theater.[6]

In 1900, the Directorate published Pogozhev's three-volume *Plan of a Legal Statute on the Imperial Theaters*, the third volume of which constituted a general history of the Imperial Theaters. Baron Drizen's *One Hundred and Fifty Years of the Imperial Theaters*, a short history of the establishment of the Imperial Theaters in the 1750s and of the centenary celebrations in 1856, appeared in 1906. The same year also saw the publication of the first volume of Pogozhev's *A Century of the Organization of Imperial Moscow Theaters* (1906–08), the three volumes of which covered the period from 1806 to 1831.[7] These informative but largely uncritical works amount to all that was published on the history of the Imperial Theaters before 1917.

During the Soviet era, the only publications on the Imperial Theaters as an institutional category were David Zolotnitskii's *The Academic Theaters on the Paths of October* (1982), which dealt with the State—formerly Imperial—Theaters after 1917, and Alexander Ushkarev's short article on the Imperial Theater repertoire during the first quarter of the nineteenth century in the collection *Theater Between Past and Present* (1989).[8]

Western studies of Russian theater during the period from the 1890s to the 1920s, its "golden age," are not rare.[9] Yet the Imperial Theaters are accorded little attention. Western histories tend to focus on the prominent innovators of the modern period such as the Moscow Art Theater, or on avant-garde experimentalists such as Vsevolod Meyerhold, the Symbolists, and the Futurists. Another category which has received scholarly attention is popular (*narodnyi*) theater.[10] Only one, unpublished study claims to deal with the Imperial Theaters, namely R. G. Thorpe's doctoral dissertation entitled "The Management of Culture in Revolutionary Russia: The Imperial Theaters and the State, 1897–1928" (1990). However, the title of Thorpe's compelling study might be considered misleading: There is only one, essentially introductory chapter on the pre-1917 period which concentrates on the 1897 and 1901 Congresses of Stage Workers, mentions an abortive attempt to merge the Moscow Art Theater with the Moscow Imperial Maly Theater in 1905, and then moves on to the period of the Provisional Government in 1917. Most of Thorpe's study concerns the *Moscow* Imperial Theaters during the decade *after* 1917.[11] Consequently, there is still no study of the St. Petersburg Imperial Theaters during the critical period from 1900 to 1920.

Four explanations for this historiographical neglect suggest themselves. First, the artistic history of the theatrical innovators and the avant-garde in Russia is more colorful, original, and alluring than the traditional, hackneyed productions of the Imperial Theaters. Most obviously, the lasting influence of Konstantin Stanislavsky, his "System," and the Moscow Art Theater which he founded with Vladimir Nemirovich-Danchenko, as well as the creative genius of the revolutionary director Vsevolod Meyerhold, who introduced Constructivism and Biomechanics to theater, have rightly attracted the attention of historians.[12] Secondly, the art of the Imperial Theaters is generally assumed to have stagnated in the late tsarist period and to have contributed very little to Russian theater's "golden age." Production techniques at the Alexandrinsky were considered outmoded and one contemporary remarked that there were many "blunders" on the Alexandrinsky stage, recalling one instance when the special effects pistol malfunctioned and fired only after its victim had fallen on stage.[13] Third, while the important history of Russian ballet during the early twentieth century is closely bound up with the history of the Mariinsky Theater, it has nevertheless been possible to study its development in isolation from the Mariinsky, particularly through the European activity of the Ballets Russes and the choreographic work of émigré artists. Fourth, the legitimate fashion for the history of popular culture has led several theater historians in recent years to concentrate on popular theater.[14]

The first three of these reasons for the neglect of the Imperial Theaters suggest that scholars of the *artistic* history of theater have not deemed them suitable for study in their own right. In that sense, the neglect of the Imperial Theaters is explicable, if not entirely defensible. It is arguable that the art of the St. Petersburg Imperial Theaters did not deteriorate to the extent implied by some historians, and we will have occasion in this study to indicate that Russian court theater was not as outmoded as has been suggested and that, in fact, it willingly co-opted many of the theatrical innovations of the Silver Age. However, the primary focus of this study will remain the institutional, not artistic, history of the St. Petersburg Imperial Theaters.

Origins and Development

The origins of the St. Petersburg Imperial Theaters are located in the history of Russian court entertainment.[15] Prior to the seventeenth century, court entertainment, such as that provided by wandering minstrels like the *skomorokhi*,[16] was staged in the Moscow Kremlin banquet hall or the monarch's private quarters. The first reliable evidence of the exclusive use of part of the royal household for entertainment concerns the construction in 1613 of a *poteshnaia palata*—a sort of recreation chamber suggesting the pursuit of revelry and frivolity—which consisted of several rooms in the Kremlin Palace and which effectively constituted the first court theater in Russian history.[17] The fortunes of court theater fluctuated according to the relative piety and priorities of individual rulers. Tsar Alexei (1645–76) initially proscribed royal amusements, but later commissioned the construction of a theater (1672) to celebrate the impending birth of his son, the future Peter I, a change prompted by increasing contact with Western culture. (Alexei's immediate favorite, Artamon Matveev, married a Lady Hamilton of Scottish descent, who communicated a passion for theatricals.[18]) On the other hand, Alexei's successor,

Fyodor (1676–82), frowned on court spectacles, and they fell into abeyance for some years.

Court entertainment was revived by Peter I (1689–1725). In addition to his own infamous pursuit of amusement,[19] Peter's reign witnessed two important developments in Russian theater history. First, a wooden public theater was constructed in Moscow's Red Square, and although it had a short existence (1702–06), as the first public theater in Russian history it established the principle that theater sponsored by the court was not necessarily for the ruler's private delectation, but could be accessible to a wider public. Secondly, during Peter I's reign St. Petersburg was founded; the Russia court was transferred from Moscow to the new capital, and the history of court entertainment entered a new phase as it was increasingly shaped by the Russian elite's cultural Westernization. In particular, during the reign of Anna (1730–40), Italian opera and ballet became increasingly popular with the leisured strata of St. Petersburg. However, court entertainment was still organized on an *ad hoc* basis only and there was as yet no permanently established theater that the court patronized.

It was in the 1750s, under Empress Elizabeth (1741–61), that the first official Russian state theater was established. Like the formation of the French state theater in the seventeenth century when the court assumed responsibility for subsidizing Molière's successful drama company, the process involved the co-optation and generous sponsorship by the court of a successful independent drama troupe, in this case the touring players organized by the popular Iaroslav actor Fyodor Volkov. Impressed by Volkov's troupe, Elizabeth persuaded him to remain in the capital. The Russian court now decided to establish and subsidize a permanent state theater based on Volkov's troupe and organized by the dramatist Alexander Sumarokov, and to that effect Elizabeth signed the famous decree of August 30, 1756 confirming that a court theater, with public access, would be financed by the state.[20] From then on, Imperial Theater seasons almost invariably commenced on August 30. In January 1759 the court added to its financial obligations towards the theater by assuming responsibility for running it. One Western historian described this as "the beginning of the famous tradition of the Russian Imperial Theatres."[21] Russians, on the other hand, always regarded Elizabeth's decree of August 1756 as constituting the inauguration of the Imperial Theaters. Thus, in 1906 the Russian theater world celebrated the 150th anniversary of the Imperial Theaters.[22]

Several years of administrative evolution were needed for the Imperial Theaters to acquire the institutional form they had at the beginning of the twentieth century. In 1766, a Directorate was founded to oversee the affairs of the Russian theater. In 1806, Imperial Theaters were formally established in Moscow and were run separately from those in St. Petersburg. In 1826, the St. Petersburg Directorate became a department of the newly created

Ministry of the Imperial Court, and in 1842 the Directorate acquired responsibility for both the St. Petersburg and Moscow Imperial Theaters.[23] Moreover, although the St. Petersburg Imperial Theaters had been established
formally in the mid–eighteenth century, the drama, opera, and ballet troupes
did not immediately acquire permanent residences, and the Alexandrinsky,
Mariinsky, and Mikhailovsky Theaters, as physical structures, only appeared
during the course of the nineteenth century. The Alexandrinsky troupe originated in Volkov's troupe, but the theater building itself, which seated 1,790
spectators, dated from 1832. Built by the Italian architect Carlo Rossi, it faces
the Nevsky Prospect; behind the theater stretches *Teatralnaia ulitsa* (Theater
Street), where the imperial Theater School and offices of the Directorate were
located opposite the buildings of the Ministries of Internal Affairs and
National Education. The building of the Mariinsky Theater, completed in
1860, was located on *Teatralnaia ploshchad* (Theater Square), opposite the
Conservatory and adjacent to *Ofitserskaia ulitsa* (Officer Street). Its auditorium contained 1,625 seats. The building of the Mikhailovsky Theater, containing 1,151 seats, was situated on Mikhailovsky Square near the Grand Hotel
Europe. It was opened in 1833 and refurbished in 1859.[24] Until 1882, these
three theaters enjoyed a monopoly on public theatrical performances in St.
Petersburg. In other words, the only public theaters in the city were the state
theaters administered by the imperial court. It was there that the courtiers,
bureaucrats, military officials, and the cultural intelligentsia of nineteenth-
century St. Petersburg acquainted themselves with contemporary drama,
opera, and ballet, although Pushkin felt that for many patrons theater was
regarded "more as conventional etiquette than enjoyable relaxation."[25]

Court Theater, Modernity and Modernism

The institutional identity of the Imperial Theaters in the late tsarist
period was thrown into sharp relief by wide-ranging changes in the theatrical landscape facilitated by a series of political, economic, and social developments that eventually brought about the demise of the Romanov monarchy.
In the late nineteenth century, the Russian autocracy confronted a range of
complex challenges created by the dynamics of the modern era. Its political
legitimacy and hegemony were being challenged on two fronts. First, in the
nineteenth century and particularly after the Great Reforms of the 1860s, the
Russian intelligentsia and an emergent civil society competed with conservative monarchy for political power. The Great Reforms of the 1860s had
widened the political and public sphere in Russia, by creating for example,
the *zemstva* (organs of local self-government introduced in 1864). The reforms
had also facilitated the growth of a Russian equivalent of the Western professional middle classes—teachers, doctors, lawyers, and so forth—and an

increasing array of organizations that were independent from the state (such as publishing houses and charities). These developments were accompanied by an expansion of economic activity and the growth of the merchant class (*kupechestvo*). These new groups were referred to collectively as *obshchestvo*, which historians generally translate as civil society. This modern and active civil society enjoyed many privileges but crucially it was denied access to the political power that its Western counterparts had gradually acquired. The recalcitrance of the autocracy in the face of the burgeoning civil society and its political aspirations fueled the revolutionary movement and exacerbated the latent conflict between state and society. What might have evolved into a predominantly liberal opposition became a predominantly radical opposition.[26]

The second challenge for the autocracy was the social upheaval inflicted by rapid industrialization, a transformation that was particularly pronounced in St. Petersburg. From its foundation early in the eighteenth century, St. Petersburg continued to grow and change, but between the 1890s and the 1920s it experienced its greatest transformation as the forces of social and economic change, followed by war and revolution, transformed the city from the jewel in the imperial crown to what one observer called "this dismantled and ruinous city."[27] The process of transformation commenced in the 1890s when the tsarist government initiated the policy of rapid industrialization. A major social consequence of this was migration and urban population increase. Between 1890 and 1914, the population of St. Petersburg increased by over one million inhabitants, an increase that derived predominantly from migration to the city, rather than from a natural decrease in the mortality rate—in fact, the death rate was higher than the birth rate at that time. The bulk of this population increase occurred between 1900 and 1914. In 1914, the population total was 2.2 million. Two-thirds of the total population—68.6 per cent in 1910—were peasants. During the harvest season, many migrated back to the villages, but this decrease in numbers was offset by an influx of migrant laborers seeking seasonal occupations in the city. The population of St. Petersburg was therefore increasingly transient and composed of *déraciné*—uprooted people.

The gap between rich and poor in the imperial capital was extremely conspicuous to contemporaries because there was minimal segregation between different groups. Inadequate transport facilities militated against the development of suburbs and consequently migrant peasants and indigenous nobles lived in close proximity. Areas where the nobility, the middle and professional classes lived, such as the Spasskaia district—where the Alexandrinsky Theater was situated—or the Kazan district—where the Mariinsky Theater was located—contained substantial numbers of ordinary workers.[28] Thus by 1900 the traditional St. Petersburg of courtiers, noblemen, government bureaucrats, diplomats, and high society socialites was experiencing a rapid and fundamental social transformation that increasingly gave it the appearance of a bustling merchant and industrial center: New prominent social types included the merchant and working classes, along with a variety of street hawkers and petty traders. These changes created a complex urban panorama of social and cultural life, and historians understandably refer to the period as one of flux and uncertainty.

These developments facilitated fundamental changes in Russian theatrical life. The pattern of change replicated that which characterized theater across Europe and inaugurated theatrical modernism. Allusion to the wider European context instructively indicates that the experience of the Imperial Theaters was not unique. Industrialization and the spread of urban life throughout Europe created new audiences in search of entertainment, as well as wealthy entrepreneurs keen to patronize the arts. The first notable consequence of this was the abrogation of the old theater monopolies in the prominent European theater capitals to enable the establishment of new theatrical enterprises: In England, the Patent monopoly was abandoned in 1843; in France, the prohibitive licensing system was abolished by Napoleon III in 1864; and in the Germanic lands, court theater monopolies were effectively abolished in 1869 when freedom of artistic activity was enshrined in law. In 1882, the Russian Imperial Theater monopoly was abolished to enable the development of commercial theatrical activity in St. Petersburg and Moscow.*

The end of the monopolies facilitated the emergence of a rich variety of new theaters across Europe, catering to increasingly diverse and experimental tastes. New theaters inaugurated the great experimentalism that characterized European theater during the two decades before the First World War. In Paris, the popular café-concert flourished and the radical Théâtre Libre of André Antoine was founded (1887). In Vienna, where the court theater monopoly had been abrogated as early as 1776, the old court theaters were challenged by new commercial and popular theaters such as Max Friedländer's Wiener Stadttheater (1872), which became a variety theater, and the Deutsche Volkstheater (1889). In Berlin, the Freie Volksbühne was established (1890).

The new theaters established in Russia after 1882 can be divided into three types. First there were the private theaters, often established by wealthy merchants of civil society devoted to the serious pursuit of art. In Moscow, the most prominent were the Moscow Art Theater of Stanislavsky and Nemirovich-Danchenko (1898–present), the Korsh Theater (1882–1917), the Nezlobin Theater (1909–17), the Kamernyi Theater (1914–50), and the Private Opera of Savva Mamontov (1885–1904). In St. Petersburg, the most

*It is perhaps noteworthy that the geographical chronology of European theater monopoly abolition (from England, through France and Germany, to Russia) roughly paralleled the geographical chronology of European industrialization.

prominent and modish new theaters included the Suvorin Theater (1895–1917),* the Nemetti Theater (1903–9), and the Drama Theater of Vera Komissarzhevskaya (1904–9).[29]

The second new type of theatrical entertainment in Russia was the more commercially oriented entertainment that flourished in this period, in particular Russian estrada, a cross between nightclub and music hall, with an emphasis on gypsy romances.[30] Russian cabaret venues also appeared, in particular the Crooked Mirror (*Krivoe zerkalo*) (1908–17) and the Stray Dog (*Brodiachaia sobaka*) (1911–15) in St. Petersburg, as well as cabaret-style "miniature theaters" such as The Bat (*Letuchaia mysh*) in Moscow.[31]

The third new type of theater belonged to the category known as popular theater (*narodnyi teatr*). Many factory owners and temperance societies financed popular theatrical entertainment as a means of combating drunkenness and other habits detrimental to a day's work. The government recognized the "social control" utility, but was careful to supervise the repertoire of such theaters to ensure that "inflammatory material" did not reach the populace.[32]

The proliferation of theatrical entertainment towards the end of the nineteenth century was accompanied by a vigorous intellectual discourse on Russian theater. Participants debated the function and future of theater, and many contemporaries even identified a theater "crisis." In fact, it was common in most European theater capitals to speak of a "crisis," although the word signified different phenomena in different countries. In France, the dilemma, as articulated in a pamphlet by Jean Dubois entitled *La Crise théâtrale* (1895), was that the combined effects of an economic slump and competition from the café-concert had led to a certain decline in theatergoing after a notable expansion during the Second Empire.[33] In Vienna, the ostensible dilemma, according to Adam Müller-Guttenbrunn's *Wien war eine Theaterstadt* (1885), was that popular French farce and operetta had led to a decline in the standards of the repertoire. His solution was to establish the Deutsches Volkstheater.[34] In Russia, contemporary reference to a "crisis" was an exaggerated term for the vibrant discourse on the nature of theater. As the critic Alexander Kugel rightly observed, Russian theater was not really suffering a fatal "crisis," and the "crisis" simply consisted of "the old becoming old, and the young growing up." In other words, Russian theater was witnessing change.[35] Indeed, other theater observers even viewed the period as a "golden age," a great era for the Russian theater.[36]

Theater debate in Russia revolved around the broad issue of realism versus Symbolism, and the question of the sociopolitical function of theater. In

---

The Suvorin Theater was also known as the Maly Theater, after the name of its original building, or the Theater of the Literary-Artistic Society, after the name of the shareholding society that ran it. The majority shareholder and effective owner was A. S. Suvorin, hence the theater came to be known popularly as the Suvorin Theater.

the second half of the nineteenth century, reformist theater activists throughout Europe renounced "artifice" in favor of "realism." Instead of the forced
theatricality of declamation and exaggerated poses, artists working with the
régisseurs of realism labored to render productions as authentic and natural
as possible: Costumes and sets were made to correspond with the subjects of
plays, and actors had to perform as though the action was not simply a stage
representation, but was really happening to them. The prominent practitioners of stage realism were the Meininger company of the Duke of Saxe-
Meiningen, Antoine, Otto Brahm and, in Russia, Konstantin Stanislavsky.
As well as staging historically authentic productions of classics such as *Julius
Caesar*, the realists staged the new "social drama" by such playwrights as Ibsen,
Strindberg, Shaw, Chekhov and Gorky—what might be termed the nascent
critical repertoire that contrasted with the lighthearted vaudevilles and melo-
dramas that had dominated European theater for much of the nineteenth
century.

There was an almost simultaneous revolt against realism by the eclectic
avant-garde, represented in Russia in various ways by theater practitioners
such as Meyerhold, Nicholas Evreinov, Alexander Tairov, and Evgenii
Vakhtangov, and by writers such as Valerii Briusov and Andrei Bely.[37] It was
Briusov who effectively inaugurated a debate on the nature of theater when
he published, in 1902, an article entitled "Unnecessary Truth" (*Nenuzhnaia
pravda*). Therein he attacked the realism of the Moscow Art Theater and
argued for an *uslovnyi teatr*, a theater of conventions. Briusov believed that
the function of theater was not to mirror reality, but to convey ideas and feelings by means of a theatricality akin to a theater of masks.[38] This was the
line pursued by Meyerhold and other practitioners, and even Stanislavsky
experimented with Symbolism in the Studio of the Moscow Art Theater. In
1908, the collected ideas of the Symbolists were published in *"Theater": A
Book about the New Theater* (*"Teatr": kniga o novom teatre*). The contributors
included Briusov, Meyerhold, Bely, Fyodor Sologub, and the future Bolshevik commissar Anatoly Lunacharsky.

Critics of Symbolism responded with a collection entitled *Theater Crisis* (*Krizis teatra*) (1908) in which less prominent writers defended realism.
Iurii Steklov (pseudonym of the Bolshevik writer and member of the Executive Committee of the Petrograd Soviet in 1917 Iu. M. Nakhamkis) argued
that the programs of the innovators associated with *"Theater"* represented "a
huge step backwards in both the interpretation of the tasks of dramatic art,
and in stage technique."[39] Theater had a responsibility to depict social realities and to avoid the esoteric and introverted path of symbolical illusions.
Theater Crisis also decried the growing commercialism of urban entertainment. Vladimir Friche, writer, revolutionary and subsequently Soviet historian of literature, argued that the theater "crisis" consisted in the fact that the
rise of "bourgeois capitalism" was rendering art dependent upon commerce.

This was evident in Western and Russian theater art of the second half of the nineteenth century. Money could be made from the sale of theater tickets; and given the fact that the public only wanted to be entertained—the bourgeois after a tiring day of speculating, the proletarian after an exhausting day in the factory—there were commercial opportunities to be exploited. The bourgeoisie and the proletariat had no time for "art," only "entertainment." Friche concentrated his analysis on German theater, but stated explicitly that the "crisis" applied equally to Russian theater. His somewhat dubious solution to the "crisis"—the threat posed to "art" by "entertainment"—was to encourage a collective theater, or a popular theater, as opposed to the intimate theater of small rich audiences—a *Festspielhaus*, as opposed to a *Kammerspielhaus*.[40]

Here there was a point of similarity between the realists and the Symbolists. The prominent Symbolist theorist, Viacheslav Ivanov, also advocated a collective theater, a theater which would return to its ancient roots in order to rediscover its social function. He proposed a "cultic theater" which would eliminate the distinction between stage and audience in order that theater might become "the authentic expression of the will of the people."[41] Theater, argued Ivanov, must return to its "ancient prototypes"—religious rites, classical tragedy, medieval mystery plays—in which the audience participated in the "collective action." Theater had to replace the church as the spiritual temple of the nation, but this could only come about if a true collective experience were achieved. To that end, the distinction between actors and audience must be abolished.[42] The closest approximation to Ivanov's ideas in practice were the mass festivals of the Civil War period which combined pre-revolutionary theories of collective theater with the exigencies of winning and maintaining the support of the population by propagating the ideals of the revolution. The huge open-air spectacles (the most famous of which was Nicholas Evreinov's *Storming of the Winter Palace* in 1920) depicted the October Revolution as the dawn of a new era in human history, and they were witnessed by thousands of spectators simultaneously.[43]

Many individuals and movements of the richly diverse theatrical world of St. Petersburg before 1917 were associated with the Russian intelligentsia. That is to say, although they did not explicitly oppose tsarism—censorship made this difficult—they were part of a movement that was implicitly challenging various facets of the tsarist order. Merchant entrepreneurs who financed theatrical enterprises such as Mamontov and Suvorin represented civil society, organizationally and financially independent from the state, and excluded from political power. The principal financier of the Moscow Art Theater, Savva Morozov, was involved with the revolutionary intelligentsia and contributed to the finances of the Social Democrats. The drama of Gorky—one of the most prominent developments in Russian theater of those years—lamented the social conditions of ordinary Russian people. Members of the avant-garde, like Meyerhold and Vladimir Mayakovsky, who scripted the first Russian Futurist plays, were political as well as artistic radicals, and both welcomed, at least initially, the October Revolution in 1917. At the same time, the theater was a subject that attracted radical members of the cultural intelligentsia who were not practically involved in theater affairs, such as Ivanov and Lunacharsky. Thus, while it would be overstating the case to assert that the new theater activism was anti-tsarist, much of it was implicitly critical of prevailing conditions in Russia, a fact that was made particularly clear by the response of many theater activists to the 1905 Revolution when they supported the reform movement (see Chapter 6).

The Imperial Theaters did not figure prominently in the "crisis" debates, nor were they generally associated with an oppositional cultural intelligentsia. Nevertheless some contemporary observers certainly identified a "crisis" in the Imperial Theaters.[44] Generally such observations were confined to the Moscow Imperial Theaters, in particular the Maly drama theater which was made to look increasingly old-fashioned by the modish successes of the Moscow Art Theater. The dramatist Alexander Kosorotov bemoaned the fact that "the public walks past [the Maly], the press is unfriendly." He blamed himself, as a writer, for the "crisis," although it was, he said, the Symbolists who hawked the *idea* of a crisis. They were the anti-realists, and for them the "crisis" was the search for "new forms."[45] So threatened did the Maly feel by the success of the Moscow Art Theater that there were attempts by the Imperial Theater administration to merge the two theaters to create a new Imperial Theater, although Stanislavsky and Nemirovich-Danchenko resisted these offers.*

The St. Petersburg Imperial Theaters were less subject to accusations of decay, although they did exist for the drama repertoire. The "failure" of Chekhov's *The Seagull* at the Alexandrinsky in 1896 was cited as evidence that the theater was out of touch with latest developments. According to one critic, the production "most clearly showed the bankruptcy of the old artistic means in the face of new tasks."[46] It was the Moscow Art Theater which successfully demonstrated how to produce Chekhov appropriately. Yet, while it is true that the Imperial Theaters did not enjoy their greatest successes with works from the Chekhovian corpus, the reasons for the "failure" of 1896 had nothing to do with the production style of the Alexandrinsky. The first night was a failure because the audience had gathered for a benefit performance for a comic actress, Elizabeth Levkeeva, fully expecting to see a conventional comedy, which *The Seagull* was not. Moreover, the fact that it was performed only five times in 1896 and then abandoned until it was briefly resurrected

*Worrall, Moscow Art Theatre, pp. 165–166, 171. One of the reasons Nemirovich-Danchenko founded the Art Theater with Stanislavsky was that he had been unable to persuade the Imperial Theater administration to implement the production reforms that soon made the Art Theater famous.

during the 1902-03 season did not mean that *The Seagull* had failed: The remaining four performances of the play in 1896 were successful with the audience,[47] and it was quite usual for a production to be performed only a few times on the Imperial stage, unless it was a phenomenal success. In fact, despite some talk of decay, the St. Petersburg Imperial Theaters remained celebrated icons of the capital city's theatrical culture. According to one critic, even during the "limp and boring" season of 1909-10, the Alexandrinsky and Mariinsky were still the "most interesting and lively" theaters around.[48] Andrei Bely, responding to fellow symbolist Viacheslav Ivanov's ideas about a prospective new theater as a new temple, remarked that, despite the efforts of the new theater activists, "The 'temple' remains the Mariinsky Theater."[49]

Nevertheless, in 1900 the St. Petersburg Imperial Theaters were confronted by a dynamic and fluctuating Russian theatrical landscape. As civil society emerged, so too did an autonomous theatrical culture that absorbed the new urban audiences, provided alternative entertainment for Imperial Theater audiences, and challenged their status as the sole providers of exemplary theater art. Moreover, the state that subsidized the Imperial Theaters was increasingly beleaguered by war and radical opposition, and eventually succumbed to a revolutionary maelstrom. The identity of the St. Petersburg Imperial Theaters and the significance of their court status in the context of these changes is the general theme of this study.

Chapter 1

"The Emperor's Theaters"

The distinguishing characteristic of the St. Petersburg Imperial Theaters was that, unlike the new private and avant-garde experimental theaters that flourished in the capital at the turn of the century, they were administered by the Russian court, the amorphous conglomeration of officials and departments that constituted the tsar's formal retinue and which had its institutional embodiment in the Ministry of the Imperial Court (*Ministerstvo imperatorskogo dvora*). As court institutions, the St. Petersburg Imperial Theaters were regarded as the property of the tsar, a fact that is readily apparent from their original Russian title, *imperatorskie teatry*. The Russian word *imperatorskii* pertains to the person of the emperor, not to the empire as a territorial unit (*imperskii*), and therefore a more accurate rendering of *imperatorskie teatry*—and one that would also express more accurately the formal status of the Imperial Theaters—would be "The Emperor's Theaters."* This proprietorial connection between the theaters and the ruling family is further apparent from the very names of the theaters: the Alexandrinsky was thus named in honor of Nicholas I's wife, the Mikhailovsky in honor of his brother, and the Mariinsky in honor of Alexander II's wife. The connection was also acknowledged by Imperial Theater artists. One of the principal choreographers and dancers of the Mariinsky ballet troupe, Nicholas Legat, remarked of himself and his colleagues that, "As members of the Imperial Ballet Company we belonged to the State, or rather, personally to the Emperor. We were his servants, his employees, as an aesthetic institution we were his property."[1]

The purpose of this chapter is to identify the formal administrative structures that bound the St. Petersburg Imperial Theaters to the Russian court and government, and to examine the manner in which the court connection

*I have chosen to retain the name "Imperial Theaters" because this is the conventional English translation.

Baron Fredericks, Minister of the Imperial Court from 1897 to 1917. *Ezhegodnik imperatorskikh teatrov.*

shaped the character of the Imperial Theaters in the late tsarist period. As we will see, the proprietorial aspect of the administrative status of the St. Petersburg Imperial Theaters was not simply a formal characteristic. In practice, it entailed the direct involvement of the Russian court in the running of the theaters, and it conferred upon them a unique and prestigious status that was manifested in a variety of characteristics and functions that were absent from other Russian theaters. That is to say, the court administration of the St. Petersburg Imperial Theaters directly bestowed upon them the routines and symbolism of Russian officialdom in a variety of identifiable ways. At the same time, however, the role of court theaters in a modernizing society was being questioned by the administration itself, and it is possible to detect a certain ambivalence in their official status at the beginning of the period in question.

Formal Structures

The formal head of the Imperial Theater hierarchy was the tsar, proprietor of the "Emperor's Theaters." Directly below him in the hierarchy was the Minister of the Imperial Court, who, from 1897 to 1917, was V. B. Fredericks, a prominent landowner from the Baltic region. Fredericks's principal assistant in charge of coordinating the day-to-day business of the imperial court was the Head of the Court Chancellery, a position held from 1900 to 1916 by A. A. Mosolov, a former colleague of Fredericks in the Horse Guards regiment. One of several departments for which the Minister of the Imperial Court was responsible was the Directorate of Imperial Theaters (*Direktsiia imperatorskikh teatrov*). The Director* was a government functionary

---

Here the term "Director," from the Russian direktor, *means "manager" and should not be mistaken for someone who directs a theater production, who was known as a* rezhissër, *from the French* régisseur. *Throughout I have maintained this contemporary terminological distinction.*

invested with full responsibility for the Imperial Theater administration and answerable to the Minister, who in turn was answerable to the tsar. Thus, as one of the Directorate's officials put it in 1900: "General supervision of the precise and punctual execution by the Directorate of its obligations lies with the Minister of the Imperial Court, who reports directly to the Sovereign Emperor on all matters relating to the conditions and results of the work of the Imperial Theaters in both capitals."[2]

The elegant offices of the Directorate were located at Theater Street in St. Petersburg, adjacent to the Theater School and the Alexandrinsky Theater. The administration had associate offices in St. Petersburg and Moscow, which were responsible for the daily running of the Imperial Theaters. The Managers (*upravliaiushchie*) of the Office of St. Petersburg Imperial Theaters—hereafter referred to as the St. Petersburg Office—from 1900 were V. P. Starzhenetskii-Lappa (to August 1902); G. I. Vuich (October 1902–December 1907); A. D. Krupensky (December 1907–14); and Baron V. A. Kusov (1914–17). The Manager was assisted in the running of the theaters by other, subordinate, officials. None of these officials, including the Manager, were members of the Imperial Theater drama, opera or ballet troupes. Thus, there existed a clear institutional and occupational distinction between theater administrators and the artists.*

The Imperial Theater organization was extensive. The Director, according to the last incumbent of that post, V. A. Telyakovsky, was responsible for its properties in both St. Peterburg and Moscow. These consisted of ten theater buildings, seven troupes, seven string orchestras, two brass bands, two choruses, two theater schools with separate ballet and drama courses, a central music and drama library, a photography department, two medical facilities, a carriage department, four electrical generating stations, a publications department (at the center of which was the editorial office of the *Yearbook of the Imperial Theaters*), and various technical departments.[3] The St. Petersburg organization included not only the three public theaters, but four private court theaters which were closed to the public, except by express invitation: the Hermitage, the Tsarskoe Selo China, the Peterhof, and the Gatchina theaters.

Three departments (*otdeleniia*) and two sections (*chasti*) were attached to the St. Petersburg Office. The general management (*rasporiaditelnoe*) department was run by a secretary (*deloproizvoditel*) and his assistant. The "household" (*khoziaistvennoe*) department's chief officials were a secretary, an executor, two architects, the manager of the equipage division, and the three Police Masters (*politseimeister*) of the theaters. The accounts (*schötnoe*)

Throughout the book the term "artists" refers collectively to the personnel involved in the production of a stage spectacle: actors, actresses, singers, dancers, composers, musicians, choreographers, writers, designers, and so forth.

department was headed by an accountant and his assistant. The technical (*montirovochnaia*) section was run by a manager, four assistants, an artist (*khudozhnik*) and librarian, a sculptor and custodian of the properties workshop, and two secretaries. The medical (*vrachebnaia*) section consisted of two permanent doctors and fifteen duty doctors. In addition to this, there were several officials (nine during the 1892–93 season) with special commissions in the St. Petersburg Office.[4] Finally, a component of the administrative machinery that was formally separate from the Office, but in practice under its control, was the Imperial Theater Production Section (*postanovochnaia chast*), which consisted of three departments—one each for scenery, properties, and costumes. These departments and sections of the Office employed hundreds of workers, all of whom were placed, in principle, at the disposal of the artistic troupes of the St. Petersburg Imperial Theaters. One of the primary functions of the administration's Offices, for example, was to keep the artists informed about their daily routines, in particular rehearsal times, through a *Journal of Instructions* (*Zhurnal rasporiazhenii*). Most importantly, the administration provided an unequaled material infrastructure which enabled the artists to create and perform in what was, at least in terms of resources, the best theatrical environment in Russia.

The Directorate and the St. Petersburg Office, along with the various departments and sections under their supervision, represented state authority in the theaters. Undoubtedly this was a source of potential conflict with artists who resented being dictated to. The friction was compounded by the fact that the artists of the drama, opera, and ballet troupes constituted a minority of the total number of St. Petersburg Imperial Theater employees. Precise figures varied from year to year, but in general the troupe numbers were constant over the period under investigation. The following statistics are averages, rounded off to the nearest whole number, based on the years 1900–10. The Alexandrinsky Theater had fifty-three actresses and forty-five actors. The Mariinsky opera had twenty-five actresses, and thirty-two actors. The Mariinsky chorus had fifty-seven female singers, and fifty-five male singers. The Mariinsky ballet had 123 female dancers, and eighty-five male dancers.[5] In 1900, out of a total number of 1,667 employees of the Directorate and the St. Petersburg Office, the total number of artists from the drama, opera and ballet troupes (including the orchestras) was 685; the remaining 982 employees were attached to the Director's office (twelve officials), the St. Petersburg Office (forty-six officials), the orchestras' administrative office (seventeen officials), the technical section (420 officials), the "household" department (431 officials), and the Theater School (fifty-six officials).[6]

The foregoing description of the St. Petersburg Imperial Theater administrative structure refers only to the court administration. It does not exhaust the agencies which contributed—if only indirectly—to the running of those institutions. In particular, the Directorate was not the official censor for the Imperial Theater repertoire, as all drama scripts and libretti had to be vetted by the drama section of the Chief Administration for Press Affairs (*Glavnoe upravlenie po delam pechati*), attached to the Ministry of Internal Affairs, before they could be performed in public, as was the case with all other Russian theaters.[7] Even after 1905, when censorship laws were eased marginally by the government and preliminary censorship was abolished for certain publications, the Imperial Theaters, as with all other theaters in Russia, were still permitted to perform only material which had obtained prior approval from the censor.[8] To ensure compliance with its instructions, the Chief Administration for Press Affairs continued to reserve a seat in each Imperial Theater auditorium for its censor well after 1905.[9] Even so, the criteria applied by the censor to performances in the Imperial Theaters were different from the criteria used for other theaters, a fact that helped to set them apart and underline their privileged status (see Chapter 4).

Likewise, St. Petersburg Imperial Theater finances were not entirely in the Directorate's control, as the theater had to rely on a grant from the Ministry of the Imperial Court and subsidies from the State Exchequer (*Gosudarstvennoe kaznacheistvo*) to supplement box-office revenues. From 1882 the Imperial Theaters had begun to receive subsidies from the State Exchequer amounting to two million rubles per annum in addition to the money they received from the Ministry of the Imperial Court—another two million rubles.[10] This ministerial largesse set the Imperial Theaters above private theaters, leading one commentator to suggest that the Imperial Theater "ought to be a model for all private (particularly provincial) theaters, since it possesses such material and artistic resources which cannot be in the hands of private entrepreneurs."[11] The Imperial Theaters were certainly richer than other theaters in Russia at the time, one of the chief reasons they were able to attract much of the best artistic talent in Russia. The *régisseur* Nicholas Petrov, for instance, makes the point in his memoirs that he had worked at the Moscow Art Theater for twenty-five rubles per month, but when he moved to the Alexandrinsky Theater, he earned 120 rubles per month.[12] It would be surprising if the substantial increase in remuneration was not a chief reason why the Alexandrinsky was able to entice the *régisseur* from the reputable Moscow Art Theater.

Yet despite contemporary impressions that the Imperial Theaters had access to limitless funds, that was not the case. Peter Gnedich, artistic leader of the Alexandrinsky from 1901 to 1908, claimed that whenever he requested anything, the answer was always that there was insufficient money; the theater was assigned a fixed amount which could not be changed.[13] At the *fin-de-siècle*, the financial situation looked relatively precarious, as the Imperial Theater accounts registered deficits that could not be covered indefinitely by State Exchequer subsidies. In 1898, for instance, the Mariinsky's opera performances alone had secured revenue of 443,000 rubles, yet Mariinsky expenses remained 200,000 rubles in excess of that—"the budget of some German principality," remarked one observer.[14] Figures show that during the 1899-1900 season, total Imperial Theater expenditure amounted to 4,048,827 rubles and 50 kopeks;[15] income from ticket sales and the court grant amounted to only 1,852,900 rubles, an overall shortfall of 2,195,927 rubles and 50 kopeks. Fortunately, this shortfall was covered by the State Exchequer, which provided 2.6 million rubles. This left the relatively small sum of 404,072 rubles and 50 kopeks to spare.[16]

Consequently, various money-saving schemes, or "austerity measures," were instituted. In 1900, for example, Alexandrinsky ticket prices were raised by between sixty kopeks for the most expensive seats and two kopeks for the cheapest seats to improve its income.[17] Yet the situation did not improve in the early 1900s. One temporary source of the problem was the Russo-Japanese War, which caused sufficient economic tightness among the population to ensure a fall in box-office takings. The St. Petersburg Imperial Theaters' deficit for 1904 amounted to 145,442 rubles, and the Directorate was compelled to reduce that shortfall by 48,798 rubles (it is not clear how the remainder of the deficit was to be paid for).[18] The initiative for savings came initially from the "*Kabinet* of His Imperial Highness," the formal title of the tsar's private office, which was part of the Ministry of the Imperial Court.[19]

From 1905 onwards, further schemes were devised to enable the Imperial Theaters to reduce their expenses and increase their income. Already in January 1905, the periodical press had announced that the Imperial Theaters of both capitals would have their income "significantly reduced" in the forthcoming year. One way of achieving this was a reduction in the number of "second" artists. In April 1905, the Directorate announced that pensions for its employees would be paid for fifteen years instead of twenty. The total pension would be increased, but presumably the State Exchequer would make a net saving.[20] By the summer of 1906, there had been a "serious reduction in the Imperial Theater budget."[21] In September 1906 ballet ticket prices were raised to the level of opera ticket prices.[22] The use of carriages for conveying artists to and from the theaters was reduced, although their use was maintained for leading artists, the "stars," such as prima ballerinas.[23] Another way of cutting costs was found by the Director of Imperial Theaters, Telyakovsky, in 1907. He observed that revenues from performances in the spring were generally insignificant, perhaps because people started to leave the city for their dachas. At the same time, the number of weekly Imperial Theater performances had increased because now they were allowed to perform on Saturdays and during most of Lent (see below). This had served to increase their expenses, but the increase was not being offset by revenues during the spring. Therefore Telyakovsky requested Fredericks's permission to conclude the season earlier than usual—on April 20, 1908, rather than in May 1908.[24]

Any improvements in the financial situation of the Imperial Theaters after the reforms of 1905–07 were set back by the outbreak of the First World War. As early as July 31, 1914, the Ministry of the Imperial Court issued a circular which announced financial cutbacks in the theaters to aid the war effort. Fredericks wrote that, "in view of military events and the consequent necessity to observe extreme economy in expenditures for the satisfaction of specific war time requirements, I address the leaders of the institutions in my Ministry with a request to take quick and most decisive measures for a significant reduction of expenditures...."[25] Fredericks specified areas where economies might be made, such as in the issuing of staff uniforms, office furniture, or work relating to parks and gardens. He did not specify measures for the Imperial Theaters, but it is inconceivable that there were no consequences for them. The *Yearbook of the Imperial Theaters* was forced to cease publication in 1915, saving the Imperial Theaters 15,000 rubles—although it was remarked that this sum was "insignificant" in terms of the overall size of the budget.[26] Another small way in which the St. Petersburg Imperial Theaters endeavored to offset negative wartime financial trends was to introduce commercial advertising in performance programs.[27]

Along with censorship and financial dependence, the Directorate had to contend with certain members of the imperial family who made it their business to interfere in the affairs of the Imperial Theaters. According to Telyakovsky, the two people most inclined to interfere were the Grand Duchess Maria Pavlovna, Nicholas II's aunt, and the Grand Duke Sergei Mikhailovich. Such interference did not occur often, but when it did, it had potentially far-reaching consequences. For example, in 1913 Maria Pavlovna decided that she would formally invite a French acquaintance, Parisian dramatist and "millionaire" Francis de Croisset, to take over the management of the Mikhailovsky Theater. De Croisset had agreed to work in St. Petersburg for nothing. According to the plan, Telyakovsky would be replaced by Krupensky, the Manager of the St. Petersburg Office. It is not clear why this change was deemed necessary. Perhaps Maria Pavlovna preferred Krupensky as an individual. Indeed, it appears that Telyakovsky was not at the very center of the consultations, the Grand Duchess evidently preferring to speak to Krupensky and Fredericks about the matter. The affair ended harmlessly when de Croisset decided that, after all, he would rather not render his services free of charge—he had requested thirty thousand francs to take up the post, and was promptly refused.[28] While the Grand Duchess's plan came to nothing, it is likely that, had her acquaintance not insisted on such high payment, far-reaching changes in the top administrative personnel of the St. Petersburg Imperial Theaters would have occurred, regardless of the Directorate's wishes. It should be emphasized, however, that the Grand Duchess's interference was often of a positive and beneficent nature. For example, during the Russo-Japanese War she organized charity concerts for invalids.[29]

The organs that administered the St. Petersburg Imperial Theaters thus formally bound them closely to the imperial court and rendered them dependent on other government ministries. They had no institutional autonomy, unlike other theaters in tsarist Russia, whose only contact with the state was indirect, namely through the Chief Administration for Press Affairs—the censor—or, in the case of the state (*kazënnyi*) theaters, through the State Exchequer.[30] The St. Petersburg Imperial Theaters were directly supervised by the imperial court, at least in a formal administrative sense. Like the Orthodox Church, which had been subjected to the secular authority since the early eighteenth century, they were departments of state. Moreover, this "court factor" (*pridvornyi faktor*), as one historian of the Alexandrinsky called it,[31] was more keenly felt in St. Petersburg than in Moscow. As the imperial capital, St. Petersburg was the center of court life and state officialdom. Moscow, geographically removed from the center of the court since the early eighteenth century, was regarded more as a business and financial center, and the court status of the Moscow Imperial Theaters was less pronounced, although in theory the theaters were still answerable to the Directorate in St. Petersburg.

Court Culture and the Imperial Theaters

The Ministry of the Imperial Court, through its department, the Directorate of Imperial Theaters, enjoyed overall formal responsibility for the running of the St. Petersburg Imperial Theaters. This was not simply a nominal fact: court administration imparted to the Imperial Theaters certain symbols and practices associated with the traditional formal sources of power in imperial Russia, namely the emperor (as we have already seen), the military and, to a lesser extent, the Orthodox Church. These key components of the tsarist state were particularly evident in St. Petersburg as the administrative center of the empire, and audiences who frequented the St. Petersburg Imperial Theaters could be left in no doubt that they were inhabiting a world closely connected to the center of power in Russia in several tangible ways that distinguished the Imperial Theaters from other theaters in St. Petersburg.

One of the most striking characteristics of the St. Petersburg Imperial Theaters was the prominence of what might be referred to as military culture, or simply the presence of militarism in the theaters. This militarism was not inherent in the theaters themselves, but rather enveloped them because St. Petersburg was a military city in general, and the Ministry of the Imperial Court in particular was staffed by recruits from the upper echelons of the military, particularly from the Horse Guards regiment. Militarism pervaded all aspects of St. Petersburg life in the imperial period of Russian history (*c*.1700–1917).[32] Perhaps this is not surprising: The city was founded for military reasons during the Great Northern War. Right down to the revolution of 1917, it was closely associated with Russian military glory. Many of its prominent buildings are military monuments (such as the Admiralty) or commemorations of military triumphs (such as the Kazan Cathedral). A large number of the city's major monuments and open spaces, such as the Triumphal Arches and the Field of Mars, have explicit military associations. Even the color of the city and the predominant architectural style—the empire style—have their origins in the culture of celebrating military grandeur: The yellow facades of many of the city's buildings were based on the gold color of imperial Rome; yellow was also used for Russian military medals. The empire style of architecture was used for the manifold barracks and manèges.

St. Petersburg was also a city of parades and military ceremonies, and the uniformed *voennyi* (soldier) adorns the pages of nineteenth-century Russian literature in a manner that emphasizes his imperial ubiquity. There was also a military ethos in government, arguably a military style of rule by the Romanovs. Individual tsars, particularly in the nineteenth century, paid particular attention to the army, participating in parades and conducting inspections, and they were obsessed with what has been called the "paraphernalia of soldiering."[33] As one historian has pointed out, it is therefore not surprising that Nicholas II considered it his "duty" to assume supreme command of the imperial army in 1915.[34] From the tsar down, a significant proportion of the imperial capital's culture was militaristic. And although official preoccupation with militarism was not a unique phenomenon in Europe—the case of Prussia (which Russian rulers drew upon) is an obvious example—it was particularly pronounced in nineteenth-century Russia, its influence highly visible in the political center of the empire.

This military culture inevitably pervaded the St. Petersburg Imperial Theaters in several ways, but most notably in terms of the people who ran them. One official based at the Moscow Imperial Theaters but writing of the Imperial Theater system as a whole observed that: "The period of the eighties and nineties was called by the press at that time the epoch of second lieutenants, since the Minister of the Imperial Court, Count Vorontsov-Dashkov, was kindly disposed towards the Finnish Life Guards regiment and, appointed Minister in 1881, shoved into theater posts the poorest officers who had served in the Turkish campaign of 1877-78." Officers of the Life Husars did even better, claimed the official, because Vorontsov-Dashkov was a commander of that regiment and appointed his colleagues to various court departments.[35] The Director of Imperial Theaters under Vorontsov-Dashkov was Ivan Vsevolozhsky, a former diplomat. His successor in 1899, and Director in 1900 when this study begins, was Prince Sergei Mikhailovich Volkonsky. The grandson of a famous Decembrist, Volkonsky was born in 1860 in the Estland *guberniia*. He studied at the Historico-philological faculty at St. Petersburg University, where his linguistic proficiency—in addition to Greek and

Sergei Volkonsky, Director of Imperial Theaters from 1899 to 1901. *Ezhegodnik imperatorskikh teatrov.*

Latin he was proficient in five living languages—enabled him to study ancient theater and contemporary drama. After graduating, he worked as a *zemstvo* official. He was given the opportunity to attend an international exhibition in the United States, where he gave lectures on art which were later published in St. Petersburg. In addition to reading lectures on Russian history and literature, Volkonsky was a keen amateur actor.[36] With his political and administrative experience, and his artistic inclinations, Volkonsky was well suited to run the Imperial Theaters. He was also liked for his open approach with the artists. When he was introduced to the Alexandrinsky troupe, he assured them that they could approach him directly with any requests, implying that they did not first have to go to the Manager of the St. Petersburg Office.[37]

In 1901, Volkonsky was replaced by Vladimir Arkadevich Telyakovsky (1860–1924), who was Director of Imperial Theaters from 1901 to 1917. The son of a military fortifications expert, Telyakovsky was a noble from the Iaroslav *guberniia.* Like many of the high-ranking bureaucrats of imperial Russia, he had trained for a military career, serving from 1879 as an officer in the Horse Guards regiment, where his commander was his step-father and future Minister of the Imperial Court, Fredericks. In 1888 Telyakovsky graduated from the Academy of the General Staff and in 1897 became a colonel. During his army years he became acquainted with two of the men whom he would have to deal with later in his capacity as manager of the government theaters, D. F. Trepov, governor-general of St. Petersburg at the time of the 1905 revolution, and A. A. Mosolov, Head of the Court Chancellery under Fredericks. In 1898 Telyakovsky was appointed by Fredericks to lead the Office of the Moscow Imperial Theaters. Three years later, in June 1901, he was promoted to the post of Director of all Russia's Imperial Theaters when a scandal involving the ballerina Matilda Kshesinskaya and Volkonsky ended with the latter's resignation.[38]

A former producer at the Moscow Imperial Theaters, Fyodor Komissarzhevsky, recalled that Telyakovsky "was such a small man physically that he seemed quite lost when sitting at the big desk in the vastness of his study in Theatre Street." Referring to Telyakovsky as the "diminutive colonel," Komissarzhevsky observed that, "Although a former colonel of Horse Guards, the Director looked more like a bank clerk than a soldier, the only military thing about his appearance being his pointed mustache. I could never imagine him on horseback...."[39] At any rate, the Horse Guards regiment, founded in 1721, provides an important key to Telyakovsky's background, education, and character. The first guards detachments in the Russian armed forces were created by a young Peter the Great in 1687. They evolved

Vladimir Telyakovsky, Director of Imperial Theaters from 1901 to 1917. *Ezhegodnik imperatorskikh teatrov.*

into elite military units that were designed "to inspire regular detachments and to award high achievement," but they were hardly meritocratic, as the officers were "chosen mainly from the rich and titled nobility." Guards not appointed from the ranks of the nobility were required to be "men of great height and physical strength."[40] Telyakovsky's diminutive stature, therefore, confirms that his noble background was the key to his entry to the regiment.*

Tolstoy provided a cutting description of the guardsman's life-style, known to him at first hand from his youth, and which Telyakovsky was exposed to:

> Military life frees [men] from their common human duties, which it replaces by merely conventional duties to the honour of the regiment, the uniform, the flag; and, while giving them on the one hand absolute power over other men, also puts them into conditions of servile obedience to those of higher rank than themselves. [...]
> [Then] there is added the depravity caused by riches and near intercourse with members of the Imperial family (as is the case in the select regiment of the Guards in which all the officers are rich and of good family), then this depravity develops into a perfect mania of selfishness. [They have] no occupation whatever, except, dressed in a uniform splendidly made and

*Telyakovsky's memoirs are silent about his background, possibly because they were written in the Soviet Union in the early 1920s, when it was not always advisable to emphasize one's noble background.

well brushed by other people, and with weapons also made and cleaned and
handed to [them] by others, to ride to parade on a fine horse which had
been bred, broken in, and fed by others. [...]
   What was considered good and important besides this, was to eat, and
particularly to drink, in officers' clubs and the best restaurants, squandering
large sums of money, which came from some invisible source; then theatres,
balls, women; then again riding on horseback, flourishing swords and jumping....[41]

Telyakovsky headed a theater administration that was practically militaristic in form. The opera *régisseur* Vasilii Shkafer referred to the Directorate's officials as a "huge phalanx" (*ogromnaia falanga*), a term with distinct
military connotations.[42] Uniforms were prevalent in the theaters—"men in
uniform, men who had nothing in common with art," as Chaliapin noted.[43]
As well as the motley collection of soldiers appointed by Vorontsov-Dashkov,
theater ushers were required to wear court uniforms, "the red outfits and the
white stockings of the valets of the court, so proper, so emblazoned with
imperial eagles," as Lev Bakst observed.[44] In 1900, the St. Petersburg Imperial Theaters alone employed 104 of these *kapeldinery*.[45] Each theater had a
Police Master, usually from the military. For example, the Police Master of
the Mikhailovsky, F. A. Pereiaslavtsev, was yet another officer from the Horse
Guards regiment.[46] According to one contemporary, the Police Master "carried out the highest administrative control in the theater."[47] In practice, his
task was to ensure the general maintenance of order in the theaters, specific
duties ranging from security of the buildings to ensuring that the heating
worked.[48] In March 1906, the Police Masters began to take additional orders
from the Palace Commandant, who was in charge of security for the imperial family, a move that reflected a general tightening of security in the theaters after the events of the 1905 Revolution (see Chapter 6).[49] The rank of
corporal accompanied the post of Police Master, and consequently the most
prominent official of the Directorate whom the artists would encounter on a
daily basis was a *voennyi*.
   According to one critic of the Imperial Theaters, militarism was even
inherent in their architecture. The critic lamented their "shameful architecture" and "barrack customs":

Constructed mainly in the reign of Emperor Nicholas I, when the spirit and
style of the barrack reigned everywhere, they bear the imprint of Arakcheev
[a powerful figure who symbolized militarism and reaction under Alexander I]. The Alexandrinsky and Mariinsky Theaters remind one of a riding
school for soldiers, and the Mikhailovsky a guardhouse, rather than temples
of art. Only the Alexandrinsky has cultural adornment on the outside—and
that is militaristic, which is completely out of place and does not particularly promote a beautiful appearance.... [In the] foyers, there are guards
everywhere, as if this was a guardhouse rather than a theater, or that audiences were gathered with some unlawful aim.... The barrack customs of the

theater are evident even when you approach it. It is all cordoned off by policemen and gendarmes, as if a search was going on inside. Of course, the audience is graded [*sortiruetsia*]. Those arriving in private carriages can drive up to their own entrance. The rest of the public are dumped at a certain distance, whatever the weather.[50]

Although this is an untypical comment on the St. Petersburg Imperial Theaters, it does illustrate a distinctive feature that set them apart from other theaters in the city; and while such practices as the critic delineates infuriated him, the fact that the negative remarks are unusual arguably underlines the fact that others were quite accustomed to them.

Thus we can identify in the St. Petersburg Imperial Theaters a concurrence of cultures—militaristic customs and a militaristic city. It is significant that no other theaters of the capital displayed such military characteristics. The fact that the Imperial Theaters did was a function of their court status, in particular the militarism that pervaded the administration in the late tsarist period.

A second notable characteristic imparted to the St. Petersburg Imperial Theaters by the fact of court administration was adherence to the Orthodox calendar. The association between the Imperial Theaters and Russian Orthodoxy, the official state religion, was evident in the policies adopted for performances during Lent, and for performances on Saturdays—the eve of the Sabbath—and the days before feast days. Until the reign of Alexander III, performances by the Imperial Theater troupes during Lent were generally permitted. Under Konstantin Pobedonostsev, the reactionary Procurator of the Holy Synod and Alexander III's grey eminence, they were strictly prohibited. Foreign or private theater troupes could perform on the Imperial Theater stage during Lent, but the Imperial Theater artists themselves could not. Instead, groups of Imperial Theater artists would tour the provinces, where performances in the Russian language were not prohibited during Lent.[51]

Gradually, this situation began to change. Toward the end of 1898, it was decided that the opera troupe could continue to perform at the Mariinsky Theater during Lent although none of the proposed operas would be of Russian origin.[52] (Nevertheless, a performance of *Eugene Onegin* was given.[53]) The drama troupe was still not allowed to perform, and while a German troupe performed German-language drama at the Alexandrinsky, part of the Alexandrinsky *troupe* toured the Baltic region.[54] Telyakovsky, perhaps thinking of the implications for revenues at a time when the Imperial Theater budget was being closely monitored, raised this issue with the tsar and Pobedonostsev, but it was not until the spring of 1906, after Pobedonostsev had retired, that permission was granted for the Imperial Theaters to function during Lent.[55] This new policy took effect from Lent 1907. The demise of Lent prohibitions therefore accompanied the demise of Pobedonostsev, who died in March 1907. All the same, official recognition of Lent was maintained, and the Imperial Theaters were still not permitted to perform during the first, fourth, or seventh weeks of Lent, unlike other theaters.

A third feature that court status accorded the Imperial Theaters and set them apart from other Russian theaters was their use by the government for special-occasion performances which underlined the Imperial Theaters' official role as celebratory emblems of the tsarist court. In particular, the Imperial Theaters were used to entertain foreign dignitaries and guests of the tsar. When the Austrian Emperor Francis Joseph I visited Russia in April 1897, he was treated to the finest display of pomp and ceremony at the Mariinsky Theater. The exterior of the theater was decorated in Russian and Austro-Hungarian flags; the roof of the building was covered in light blue electric lamps, and was crowned by a huge phosphorescent lyre (the ensign of the Imperial Theaters), and the pediment sported a large, electric-lighted double-headed eagle. The audience of dignitaries in attendance was treated to the first and second acts of *The Sleeping Beauty*. At the beginning and end of the performance the Mariinsky orchestra played the Austrian anthem. Gala performances by Imperial Theater artists were also given at Peterhof for foreign guests, including, in the summer of 1897, the King of Siam, Kaiser Wilhelm II, and the President of the French Republic.[56] Similarly, the Directorate arranged a gala performance of *The Hump-Backed Horse* at the Mariinsky on September 18, 1916 in honor of the visit to Russia of the Japanese Prince Kan-in. During the performance, officials from the Japanese embassy and the Russian imperial court occupied the parterre; Telyakovsky occupied the Director's box.[57] Such events enabled the government to showcase the finest achievements of Russian theater culture to foreigners.

The presence of foreign dignitaries was not the only occasion when the Imperial Theaters were used by the court/government to formally mark an event. In December 1908, the Mariinsky Theater was the venue for a celebration of the seventy-fifth anniversary of the Russian national anthem, composed by A. F. Lvov. The evening of December 20 began with the performance of various overtures, and vocal and instrumental numbers, mostly composed by Lvov, followed by a rendition of the anthem. After this concert, the opera *A Life for the Tsar* was given. One half of the auditorium was reserved for members of the Russian Assembly (*Russkoe sobranie*) and other patriotic societies, the other half for tickets made available for general sale. The same program was performed at the Bolshoi in Moscow on the same evening. Of particular interest is Telyakovsky's decision to invite members of the Russian Assembly to the performance. The Russian Assembly was a right-wing cultural association, founded in St. Petersburg in 1901 by the aristocrat D. P. Golitsyn. The majority of its members were conservative-monarchist military officers or government and court officials. Their invitation to an event in celebration of the national anthem provides a clear insight into the administration's perception of the association between the imperial ruling elite and the Imperial Theaters (see Chapter 3).[58] Of course, the three hundredth anniversary of the Romanov dynasty was celebrated in the Imperial Theaters. On the evening of February 21, 1913, the Mariinsky Theater performed the national anthem, followed by *A Life for the Tsar*. The Alexandrinsky presented the anthem, followed by the premiere of *The Election to the Realm of Tsar Mikhail Fedorovich Romanov*, written by A. N. Chaev, followed by *Koz'ma Zakhar'ich Minin-Sukhoruk*, a scene from a dramatic chronicle by A. N. Ostrovsky. These performances were repeated over several evenings. The Mikhailovsky Theater, as the home of the French troupe, did not mark the occasion.

A fourth noteworthy characteristic imparted to the Imperial Theaters by their association with the court was the elevated status of their artists, who were encouraged to regard the Imperial Theaters as privileged. The importance of this is evident from the history of commemorative badges, something which might at first glance seem trivial but in fact highlights the extent to which status and prestige—especially prestige accruing from a physical sign of close connection to, or favor with, the court—were important parts of Imperial Theater culture. For example, in 1888 the idea of creating a badge of distinction for certain Imperial Theater artists was conceived and in 1895 the badge appeared. The design, according to a description published in the *Yearbook of the Imperial Theaters*, consisted of a light blue enamel lyre with gold ornamentation and a gold star at the top. The lyre was cradled by a laurel wreath entwined with ribbon and topped by the imperial crown. It was five centimeters high and four centimeters wide, and was to be worn on the left-hand side of the chest. Upon its appearance, the badge was awarded to eight artists, seven of whom were the tsar's soloists, a special title conferred by the crown for distinguished service to Russian art.[59] Imperial Theater artists who served during the reign of Alexander III were awarded medals in memory of the deceased emperor.[60] Twenty-five Imperial Theater artists were presented with medals of light blue enamel with a relief crown by the Ministry of the Imperial Court to wear on their chests in recognition of their participation in Nicholas II's coronation cantata and gala performance.[61] In 1913, a jubilee badge was introduced to celebrate the three-hundredth anniversary of the Romanov dynasty. Only certain officials and artists were permitted to wear the badge. Applications had to be submitted to the Court Chancellery and to the "Committee for the Organization of the Celebration of the Three Hundredth Anniversary of the Reign of the House of the Romanovs." The St. Petersburg Office requested that Telyakovsky, Krupensky, and V. A. Kusov be permitted to wear the badge.[62] They were later permitted to do so. The Directorate applied for badges on behalf of the troupes, but only certain members were granted permission to wear them.[63] The fashionable desire for commemorative badges persisted throughout the year. Some applicants were unsuccessful. For example, Fredericks stipulated that the Police Master of the

Mariinsky, A. I. Bestuzhev-Riumin, did not belong to the category of people permitted to wear the badge.[64]

These hierarchies were not replicated elsewhere in Russian theater. In themselves they are not remarkable; but they served further to distinguish Imperial Theater artists from other artists, and in a manner that emphasized their relative proximity to the court. It was not until after the revolution of 1917 that similar state honors were awarded to artists of other theaters (though by then theaters like the Moscow Art Theater had themselves become state theaters).

Finally, even as physical structures, the St. Petersburg Imperial Theaters bore many of the hallmarks of court culture and were in a sense symbolic monuments of the tsarist order. One might reasonably refer to them as "power symbols." Their symbolic properties were located in the architecture of the auditoria, whose opulent splendor constituted a symbolic manifestation of the wealth and grandeur of the power that created and financed them. They were replete with velvet and gold decor, brilliant chandeliers, portraits of the tsars, and double-headed eagle insignia, although the slightly more spartan, auburn interior of the French Mikhailovsky was rather more demure than the gilded ostentation of the Alexandrinsky's scarlet interior, or the ornamental lustre of the Mariinsky's azure auditorium. Unlike other, private theaters, the Imperial Theaters had royal boxes, perhaps one of the most obvious examples of their symbolic status. The fact of royal attendance itself distinguished them further. The royal boxes were like miniature theaters in themselves, with elaborate proscenium arches and curtains that framed their inhabitants in a manner that suggested they were on display as much as the Imperial artists.

The theater buildings were designed by Western architects of the neoclassical school and blended splendidly with the regular facades of the imperial capital. The Imperial Theaters, particularly the Alexandrinsky, are impressive examples of imperial classical, non–Slavic architecture. Like most St. Petersburg architecture, they do not invoke in any way indigenous Russian styles of construction. Therefore, their architecture can be viewed as part of the broad divide in late imperial Russia between the Westernized elite and the Russian masses. This point, however, should not be exaggerated. St. Petersburg architecture generally represented imperial authority and the Imperial Theaters were only prominent constituent parts of that political ensemble of bricks and mortar. Yet such architectural characteristics generally set the Imperial Theaters apart from other public theaters in St. Petersburg, whose decor and architecture was rather more diffident. The interior of the Suvorin Theater was compared by contemporaries to the Mikhailovsky, the least flamboyant of the Imperial Theaters; the Nemetti Theater was built in the *style moderne*, providing a notable contrast to the empire classicism of the Imperial Theaters, which was particularly pronounced in the Alexandrinsky's architecture; and the Vasileostrovsky Theater, which catered chiefly

View of the Alexandrinsky from Theater Street. On the right are the buildings of the Imperial Theater School and the offices of the Directorate of Imperial Theaters. Vospominanya (Moscow-Leningrad, 1965).

to migrant laborers, was a much more mundane, wooden structure without a conventional foyer, where audiences sat on stools and benches, in contrast to the comfortable armchairs of the Imperial Theater parterre.[65]

The Pogozhev Commission

Militarism, Orthodoxy, special-occasion performances, special occasion badges, and architecture helped to distinguish the Imperial Theaters from other theaters in St. Petersburg and served to identify them with the formal loci of power in tsarist Russia. This close association between theater and state was reinforced in 1900 when the Directorate published a three-volume legalistic document, composed by one of its senior officials, entitled *Plan of a Legal Statute on the Imperial Theaters* (*Proekt zakonopolozhenii ob imperatorskikh teatrakh*). The *Proekt* essentially constituted the codification of the existing rules and regulations governing the administration of the Imperial Theaters. It covered the whole range of associated areas, from the powers and responsibilities of the Director to the various levels of pensions for artists and employees of differing ranks. The *Proekt* dealt with both the St. Petersburg and Moscow Imperial Theaters, but explicitly distinguished between them in terms of the organizational and statistical information it provided. Despite the Herculean efforts of its author to produce the three lengthy volumes (which added up to one and a half thousand pages) in a relatively short space of time, the *Proekt* was never adopted as a governing statute for the Imperial Theaters: It does not appear in the *Complete Collection of Laws of the Russian Empire* (*Polnoe sobranie zakonov Rossiiskoi imperii*); and although the theatrical press reported its publication in 1900, informing readers that it only had to be ratified by the State Council to become law, no subsequent mention of the *Proekt* is made in any of the contemporary sources. In fact, Imperial Theater regulations remained uncodified.* Consequently, the *Proekt* does not provide a reliable description of the administration of the Imperial Theaters, although it is clear from other contemporary sources that the present study has utilized to reconstruct the history of the St. Petersburg Imperial Theater administration that most of the *Proekt* is descriptive rather than prescriptive. That is to say, it clarified the structures and functions of the administration as they existed before 1900 and as they continued to exist after 1900.

The fundamental significance of the *Proekt*, however, lies not in its detailed exposition of Imperial Theater administrative structures and regulations, but in its implicit commentary on the official status and function of the Imperial Theaters in Russian society. Particularly valuable in this respect is the lengthy Introduction, in which its author discusses the reasons for producing the *Proekt*. It is in the *Proekt*, particularly its *raison d'être* as articulated by its Introduction, that a dual function and meaning (and implicit ambivalence) of the Russian court theaters that runs through their history in the late tsarist period first becomes evident. That is to say, while the *Proekt* confirmed that the Imperial Theaters were expected to function as embellishments of the imperial court, it also identified what was intended to be a wider function that appears similar to the role played by national theaters that had evolved from court theaters elsewhere in Europe in the eighteenth and nineteenth centuries. The fact that the *Proekt* was not incorporated into Russian law does not negate the significance of its author's statements on the general status of the Imperial Theaters; they remain the most comprehensive remarks bequeathed by late imperial Russian officialdom regarding the official status and function of Russian court theater.

The *Proekt* was conceived and written by Vladimir Petrovich Pogozhev (1851–1935). He was the Manager of the St. Petersburg Office between May 11, 1882, and February 24, 1900, with additional elevated status as a "special official" in the Directorate from 1897 to 1900. He was also a theater historian; in fact, the whole of volume three of the *Proekt* is a history of the Imperial Theaters to the end of the nineteenth century. But in 1900, after almost two

---

Statutes on the administration were drawn up during its formative stages in the late eighteenth and early nineteenth centuries, and subsequently there were separate germane articles of legislation relating to the Imperial Theaters, such as the 1882 abrogation of their monopoly on performances, but they were never gathered together as one code.

decades at the helm of the St. Petersburg Office, Pogozhev was principally an administrator, a classic theater bureaucrat. According to the *Yearbook of the Imperial Theaters*, Pogozhev retired from the service of the St. Petersburg Office on February 24, 1900.[66] Quite why he left the post at this time is uncertain—he was in the middle of writing the *Proekt*, which he composed between September 1899 and May 1900. It is unlikely that there was any altercation with the Directorate because it duly published the *Proekt*, for consultation, and Pogozhev continued to act as the Directorate's semi-official historiographer, writing in particular the early organizational history of the Moscow Imperial Theaters, as well as several historical articles for the *Yearbook of the Imperial Theaters*. The likely explanation for his resignation as Manager of the St. Petersburg Office is that he was preparing for his promotion to membership of the Council (*sovet*) of the Ministry of the Imperial Court, which came in March 1900.[67] Thereafter Pogozhev appears to have withdrawn from any involvement in the administration of the Imperial Theaters, despite continuing to write about them.

The origin of the *Proekt* is explained by Pogozhev in his Introduction to the work. On January 20, 1899, Pogozhev submitted a memorandum to the then Director of Imperial Theaters, I. A. Vsevolozhsky, urging him to establish a commission to review the status of the Imperial Theaters. Vsevolozhsky agreed to Pogozhev's proposal to establish such a commission and to his suggestion that it commence its deliberations in March 1899 with the intention of completing its task and publishing the *Proekt* by September 1900 (which it did). The commission, which was granted the right to consult whomsoever it wished, consisted of ten officials from the Directorate and the Ministry of the Imperial Court, namely: Pogozhev, the commission's chairman; Telyakovsky, the Manager of the Moscow Office of Imperial Theaters; Gershelman, an assistant in the St. Petersburg Office; Molchanov, head of the technical section of the St. Petersburg Office; Pisniachevskii, the Inspector of the St. Petersburg Theater School; Zlobin, an official in the Chancellery of the Ministry of the Imperial Court; Strukov, an official from the "*Kabinet* of His Imperial Highness"; Kokovikhin, an assistant of Strukov, invited for legal consultation; Riudman, an official from the *kontrol* (inspection unit) of the Ministry of the Imperial Court; and Petrov, an assistant in the technical section of the St. Petersburg Office, who acted as the commission's clerk. An eleventh member, leader of the court orchestra Baron Shtakelberg, joined the commission a month later in April 1899.[68] Thus, as one contemporary observer put it, the *Proekt* was "not only formulated in the depths of the Chancellery [of the Ministry of the Imperial Court], but was encircled by the mystery of the Chancellery."[69] Perhaps the most notable feature of the commission is the absence of Imperial Theater artists (with the insignificant exception of Shtakelberg), a fact that underlined the extent to which the *Proekt* was a product of the administration and thereby reflected the views and priorities of Imperial Theater officialdom.

In May 1899, the commission published a list of what it considered to be the twelve most important reforms that should be incorporated into the new statute. The most important task was the "legal formulation of the tasks of the Imperial Theaters," that is, the formal codification of the rules and regulations. The second most important issue to be considered—although it appears rather trivial—was a change in the names of the central and local administrative organs of the Imperial Theaters. The remaining points on the list largely related to ways in which the Imperial Theaters could save money and plan the repertoire more effectively.[70] When the *Proekt* was published, the feature that provoked most interest was the proposal that money be saved by altering the way in which drama troupe artists were paid: They would receive a much smaller annual salary, on top of which they would be paid according to the number of performances they participated in, a system known as "one-off payment" (*razovaia uplata*).[71] This reflected general concern that the main issue confronting the Imperial Theaters at the time was rising deficits, as noted above.

The real significance of the *Proekt* is revealed in the opening sentence of the Introduction:

> At the present time, the Imperial Theaters are living through an epoch in which those people at the helm of theater affairs—and the sincere lovers of theater who are certain of the supreme significance of its mission—are beginning to think seriously about the future fate of the institution which has honorably served Russian education [*prosveshchenie*] for a century and a half.[72]

The dilemma for the Imperial Theaters had developed after the assassination of Alexander II in 1881 and the ensuing administrative changes. Under the new tsar, Alexander III, the new Minister of the Imperial Court, Illarion Vorontsov-Dashkov, and the new Director of Imperial Theaters, Ivan Vsevolozhsky, a program of reform in the Imperial Theaters was initiated. Pogozhev identified two waves of reforms. The first occurred in 1882–83, the centerpiece of which was the end of the Imperial Theater monopoly on performances in the two capitals. The other key features, according to Pogozhev, were an increase in the opera budget to augment the orchestra and chorus and raise standards; the augmentation of the artistic troupes and a rise in artists' wages; a rise in wages for the staff of the Directorate; and a rise in authors' fees. Unfortunately, these increased expenditures had not been met by increased income and the deficits increased. This resulted in the second wave of reforms, which lasted from 1884 to the end of the 1890s, and which focused on curbing the expenditure of the Imperial Theaters by closing down the Italian opera troupe in 1885 and the German drama troupe in 1890.[73] By the time Pogozhev conceived his *Proekt*, however, the financial position of the Imperial Theaters was still precarious and further money-saving ideas were required, a problem that was addressed by the administration regardless of the *Proekt*, as we have already seen.

Yet in addition to the general concern about the Imperial Theater budget, there was a more fundamental issue confronting officials: What was the function of the Imperial Theaters? This question initially had been posed by Vsevolozhsky in a paper presented to Vorontsov-Dashkov in March 1882. According to Vsevolozhsky, the Ministry of the Imperial Court needed to answer two questions at the time of the abrogation of the Imperial Theater monopoly: First, what does the Imperial Theater mean for the state, and second, what does it mean for the court? According to Pogozhev, Vsevolozhsky's answer to his own first question was that the Imperial Theater was first and foremost a "state pedagogical institution, meeting the educative tasks of the government." But, in answer to his second question, Vsevolozhsky insisted that it was also a "court institution ... a constant point of contact between the tsar's generosity and the aesthetic tastes of his subjects." Vsevolozhsky concluded that the Imperial Theaters must retain these two characteristics: They must be "model" (*obraztsovyi*) theaters, and "brilliant institutions, corresponding to the dignity [*dostoinstvo*] of the Imperial Court"; simultaneously a "state, model theater" and "an attribute of the brilliant decor [*obstanovka*] of the Imperial Court."[74] Thus the court, through its patronage of theater art, arrogated for itself, at least theoretically, the leading role in Russian theater culture. The official position appeared to be that there could be no better theater because there could be no better patron.

Pogozhev's memorandum of January 1899 to Vsevolozhsky reiterated the Director's 1882 definition of the Imperial Theaters' function. "The Directorate of Imperial Theaters," he began, "has a unique status among governmental institutions. The external significance of the Directorate seems bifurcated." Pogozhev explained that the Imperial Theaters appeared to have two separate—though not necessarily incompatible—functions. The Directorate was "a state institution which, by means of clear artistic methods, fulfills part of the general educative tasks of the government." But it was also a "court institution, that is, one of the components of the outwardly brilliant decor of the Russian Imperial Throne."[75]

Why was the status and function of the Imperial Theaters an issue for Pogozhev? The answer lies in the wider context of developments in Russian theatrical culture in the late tsarist period. The new theaters that had emerged after 1882 challenged the traditional status of the Imperial Theaters as the exclusive purveyors of dramatic and musical entertainment. The weekly journal *Theater and Art* (*Teatr i iskusstvo*) summed up the dilemma when discussing the (unrealized) idea of creating a new Imperial Theater in Odessa: "Our epoch is not the same as that when the state theaters were created. The need for theatrical presentations, constituting a distinctive feature of the upper classes of society, has been democratized, it has become more general...."[76] Given the increasing competition from new theaters, and the wide variety of entertainments to choose from, was there any justification for the Imperial Theaters retaining their privileged status? "In the end," wrote Pogozhev, "the Imperial Theater lost its historical physiognomy of the grandest of the landowner [*pomeshchichii*] theaters and already a second decade [after the end of its monopoly] it awaits elucidation of the principles of its existence, definition of the precise terms of its activity, and their systematic legislative consolidation."[77] Thus, Pogozhev was calling for clarification of their function. The central issue was "the absence of a precisely defined, leading idea and stable system in the administration of the Imperial Theaters," as well as the "obsolescence, confusion and incompleteness of the [existing] legislation relating to the Imperial Theaters."[78]

Pogozhev's considered response was simply to give renewed emphasis to the idea of a dual function for the Imperial Theaters. Article one of the *Proekt* states: "The Imperial Theaters function as an academy of all types of stage art in Russia and, as such, constitute a state institution fulfilling the general educative tasks of the Government by means of model productions. At the same time, the Imperial Theaters form a Court Establishment [*Pridvornoe Ustanovlenie*], working for the maintenance of the outwardly brilliant decor of the Russian Imperial Court."[79] This definition of the function of the Imperial Theaters was redolent of the idea of national theater that had emerged in European theater capitals in the eighteenth and nineteenth centuries. Vienna had led the way in the eighteenth century. In 1776, Joseph II had abolished the monopoly of the two court theaters in the city, somewhat earlier than comparative monopoly abolitions in other theater capitals in the nineteenth century. At the same time, he announced that one of the Viennese court theaters, the Hofburgtheater, would become a national theater. According to an historian of Viennese theater, Joseph's announcement was a response to the rise of the educated bourgeoisie and the consequent need for theatricals that would be accessible to a wider audience. The traditional court theaters had housed foreign companies which made them less accessible because of the language barriers. Moreover, the national theater would be a non-commercial theater, sponsored by the state. The idea of a national theater was associated further with the notion of Enlightenment cultural education and, in particular, with the promotion of national culture.[80] In other words, a national theater would represent the culture of a whole "nation," not just a court circle. Historically, such theaters have been designed to assert the cultural-national identity, in particular the language, of groups subordinated to imperial powers.[81]

The Imperial Theaters were never explicitly defined as national theaters, yet in its emphasis on the educative value of the theaters, and the tentative assertion of a Russian nationality in the art of the theaters, the *Proekt* was a move in that direction. Pogozhev states that a theater can fulfill one of three functions: it can be a purely commercial undertaking, when the principal objective is to make a profit; it can be purely for entertainment purposes, following public taste without regard to quality or financial profit; or it can be an institution with "higher educative tasks" in which the objective is to focus on the quality of the repertoire and monetary gain is a secondary consideration.[82] There was no doubt which function the Imperial Theaters were designed to fulfill:

> The choice of the third principle set out above, in all its purity, points to the logic of the state structure of the great Russian Monarchy, with the history of the Imperial Theater with its undoubted services to the education of Russian society [*obshchestvo*], with which are marked 200 years of the existence of court theatrical entertainments.[83]

The use of the word *obshchestvo*, which was making its way into Russian educated vocabulary during the period, is instructive. The term broadly referred to civil society. Pogozhev was certainly not claiming that the Imperial Theaters were part of civil society—by definition they were institutionally separate from it (*pridvornyi*, not *obshchestvennyi*). Rather he was identifying a relationship—whether it existed or not in practice—between court institutions and civil society that had not previously been articulated. It would be injudicious to overstate this point: The word *obshchestvo* does not appear frequently in the *Proekt*. Yet Pogozhev's remarks point to the fact that Imperial Theater officialdom was cognizant that it had to assert a specific function for the Imperial Theaters and to defend their status in the face of a larger theatrical world.

A cardinal feature of national theaters is that they promote indigenous, national artistic endeavor. Again, this was not a prominent feature of Pogozhev's *Proekt*, but its background presence merits attention. Pogozhev underlined the importance of the Imperial Theaters as citadels of Russian national culture in two respects. First of all, the *Proekt* stipulated that the Imperial Theater repertoire must focus chiefly on the works of Russian dramatists and composers and that foreign works translated into Russian must not amount to more than one-third of the total number of works produced per season. The number of Russian opera productions must be no less than ten per season, and there must be at least thirty performances of Russian operas per season. There was also an emphasis on the classics, both Russian and foreign—underlining the educative role of the theaters—the number of which should be strengthened: Each season no less than ten "major plays" from the classical repertoire should be produced.[84]

A second way in which Pogozhev emphasized Russian-ness in the Imperial Theaters was indirect, namely the slightly disparaging manner in which he referred to the Mikhailovsky, the home of a French drama troupe. Pogozhev's remarks on the Mikhailovsky were made in the context of considering ways in which further savings could be made in Imperial Theater expenditures. One idea mooted was that theaters under the Directorate's authority could be leased to private entrepreneurs who wanted to establish their own theater companies. The problem with this idea, of course, was that it would make the theaters commercial. "The single exception that can be permitted to be handed over to private enterprise," wrote Pogozhev, "is the French theater in Petersburg, as a theater with more modest aims than the model theaters."[85] "It is impossible," he claims further, "to consider the French theater in Petersburg a significant model theater." Nevertheless, he continues, "in its capacity as a Court theater, it is essential as a traditional part of the splendor of the Imperial Court. This is not to deny that the French theater at the present time is a useful model for Russian theater, if not in the sphere of repertoire, then in forming a school of stage performance and declamation."[86] There is in these remarks a clear sense that the Russian troupes were considered superior to the French troupe. The emphasis on the role of the Mikhailovsky as a "court" theater implies a restricted role, and the reference to "declamation," in the context of an era in which declamation was increasingly regarded as outmoded and anti-realistic, is equally scathing.

This, of course, does not amount to an explicit statement to the effect that the Imperial Theaters *were* national theaters; but the undercurrents are unmistakable. It is also noteworthy that the first (and only) histories of the Imperial Theaters as a distinct institutional category begin to appear in this period (from the 1880s through to the 1900s), as noted in the Introduction to this study. There was, in other words, a growing awareness of Russian theater in general and the specific role of the Imperial Theaters in particular, allied to a wider sense of national, cultural renaissance.

The Pogozhev Commission, therefore, indicated what the administration regarded as the function of the Imperial Theaters in a changing theatrical landscape in Russia. This fact is in itself significant: The representatives of court power actually theorized about the cultural institutions they had dominion over. It is important not to forget that the *Proekt* largely consisted of a detailed exposition of the various rules and regulations of the Imperial Theaters, and that it was never adopted as a legal statute. However, the fact that it was drawn up in the first place is significant. It confirmed that the Imperial Theaters were considered embellishments of the court, but that they also had, in theory, a wider national-educative function. The *Proekt* further highlighted a latent dilemma for the Imperial Theaters: were they to be defined in terms of their unique court status; or must they establish and develop a wider role? In the meantime, Pogozhev concluded they must be exemplary "national" theaters that nevertheless remained part of the state and adornments of the court.

* * * *

The objective of this chapter has been to illustrate the manner in which the St. Petersburg Imperial Theaters were formally connected to the tsarist court/government, how that connection determined certain general characteristics of the theaters, and how the administration viewed the role of the theaters in 1900: in other words, how culture and power were formally intertwined. The connections between the state and the theaters were not merely nominal. The theaters were administered and financed by the state, and they were imbued with several characteristics that symbolically identified them with power in tsarist Russia and clearly distinguished them from private and popular theaters. Therefore it remains justifiable to refer to them as court/government/state institutions. There was almost a "program" for the Imperial Theaters in the sense that they were required by the state to uphold the reigning values of tsarism such as Orthodoxy; and the Pogozhev Commission confirmed that they were to function as embellishments of the court. That was their special feature in the context of a changing Russian theatrical landscape. In that sense the Imperial Theaters were constituent parts of the state's political paraphernalia. At the same time, the Pogozhev *Proekt* indicated that the administration saw a wider, less exclusive role for the Imperial Theaters than their court status might have implied. They were to be both court institutions and "national" educators, guardians of art in the face of the rise of commercial entertainment.

Chapter 2

The Directorate
and the Artists

The fact that the St. Petersburg Imperial Theaters were part of the Russian court's apparatus meant that they possessed several characteristics which set them apart from other theaters in the capital. Yet how far did court administration affect the central task of the St. Petersburg Imperial Theaters as cultural institutions, namely the creation and performance of dramatic, operatic, and balletic art? Conventional wisdom holds that the artistic development of the Russian Imperial Theaters was impeded by the fact of court supervision. That is to say, the relationship between the court department responsible for overseeing the affairs of the theaters, the Directorate of Imperial Theaters, and the drama, opera, and ballet troupes was antagonistic. Indeed, insofar as there is a central theme in the small Imperial Theater historiography, it is that court status rendered the Imperial Theaters oppressed, rigorously controlled institutions, identified with the conservatism of the court rather than with the rich experimentation and innovation of the wider Russian theatrical world.

The Directorate of Imperial Theaters was established in 1766 with responsibility for the affairs of the Russian state theater. It has been portrayed by historians of Russian theater as a bureaucratic institution that wielded its authority to the detriment of Russian theater culture, particularly during the late imperial period. There is a consensus that the artistic evolution of the Imperial Theaters was held back by their subjugation to the Ministry of the Imperial Court, that the Directorate was "conservative," and that it failed to understand the creative requirements and sensibilities of the artists. In fact, the reputation of the Directorate is not dissimilar to that of the four infamous First Gentlemen of the Bedchamber, who personified the meddling of the French court in the affairs of the Parisian royal theaters—particularly the Comédie-Française—before 1789.[1]

A typical example is Volkov's assessment that "the bureaucratic apparatus of all the theater offices [the Imperial Theater administration] and irresponsible influences frequently paralyzed any reform initiatives, and condemned the Imperial stage to routine and conservatism. This was particularly felt in Petersburg."[2] Bogdanov-Berezovskii argues that the Imperial Theater administration was conservative and displayed a marked preference for the older Russian composers and for the classics, particularly those works which were regarded as apologies for orthodoxy and autocracy, such as *A Life for the Tsar, Ruslan and Liudmila, Prince Igor*, and *Khovanshchina*. The newer operas of Rimsky-Korsakov, such as *Kashchei the Immortal* and *The Golden Cockerel*, as well as the works of young composers from the modernist school like Igor Stravinsky's *The Nightingale, The Firebird*, and *Petrushka*, and Sergei Prokofiev's *The Gambler*, were ignored. "This, in the end, finds its expression in the strengthening of bureaucratic oppression in the administration of the [Mariinsky] troupe, in the suppression of artists' initiative, in the encouragement of 'leading artists' [*prem'erstva*]," concluded Bogdanov-Berezovskii.[3] Writing of the Mariinsky opera and ballet during the pre–1917 period, Kenigsberg suggests that the "development of Russian art was not assisted by the bureaucratism of the theater management...."[4] The Soviet *Theater Encyclopedia* contends that artists at the Alexandrinsky were "compelled by the policy of the Directorate, as well as by the tastes of influential bourgeois audiences, to waste their talent performing feeble plays."[5] Gorchakov, who refers to the bureaucrats who administered the Imperial Theaters as "complete autocrats," writes that: "On the crown stage, this kind of corporal-of-the-guard director was a protector of clichés and routine."[6] Slonim, in his history of Russian theater, writes of "bureaucratic red tape and a formal hierarchy, which undermined the Imperial Theaters...."[7] Clowes, in an essay on the Moscow Art Theater, claims that the Moscow Art Theater "was conceived as an alternative to government-run theaters, which were top-heavy with bureaucracy and short on innovative spirit."[8] The verdict is unambiguous: The development of Russian theater culture was hindered by the court administration of the Imperial Theaters.

Yet, in what appears to be a paradox, the St. Petersburg Imperial Theaters produced exemplary dramatic, operatic, and balletic art, much of which achieved world renown. In addition to the resources at their disposal, this was a function of the presence in the troupes of some of the most outstanding individual talents of the period, who either spent their whole careers or considerable parts of them in the Imperial Theaters. The superlative talents of Russian Silver Age culture who were based in the Imperial Theaters included actors (Konstantin Varlamov, Vladimir Davydov); actresses (Maria Savina); singers (Fyodor Chaliapin,* Ivan Ershov); dancers (Tamara Karsav-

---

Chaliapin was officially based in Moscow, but regularly performed in St. Petersburg.

ina, Matilda Kshesinskaya, Olga Preobrazhenskaya, Anna Pavlova, Vaslav Nijinsky); choreographers (Marius Petipa, Mikhail Fokin); conductors (Eduard Napravnik); *régisseurs* (Alexander Sanin, Vsevolod Meyerhold); and set designers (Lev Bakst, Konstantin Korovin, Alexander Golovin). This chapter explores that ostensible paradox (the coexistence of a repressive Directorate and a flourishing artistic culture) by examining the relationship between the Directorate and the St. Petersburg Imperial Theaters. Was the Directorate a negative influence in the affairs of the theaters or, contrary to the consensus, was the Directorate a positive influence that enabled them to flourish? Or, alternatively, did the Directorate largely refrain from interfering in the artistic affairs of the theaters? Did the above-mentioned talents flourish *despite* the administration? What exactly was the relationship between the Russian court and its St. Petersburg Imperial Theaters in the late tsarist period?

The relationship between the Directorate and the artists was influenced, inevitably, by the personality and conduct of the individual Director. As noted in the previous chapter, the last Director, Telyakovsky, was a soldier by training, not an artist, although he was keen to stress in his memoirs an affinity with the arts, recording that he had played the piano from the age of six and that as a child he had met such musical luminaries as Peter Tchaikovsky, Anton Rubinstein, and the Mariinsky opera artist F. P. Komissarzhevsky.[9]

Assessments of Telyakovsky by contemporaries range from the openly sycophantic, through the reluctantly complimentary, to the implicitly dismissive and condescending. The prominent Moscow Maly Theater actor and dramatist Alexander Sumbatov-Yuzhin was consistently complimentary towards him, congratulating the Director upon his appointment in 1901[10] and referring to his "truly artistic and enlightened administration of the Imperial Theaters" on the tenth anniversary of his Directorship.[11] The *régisseur* Fyodor Komissarzhevsky (son of the above mentioned F. P. Komissarzhevsky and brother of Vera Komissarzhevskaya) recalled that the Imperial Theaters were indebted to Telyakovsky for a "modern—and higher standard of productions.... He introduced work by modern writers and musicians into the repertoire...," and despite doubts about Telyakovsky's suitability when he was appointed, "he proved a success, and was, like C. B. Cochran in London or Reinhardt in Germany, that rare combination, a sound business man who possessed artistic ideas."[12] Chaliapin was impressed by Telyakovsky, even though he generally felt uneasy about working in what he called the Imperial Theater atmosphere of "men in uniform." "It was quite clear to me that he [Telyakovsky] not only understood, but had real knowledge of the art he served so well."[13]

Yet others expressed anxiety about the fact that Telyakovsky had a military rather than artistic background. It was remarked by some that "the man who was in charge of horses will now be in charge of actors."[14] His military background resulted in the new Director bringing to the administration what

Gnedich called a "tone of regimental discipline," evidenced, for example, in his attitude to the management of the artists—in contrast to his predecessor Volkonsky's relaxed and informal approachability, Telyakovsky informed artists that they could meet him between twelve and two P.M. on Tuesdays and Fridays.[15] Rimsky-Korsakov, on returning from Paris in May 1907, remarked disdainfully that "in Paris, the director of the theater is at the same time the chief regisseur [*sic*]. He's always appointed from among the former artists, which can only prove beneficial to the whole enterprise. It's not like this in our country, where people totally unrelated to music are often appointed to the directorship of the theaters."[16] In March 1913, when false rumors spread that Telyakovsky was to resign in connection with Maria Pavlovna's abortive attempt to bring Francis de Croisset to the Mikhailovsky and elevate Krupensky to the position of Director, an anonymous theater journalist reminded readers that, "according to Freud's theory a dream is the disclosure of our secret and unconscious desires," intimating that, while there might have been no truth in the rumors, they existed because many people *wanted* Telyakovsky to resign.[17] Telyakovsky was unperturbed, indeed mildly amused, by such rumors, merely noting their existence in his diary without comment.[18]

Seeking to balance competing impressions of Telyakovsky, the historian might reasonably conclude that the man was respectfully tolerated by people who nevertheless did not consider him ideally suited for the position of Director. Such judicious balance is found in the retrospective assessments of two of the most prominent artists of the time. The Mariinsky's chief conductor, Eduard Napravnik, wrote:

> Fairness demands that it be pointed out that V. A. Telyakovsky, a benevolent, equitable, accessible man, gaining in his long administration significant experience, would have been quite able, had he wanted to, fully to serve a single healthy principle—to administer the theaters in friendly cooperation with people competent in all specializations. Incidentally, there reigned the "principles": "First of all revenues, and then everything else" or "First of all quantity, and then quality."[19]

Likewise, the celebrated set designer Alexander Golovin was disinclined to throw vitriol at his former superior: "A soldier by education, he was, however, 'in his place' in the role of leader of the Imperial Theaters. Perhaps he lacked specialist knowledge, but he had, at any rate, good taste, which often helped him out."[20] In other words, while history will correctly refrain from considering Telyakovsky in any sense the architect of the Imperial Theaters' artistic achievements of the late tsarist period, the absence of outright hostility among most contemporaries (either commenting at the time or reminiscing) signifies that he did not play a malevolent role in the creative work of the theaters.

Of course, such personal experiences, impressions and judgments only provide a flavor of the relative esteem or disregard in which the "diminutive colonel" was held. While they certainly provide some clues about the relationship between the administration and the artists, we will need to examine in greater detail the history of the Directorate under Telyakovsky in order to illustrate its specific functions and ascertain the extent to which it could have impeded the artistic development of the St. Petersburg Imperial Theaters.

The primary function of the St. Petersburg Imperial Theaters was to entertain their audiences by staging exemplary performances of drama, opera, and ballet. If there is any validity to the proposition that the Directorate interfered unreasonably in the affairs of the theaters, and to the detriment of their art, this is where it would be evidenced most. So how was the artistic activity of the Imperial Theaters organized? What was the "balance of power" between the officials of the St. Petersburg Office and the artists? How far, and in what ways, did the Directorate participate in the primary function of the theaters?

First, it is necessary to note that each troupe—drama, opera, and ballet—had a leader, approved by the Director. Drama troupe leaders tended to be appointed from outside the troupe itself, while opera and ballet troupe leaders tended to be established artists from within the troupe. The leader of the Alexandrinsky from January 1901 to 1908 was Gnedich. His official title was Manager of the Troupe (*upravliaiushchii truppoi*): This was a new title, as Gnedich's predecessor, Evtikhii Karpov, had been known as the Chief *Régisseur* (*glavnyi rezhissër*), a title indicative of the tasks allotted to the leader, who was essentially an *artistic* leader. He was the official authority for all artistic matters arising within the theater, although his decisions were formally subject to approval by the St. Petersburg Office. Gnedich was succeeded by Nestor Kotliarevskii, whose official title from the 1909-10 season was Superintendent of the Repertoire and the Troupe (*zaveduiushchii repertuarom i truppoi*), again emphasizing the specifically artistic nature of his task. The Mariinsky opera troupe was led by the *régisseurs* A. Ia. Morozov and G. I. Monakhov, who were joined during the 1906-07 season by Vasilii Shkafer. The following season, Shkafer was replaced by Meyerhold and Peter Melnikov. By the 1909-10 season, Monakhov had departed, and the Chief *Régisseur* was Ioakim Tartakov. The official artistic leader of the Mariinsky ballet troupe, known as its first ballet master, was the legendary Frenchman Marius Petipa, who dominated the Russian ballet during the second half of the nineteenth century. Although Petipa had effectively retired by 1903, he retained the title of first ballet master until his death in 1910. In the early twentieth century, he was assisted by a second ballet master, successively Lev Ivanov, A. Koppini, Alexander Shiriaev, Nicholas Legat, and Nicholas Sergeev. After Petipa's death, Legat became first ballet master.

These people directed, orchestrated, and choreographed Imperial Theater productions. According to Gnedich, troupe leaders, as well as certain influential individuals not formally in charge of troupes, even "recommended or dismissed staff, they planned the repertoire."[21] Yet, as we will see, these were officially the prerogatives of the Directorate, and Napravnik wrote that, in fact, the Director "was granted unlimited power over all and with all, including the colossal budget of the Petrograd and Moscow Theaters."[22] The key question here is: to what degree was the Directorate involved in creative processes? We will explore this question by looking at three key areas of activity involved in creating the art of the theaters, namely recruitment and supervision of the artists, selection of the repertoire, and the artistic and technical details of staging a performance.

Recruitment and Supervision of Artists

Although the Head of the Court Chancellery, Mosolov, often received aspiring artists with notes from Rasputin asking him to "fix it" for them,[23] it was the Directorate that was responsible for securing contracts with artists and for controlling their activities within the Imperial Theater organization. This was recognized by most artists wishing to enter the service of the Imperial Theaters. For example, when there were rumors of a vacancy for a conductor at the Moscow Bolshoi in March 1908, Telyakovsky received a letter from I. O. Palitsyn, who humbly wrote: "I allow myself to remind [you] of my existence."[24] In March 1913, a singer named Ivanova-Petrovskaia approached Telyakovsky with a letter of recommendation from Fredericks. An impromptu audition was held, but the Director felt that, although she had a nice voice, Ivanova-Petrovskaia was not sufficiently "dramatic" and therefore was of "little use to us" (*"malo nam nuzhny"*).[25] But the Directorate did not simply wait for aspiring artists to approach its Offices. It also approached them, particularly those talented and successful artists who might greatly augment the creative profile of the theaters. By way of example, it is apposite to recount the manner in which Telyakovsky recruited Chaliapin back to the Imperial Theaters at the end of the 1890s. Chaliapin had performed at the Mariinsky Theater from 1894 to 1896, but had been lured to the Private Opera of Mamontov in Moscow. Chaliapin then proceeded to establish a reputation for himself, and Telyakovsky, who had recently been appointed Manager of the Moscow Office, resolved to coax him back to the Imperial Theaters. Evidently taking into account the singer's predilection for alcohol, Telyakovsky arranged for his assistant to treat Chaliapin to an intoxicating breakfast at the Slavianskii Bazar on December 12, 1898. After breakfast, the two men repaired to Telyakovsky's flat where the Manager persuaded Chaliapin to rejoin the Imperial opera for double the remuneration he received from Mamontov. Telyakovsky was behaving somewhat irresponsibly, for he knew that an Imperial Theater artist then was paid 3,600 rubles per annum, whereas meeting the offer made to Chaliapin would entail a salary of 9,000, and eventually 11,000, rubles per annum. The Director in St. Petersburg, Vsevolozhsky, disapproved of such a payment, but he knew that Telyakovsky could use his connection with the Minister of the Imperial Court to get his own way, and so he concurred with the proposal. Meantime, when Chaliapin sobered up, he changed his mind. He explained to Telyakovsky that he did not really want to leave Mamontov's Opera. However, he was promptly reminded of a forfeit—15,000 rubles—that he was obliged to pay in the event of the contravention or nullification of his contract. Chaliapin failed to raise the money, and duly returned to the Imperial Theaters.[26]

The Directorate's methods of recruitment occasionally provoked disquiet. Telyakovsky was criticized for going to Paris to recruit actors for the French troupe, although the complaint was less about his enthusiasm as a recruiter than his taste for French drama.[27] In 1910, Napravnik was incensed to learn from the newspapers that Albert Coates had been invited by Telyakovsky to work as a conductor at the opera.[28] Napravnik had nothing against Coates; but he had expected Telyakovsky to mention that he was recruiting a new conductor! Telyakovsky also procured for the Imperial Theaters the services of such eminent artists—many of whom had been members of the innovative *World of Art* (*Mir iskusstva*) group—as Bakst, Benois, Fokin, Golovin, Meyerhold and Rakhmaninov. The fact that the Directorate employed such prominent and talented artists belies the suggestion that it was "short on innovative spirit." Of course, someone like Meyerhold was compelled to tone down his artistic radicalism in the Imperial Theaters, and he confined his avant-garde work, under the pseudonym "Dr. Dapertutto," to clubs and studios at that time, but nevertheless his lavish Petersburg spectacles produced with Golovin were considered spectacular, definitive achievements and ranked high in the pantheon of late imperial culture. Such productions as *Don Juan* and *Masquerade* confirmed the St. Petersburg Imperial Theaters as the leading artistic institutions of the late imperial period, and by hiring the talented personnel to produce them the Directorate under Telyakovsky signaled a progressive and ambitious approach to Russian theater culture. Indeed, the hostility shown Meyerhold by many Imperial Theater artists indicates that, in fact, they were more conservative than the Directorate.[29]

As the effective employer of Imperial Theater artists, the Directorate enjoyed the contractual right to direct their activities within the theaters, such as which roles they might play and in which productions. The final clause of the artists' contract read:

> The artist must always be prepared to fulfill the instructions of the Directorate, even when he is not engaged in the advertised performance, and in

the event of a sudden change of performance he is obligated, absenting himself from home, to leave a note by which he can be tracked down. In the event of the cancellation of a performance caused by the non-observance of this rule, the artist is subject to a fine to the measure of / / part of full pay.[30]

The Directorate and its Offices were responsible for enforcing the terms of an artist's contract, for maintaining discipline in the theaters, and for keeping the general work of the troupes within the confines of its instructions. There are many examples. In January 1905, the

Contemporary sketch of Telyakovsky and Chaliapin. *Vospominaniia* (Moscow-Leningrad, 1965)

Directorate felt it expedient to remind artists that, according to their contracts, they were not allowed to perform on private stages (though permission was often granted for this; for example, Meyerhold remained active in experimental theaters while still employed by the Directorate).[31] The St. Petersburg Office expressed concern that two performances in October 1908 at the Alexandrinsky started nine minutes and six minutes late respectively, and consequently an announcement was issued to the effect that the leader of the drama troupe was responsible for ensuring that performances began at eight o'clock precisely. In October 1908 the administration complained that, once again, the change of scenery at the Alexandrinsky had been accompanied by "noise and clatter," and it advised that silence be maintained at such times.[32] In September 1909 the St. Petersburg Office informed artists that during the 1908-09 season it had received fifty-nine reports from the drama troupe leader, and eighteen from the opera troupe leader concerning the absence, "without valid reason," of artists from rehearsals at which they had been instructed to appear, and in addition to these absences there were valid absences caused by illness. The Office reminded artists that this rendered the creative work of the theaters difficult, and it reminded them that absence or lateness—over one quarter of an hour—merited financial punishment.[33] Finally, perhaps the greatest affront to artists' egos was the Directorate's injunction that curtain calls during intervals be restricted to three because they slowed down the performance and hampered costume changes.[34]

Instructions and injunctions such as the ones presented above were intended to improve the quality of performances. The appeal to make less noise during scene changes, or to make sure performances started on time,

Contemporary sketch of Telyakovsky, complete with Horse Guard regimental spurs, setting off for Paris to recruit new artists. *Vospominaniia* (Moscow-Leningrad, 1965)

might serve to remind artists that they were supervised by an imperial court department, yet they cannot be construed as evidence that the Directorate impeded the artistic creativity of the theaters. On the contrary, they indicate a concern for precision and perfection in Imperial Theater performances.

Selecting the Repertoire

The repertoire is the soul of a theater, its *raison d'être*, and is therefore of fundamental importance to the artists. The St. Petersburg Imperial Theater repertoire was ultimately decided by the Directorate and, in practice, the theater troupes exercised a minimal degree of influence over its content. The administration's hegemony over the repertoire was emphasized by the fact that, when a work was selected for production, performance rights were given to the Directorate, not to an individual theater.[35] Individual theaters were not permitted to introduce a new work to the repertoire or proceed to its rehearsal until the Director had established with its author that it would be produced[36] (though this did not always deter the theaters from proceeding with preliminary preparations—in May 1908, Rimsky-Korsakov asked Telyakovsky to inform him whether certain operas of his could be performed because the roles, he said, had already been allotted[37]).

The Directorate did not have a systematic procedure for selecting the repertoire. The Director often decided that he wanted particular works performed and simply instructed the theaters to produce them. However, it is clear that the administration welcomed a dialogue of sorts on what should be staged and there was constant exchange about the repertoire between officials, authors, composers, and theater artists, many of whom were themselves amateur dramatists. For example, Sumbatov-Yuzhin, a leading actor at the Moscow Maly, also wrote plays and petitioned Telyakovsky to have them staged in both Moscow and St. Petersburg.[38] The Alexandrinsky actor Nicholas Khodotov even read a play he had written to Telyakovsky, who liked it and promised to recommend it for the Moscow stage.[39] The whole process of petitioning, humorously illustrated by a cartoon in *Theater and Art*, which depicted a dramatist clutching a copy of his work while bowing and fawning to Telyakovsky,[40] had its critics. Rimsky-Korsakov in particular complained about having to ask the Directorate to produce his operatic works, gaining the sympathy of *Theater and Art*, which asked

> Why must authors seek the stage? One would think that, on the contrary, the stage should seek authors.... The theater administration is a subordinate and dependent organ. If authors ceased to provide works for the stage, then the theater administration would remain only to receive salaries, and it could do no business. Meanwhile, the work of the author remains thus, independent from the administration and even the stage which it manages.[41]

Yet, while the Directorate's control over the repertoire obviously denied the theaters repertorial autonomy, it did not necessarily hinder the creativity of the troupes. The Directorate, contrary to the allegations of some critics, took its role seriously and displayed an interest in "quality control" of Imperial Theater art. For instance, it was assisted in the task of selection of the repertoire by an advisory organ, the Theater-Literary Committee (*Teatralno-literaturnyi komitet*), established in 1855, and from 1891 consisting of two separate committees, one each for St. Petersburg and Moscow. Its task was to comment on the literary merit of plays which had already been passed by the censor and which the Imperial Theaters were interested in staging. It was not concerned with opera or ballet.[42] The Committee's role was purely advisory and its approval of a play did not guarantee acceptance by the Directorate. For example, Karpov had a play unanimously approved by the Committee, but it was never staged.[43] In 1903, the Directorate even attempted to establish a formal consultative Repertoire Council in the Alexandrinsky to allow the artists a greater say in what was produced, but that project was scuppered by the opposition of theater elders, such as Maria Savina, as it was in 1905 when an attempt was made to revive the Council (see Chapter 6).

Although the administration conveyed the impression that it was concerned to produce only works of merit, there is some evidence that attempts were made to influence the content of the repertoire through bribery. In 1908, Gnedich, according to his own account, procured through one of his colleagues a financial loan from an anonymous benefactor. Gnedich soon learned from his colleague that the benefactor (who turned out to be a certain Count Zubov) had written a play and would like him to read it. Gnedich obliged, but took no further action with the play, which he considered to be mediocre. Then in the autumn, Telyakovsky suddenly confronted Gnedich. According to Telyakovsky's comments at the time, he was concerned about the fact that certain "documents" indicated Gnedich had accepted a bribe of three thousand rubles from Zubov. Telyakovsky was somewhat perturbed because this was not only a "disgrace" for Gnedich, but reflected badly on the Directorate as a whole.[44] According to Gnedich's account, however, Telyakovsky was less concerned about the possibility that a bribe had been accepted than he was about the fact that Gnedich had not honored his part of the alleged deal. Gnedich claimed that Telyakovsky confronted him with the following: "You took money from count *** [*sic* in Gnedich's memoirs], but his play has not been staged.... He did you a favor, and you refuse him a production," to which Gnedich retorted that he had received no favor because he was paying interest on the "loan." Whether or not Gnedich did take a bribe, and whether or not Telyakovsky was alarmed simply because one of his subordinates had reneged on the "agreement," the whole episode highlighted the issue of corruption in the Imperial Theaters. Gnedich was given the benefit of the doubt. A letter signed by various authors, including Viktor Ryshkov, Vladimir Tikhonov, and Sumbatov-Yuzhin, appeared in *The New Times* (*Novoe vremia*) and *Theater and Art* testifying to his integrity and asserting that there could be no truth in the rumors that he had accepted bribes. And although Telyakovsky appears here in a negative light, he was probably no more corrupt than anyone else. Zubov was a close friend of Fredericks and it is possible that the Director simply wanted to avoid offending his superior by producing his friend's play. Nevertheless, Gnedich claimed that *Telyakovsky* had initially decided the play should *not* be produced. As a result of this episode, Gnedich decided he could no longer serve the Directorate, and resigned on October 31, 1908.[45] It is probable that he resigned with his integrity intact. He was a respected figure, not known for maladroitness or intrigue. Alexandrinsky artists paid tribute to his twenty-fifth anniversary as an author, and in an address the actor Dalmatov referred to his "exemplary attitude towards the artists."[46] Moreover, it is worth noting that Gnedich explained his reasons for resigning in a published letter which amounted to an attack on the Imperial Theater administration:

> Our stage is oppressed by officialdom. While the Office, besides standing at the head of the troupe, will accept or not accept a play, invite or dismiss artists, buy furniture, order scenery and so on, it is impossible to carry out business properly. Each stage must have one responsible person for all, and not an executor of Office orders, which instead of saying definitely yes or no, says neither yes nor no.[47]

Telyakovsky, for his part, claimed that he did not understand what all the fuss was about. In an interview about Gnedich's resignation, the Director provided an insight into how he viewed Gnedich and, by implication, the majority of Imperial Theater personnel:

> I don't understand why the public was agitated this time, as though some first-rate artist had been dismissed. A *bureaucrat* [*chinovnik*] has tendered

his resignation, and not at all a stage figure. I can call a person under my direct command nothing other than a bureaucrat. Do such misunderstandings arise between a superior and a subordinate only a little? What is our internal order to the public?[48]

In its role as arbiter of the Imperial Theater repertoire, the Directorate clearly was in a position to prevent artists producing certain works if it wanted to. Yet the evidence suggests that the Directorate under Telyakovsky was willing to broaden participation in the selection process. Moreover, between 1900 and 1917, the Alexandrinsky Theater produced a total of 394 *different* plays, and between 1900 and 1911 the Mariinsky Theater produced a total of sixty-six operas and fifty-one ballets. With such large numbers of productions, it is difficult to see how the Directorate can be blamed for hindering the development of the repertoire. Few major works that were produced elsewhere were not produced in the St. Petersburg Imperial Theaters.

Staging the Repertoire

According to the contract which Imperial Theater artists signed upon entering those august institutions, the Directorate was required to provide the necessary equipment for a production, such as the scenery and properties, as well as such essential thespian items as costumes, head gear, gloves, and shoes.[49] In terms of scenery, the Directorate ensured a reasonable supply of new material. It is true that many of the same sets were used in different, and eclectic, productions, but it is equally true that much time and money was spent creating new sets. In 1897, *Theater and Art* reported that the Directorate was paying full attention to improving the set design department (*dekorativnaia chast*) of the St. Petersburg Imperial Theaters, having ordered for the forthcoming season seventy sets, more than forty of which would be new.[50] The critic Iurii Beliaev remarked that the new scenery for the Alexandrinsky's production of *The Merchant of Venice* must have been expensive, belying any notion that the Directorate was unwilling to spend money on productions.[51] Some prominent productions had money and effort lavished on them to almost unprecedented degrees, such as *Masquerade*, for which Golovin reportedly made ten new backdrops and four new curtains.[52]

It is also difficult to sustain the argument that Imperial Theater production techniques were failing to keep pace with innovations pioneered by private theaters. In fact, at the beginning of the twentieth century, the Imperial Theaters were beginning to reform artistically. Pogozhev had reiterated their function as model theaters in 1900 in the context of competition from private theaters; yet the administration was not reluctant to learn from private theaters. In particular, Stanislavsky and the Moscow Art Theater's commitment to stage realism and historical authenticity in productions inspired the government stage to follow suit. In 1900 the set designer Apollinarii Vasnetsov traveled to the Novgorod and Arkhangel'sk regions to study the area's architecture for a new production of *Sadko* at the Mariinsky Theater. The Mariinsky *régisseur* Osip Palechek also began to adopt a more authentic approach to staging, for instance in his 1900 version of *Eugene Onegin* when, for the first time on the Imperial stage, he "individualized" the sets for the Larin and Petersburg balls—earlier productions had used similar sets, according to Gozenpud. Similarly, at the Alexandrinsky Gnedich endeavored to apply the Moscow Art Theater's principles of stage realism, as did Sanin, who had in fact worked with Stanislavsky at the Art Theater.[53] Imperial ballet in particular entered a new reform phase during the period in question (see Chapter 5). Such aesthetic developments were initiated by the artists, but they could not have occurred without the (at least tacit) cooperation of the Directorate.

Individual Directors often made direct contributions to Imperial Theater productions. During his administration, Vsevolozhsky, Director from 1881 to 1899, produced over one thousand drawings and paintings for ballets and operas, including costume designs for Tchaikovsky's ballets and for his operas *Yolande* and *The Queen of Spades*, many of which were used.[54] Telyakovsky was less active in this respect, tending to influence artistic content indirectly. An early example from Telyakovsky's tenure as Manager of the Moscow Office of Imperial Theaters is that in 1900 he denied Alexander Lensky, a leading actor and *régisseur* at the Maly Theater, full control over his production of *Romeo and Juliet*. Lensky believed that the *régisseur* should control the work of the set designer (*dekorator*), but Telyakovsky disagreed, insisting that they should be independent of one another. Telyakovsky's will prevailed, and to add injury to insult, Lensky's costume designs were rejected in favor of those by Mrs. Telyakovskaya, whom Benois described as "the *invisible directrice* ... the real source of her husband's inspiration...," a remark supported by Golovin, who noted that Telyakovsky often followed his wife's advice. Valts, a set designer from the Moscow Bolshoi Theater who became acquainted with Telyakovsky when the latter was Manager of the Moscow Office, likewise observed the influence of the Director's spouse: "Telyakovsky's wife considered herself an artist and loved to demonstrate her knowledge of art. She drew costumes for new productions and watched over them being carried into fulfillment."[55]

In general, however, the administration was not involved in the details of staging a performance. Despite having overall responsibility for such matters, the Directorate and its Offices delegated the daily tasks of artistic creativity to the artists, who worked under the guidance of their troupe leaders. By way of illustration, it is apposite to recount an example of Gnedich's duties as artistic leader of the Alexandrinsky. During the 1905-06 season,

Contemporary sketch of Telyakovsky at home with his wife and children, who are depicted designing costumes for Imperial Theater productions. The sketch is a scathing comment on what many considered to be the substandard contributions of Mrs. Telyakovskaya. *Vospominaniia* (Moscow-Leningrad, 1965)

Ostrovsky's *The Heart Is Not a Stone* was revived under the direction of Sanin. During a rehearsal, Konstantin Varlamov, who was playing the part of Inno-kentii, approached Gnedich and announced his withdrawal from the pro-duction. Although Varlamov had played this part for many years, he could not concur with Sanin's instruction that he clamber up a hill to reach monastery gates. Varlamov insisted he was not doing this for any "devil!" "All this century I've sat on a little stone at the front [of the stage]." It transpired that Varlamov's dissent derived from the fact—which he probably did not wish to confess to Sanin in full view of his colleagues—that he would be unable to hear the prompter from the "hill." According to Viven, Varlamov was the only artist who never knew his lines by heart! Gnedich discussed the matter with Sanin, and they agreed to resolve the problem by deploying a second prompter.[56]

The artists, then, determined the staging details, although the Direc-torate could interfere at whichever stage or level of a production it desired. It could no more take charge of every detail of a theater performance than a government can regulate its citizens' every action. The Directorate governed the framework of a production and interfered where it chose to. As Telyakovsky remarked to Napravnik when he offered him the post of leader of the Mariinsky opera troupe—which Napravnik declined to accept—"[y]ou will report to me, and I will ratify."[57] Even then, Telyakovsky conceded that it was possible to manipulate the Director. Writing of the Mariinsky bari-tone and *régisseur* Ioakim Tartakov, he claimed that, "if I knew him well, then Tartakov got to know me even better and was expertly able to get what he wanted, always pretending to be someone fulfilling my own wishes."[58] Gnedich even claimed that he could ignore the instructions of the Director. Telyakovsky once said to him: "You don't carry out my instructions." "They don't permit me to carry them out," replied Gnedich. "Who?" asked Telyakovsky. "The interests of the repertoire," retorted Gnedich.[59]

There were, of course, instances of administrative interference in the staging of performances which led to serious disruption and grievances among artists. During the Directorship of Volkonsky, Sergei Diaghilev and other members of the *World of Art* group were offered the chance to produce Delibes's ballet *Sylvia* on the Imperial stage. Diaghilev claimed that Volkon-sky promised him complete control over the production. However, some of Volkonsky's assistants in the St. Petersburg Office complained about such a degree of creative autonomy (which presumably reminded them of their own dispensability when it came to artistic matters), and the Director was compelled to retract his promise. According to Benois, Volkonsky nevertheless assured Diaghilev that, in practice, he would exercise full control over the production, although everything would have to be done in Volkonsky's name. Diaghilev protested by relinquishing the editorship of the *Yearbook of the Imperial The-aters*, which had led to his initial involvement with the Imperial Theaters.

Diaghilev had now severed all connections with the state theaters.[60] When Sanin asked Mikhail Fokin to choreograph a dance for Alexei Tolstoy's *The Death of Ivan the Terrible* at the Alexandrinsky, Fokin warned him that the administration might not approve because he was not yet a ballet master. Indeed, Krupensky duly informed Sanin that he had no right to choose his collaborators without official approval. Sanin felt so affronted that he resigned from the Imperial Theaters.[61]

In both these cases, the preferences of bureaucrats evidently had disrupted, prohibited, and frustrated artistic activity, supporting the argument that the Directorate was authoritarian and artistically repressive. Likewise, Napravnik was frustrated to some extent by the behavior of the Directorate, lamenting to a colleague, "How can I maintain discipline among the artists. Yesterday I say to a singer that I will not allow her to sing some role if she once again comes to the rehearsal not knowing the part, but she replies to me, in front of all the personnel: 'But Vladimir Arkad'evich [Telyakovsky] told me that I will sing this role.'"[62] Another example relates to the 1911 revival of Gluck's opera *Orphée et Euridice*. Letters from 1908, when the production was conceived, show that Telyakovsky ordered a specific, new French edition of the opera be used, with a new Russian text, to the disdain of those artists who preferred the original.[63] Some examples of official interference were absurd, like Krupensky's injunction to female ballet dancers to shave their armpits.[64] In January 1911, Nijinsky appeared in a performance of *Giselle* wearing a pair of tights that revealed his "form" too daringly, creating a "sensation" in the auditorium, and shocking the occupants of the tsarist box, the Dowager Empress Maria Feodorovna and Grand Duke Sergei Mikhailovich. Telyakovsky's response to the general outrage led directly to the suspension and resignation of the famous dancer from the Mariinsky in the same month.[65]

To conclude this section, while the Directorate had overall formal responsibility for the recruitment and supervision of the artists, the selection of the repertoire, and for providing the resources and guidelines for a production, in practice decision making in staging was dispersed among the artistic personnel of the theaters.

The "Dictatorship of Savina" and Others

In identifying the key areas of the Directorate's activity in the St. Petersburg Imperial Theaters, it has been argued that, on balance, its influence was not injurious to the artistic development of the theaters and in some cases (such as the recruitment of talented artists) it was wholly positive. An important dimension of the relationship between the Directorate and its theaters that remains to be discussed is the role of certain influential artists who were often in a position to instruct the Directorate. The history of these individuals suggests that the day-to-day running of the theaters involved diffuse localities of personal power, and therefore that the relationship between the administration and the artists was much more complex than the picture of an all-powerful Directorate suggests. Particularly in the selection and staging of the repertoire, the influence of leading artists was paramount and often superseded official channels. Challenges to the authority of the Directorate issued not from the formal leaders of the theater troupes, but from specific, powerful individuals, whose influence can be explained only in terms of contacts, personalities, and popularity. Occasionally, those individuals were the formal leaders of the troupes, but it was not that capacity which determined their influence.

At the Alexandrinsky Theater, the circumvention of official power was most clearly evidenced in the so-called "dictatorship of Savina." Maria Gavrilovna Savina (1854–1915) was the leading actress at the Alexandrinsky, and her influence is explained both by her popularity as a comic actress and by her marriage to a relative of Vsevolozhsky, Director of Imperial Theaters from 1881 to 1899. She was, according to one of her colleagues, the "center" of the Alexandrinsky.[66] Savina had started acting at the Alexandrinsky in 1874. In 1899, the tsar presented her with the prestigious title of tsar's soloist.[67] In January 1900, she celebrated her jubilee with a benefit night, which had followed upon a triumphant tour abroad which served to greatly strengthen her "dictatorship." In the words of one of Savina's biographers, "her hands were fully free, and she could sweep from her path all that hindered her creative plans and intentions. The situation of Savina in the theater was unassailable, and a change of Directors, of managers of the troupe, of *régisseurs* could not shake it."[68] One student on the imperial drama course recalled that Savina "had great influence on theater affairs, and did much that she wanted. At her instruction, *régisseurs* were invited and dismissed."[69] E. I. Time's acting career at the Alexandrinsky was initiated by Savina, who had admired her thespian abilities at an exhibition performance and had persuaded Gnedich and Telyakovsky to invite her to join the troupe in 1908.[70] The actor Gorin-Goriainov likewise joined the troupe in 1911 at Savina's initiative, having made a positive impression on her when she performed in the town Mineral'nye vody in the summer of 1910.[71] Her colleague Nicholas Khodotov remarked that, such was Savina's influence, contemporary dramatists felt it their "duty" to acquaint her with their work, confident that this was an assured route to having their work produced at the Alexandrinsky.[72] Although many secretly hated her, and Volkonsky even considered her "the personification of spite,"[73] Savina commanded unequaled respect at the Alexandrinsky. Viven recalls that, when an elder artist entered a room where everyone was seated, all would remain sitting except for a younger troupe member who gave up his seat. When Savina entered such a room, everyone stood, and did not sit until she sat.[74] Savina's confident arrogance revealed itself in her comments to Gnedich upon his appointment as artistic leader of the Alexandrinsky troupe in 1901. She pointedly informed the new recruit that she had served in the theater before his arrival and would continue to serve after his departure—"they [new artists] don't stay in this place for long."[75]

Telyakovsky admitted in his memoirs that Savina was the other Director of the Imperial Theaters.[76] Despite formal courtesies, he secretly detested her. Khodotov recalls that "Telyakovsky spoke of her with hate behind her back, humored her to her face, and intrigued against the hated 'Mashka' among the artists."[77] Telyakovsky, and others, found it difficult to control the temperamental Savina. Her reputation by the twentieth century was so formidable that she could get her own way without difficulty. Gnedich claimed that this was possible because leading artists were able to appeal to the Minister of the Imperial Court or even to the tsar. Alternatively, they could threaten to resign. After all, "for the theater and the takings, prima donnas are, of course, more essential than a manager [*direktor*]."[78]

Perhaps the single most influential individual at the Mariinsky opera was the senior conductor, the Czech Eduard Frantsevich Napravnik. As one journalist proclaimed, "To speak of the opera is to speak of Mr. Napravnik."[79] Shkafer claimed that "E. F. Napravnik was worshipped; his authority in the theater was considered unshakable."[80] So well known was he that Dostoevsky refers to him in *The Brothers Karamazov* (book II, chapter two), a reasonably significant measure of the conductor's cultural profile. When Napravnik died in November 1916, it was proposed by the city Duma that the Russian word for "conductor" be changed by substituting the Slavic word "napravnik" for the German word "kapelmeister" (which had also come by then to mean an orchestral conductor, or *dirizhër*). The proposal was dropped the following year when it was pointed out that the Czech word "napravnik" meant "vassal."[81]

Telyakovsky greatly respected Napravnik and consulted him about the opera repertoire, even when Napravnik was not conducting due to illness.[82] Napravnik was not so enthusiastic about Telyakovsky—"Telyakovsky was quite polite towards me, but no more"[83]—though he was not as hostile to him as others were. Like Savina, Napravnik was one of those figures whom people approached with their artistic suggestions. For example, in February 1905, Chaliapin wrote to Napravnik asking him to conduct him in the opera *The Demon*. Napravnik replied that his continuing illness made it impossible for him to conduct at that moment. The dancer Olga Preobrazhenskaya, in September 1906, asked Napravnik to suggest suitable pieces of Tchaikovsky's work for dance variations, claiming that no one else could advise her.[84]

The most powerful figures at the Mariinsky ballet were Matilda Kshesinskaya, the tsar's former mistress, and Nicholas Legat. Kshesinskaya was known as "Matilde d'or"—golden Matilda.[85] Her influence derived both from her unrivaled status as a dancer—while some of her famous colleagues such as Pavlova and Karsavina achieved the status of *prima ballerina*, Kshesinskaya held the title *prima ballerina assoluta*—and, no doubt, from her intimate relationship with the tsar's uncle, Grand Duke Vladimir Alexandrovich. One contemporary remarked that "officials fawned and ingratiated themselves before her."[86] In fact, such was her influence that she forced the resignation of Volkonsky, Telyakovsky's predecessor.

Volkonsky experienced only misfortune in his relations with the famous dancer. In 1900 he proposed that a visiting Italian dancer, Henrietta Grimaldi, take Kshesinskaya's part in her favorite ballet, *La Fille Mal Gardée*. Kshesinskaya protested, but Volkonsky insisted that she make way for Grimaldi. "Things could obviously not rest there, and I took my own steps," wrote Kshesinskaya. Volkonsky soon received an order from the Minister of the Imperial Court ordering him to obey Kshesinskaya's wishes. "I owed this new favour to the tsar, who intervened on my behalf...."[87] Kshesinskaya used the same influence to obtain, in February 1900, a benefit performance to celebrate her tenth anniversary on stage, something granted only for a twentieth anniversary.[88] Her power was confirmed when she refused to wear a farthingale during one of the ballets. The Directorate fined her for disobeying orders, as it was entitled to do. At Kshesinskaya's insistence, the tsar instructed Volkonsky to annul the relatively insubstantial fine, and when this was done Volkonsky used the event as an excuse to resign, having felt that his authority was being undermined.[89] This incident contrasted starkly with the experience of the ballet dancer Bakerkin, who was fined twenty-five rubles by Volkonsky because he appeared in *Giselle* wearing a costume of "diamond decorations not corresponding to the design of the costume."[90] Bakerkin was not an influential artist and had little option but to pay his fine.

In January 1904 Kshesinskaya took early retirement to spend more time at her Strelna dacha, although she returned to the stage for the 1904-05 season. Even then, she used her influence to dictate her own activity.

> I refused to sign a contract, as the Director would have liked, and only agreed to appear in certain performances, like a guest artist. In fact, I wanted to remain perfectly free, and told the Administration [the Directorate] that no contract could bind me and no attack frighten me; but that I would always be ready to be of service. So I returned to the stage on these terms, and was never to retire.[91]

The most influential figure at the Mariinsky ballet after Kshesinskaya was Nicholas Legat. In his early years as a dancer at the Imperial Theaters, Legat had asserted himself against the Directorate. In his memoirs, he relates how he hated dancing ballet parts in operas because it was not considered authentic ballet. On one occasion, he had to dance in Weber's opera *Der Freischütz*. The dance part at the end involved four couples, of whom the male dancers were the Legat brothers, Gerdt and Bekefi, who all wore identical costumes. One night, the Legat brothers painted their faces like Bekefi's in order to create the impression that three Bekefis had appeared on stage. They did this without the knowledge of their female dance partners, who were visibly confused when the piece was performed. The auditorium responded with uproarious laughter, shouting "Bekefi!" and when the said dancer advanced to bow in response to the calls, the Legats moved forward too. Volkonsky severely reprimanded Legat for this incident, but the dancer managed to persuade the Director to relieve him of that particular part and, ultimately, parts in operas. Legat had successfully struggled in public against the *proizvol* (arbitrariness) of the Directorate and went on to exercise great influence in the ballet. As Legat himself explained, "a few of us achieved positions where, in the end, we could (and did) practically dictate to the Director of Imperial Theatres what we should do, or not do, in which ballets we should appear, and in which we shouldn't (that is, wouldn't)." Like Kshesinskaya, Legat enjoyed the favor of Nicholas II—the tsar was "always very kindly disposed to me"—and felt that he could rely on his "gracious patronage" if needed.[92]

* * * *

This chapter has considered the relationship between the Directorate of Imperial Theaters and the troupes (an immediate point of contact between power and culture, state and theater) in order to explore the argument that the court administration was repressive and impeded the artistic evolution of the theaters under its authority. After considering the reputation of the last Director, we focused on the key areas of the Directorate's activity relating to the art of the theaters: recruitment and supervision of artists, selection of the repertoire, and staging of the repertoire.

It is evident that the Directorate often irritated the artists. Napravnik resented the fact that Telyakovsky did not inform him that he was employing a new conductor for the Mariinsky opera; Rimsky-Korsakov believed it was inappropriate that authors had to approach the Directorate if they wanted their works performed; Gnedich resigned from the Alexandrinsky because he considered the Directorate corrupt, the theater "repressed by officialdom"; and Diaghilev's production of *Sylvia* at the Mariinsky was scuppered by a dispute between the administration and the artists about overall control of the production.

Such incidents have forged the image of a repressive Directorate that impeded the artistic creativity of the Imperial Theaters. Yet the real picture is more complex. The Directorate made several positive contributions to the artistic evolution of the St. Petersburg Imperial Theaters in the late tsarist period, not least by actively recruiting some of the best artistic talent of the

Silver Age, and many of its supervisory injunctions—for instance, requesting that artists make less noise during scene changes, or that they turn up to rehearsals on time—were hardly inconsistent with the pursuit of superlative art. Moreover, the details of staging a performance were generally in the hands of the theater troupes, a fact underlined by the presence of powerful individuals such as Savina (the "other Director of Imperial Theaters") and Kshesinskaya (who actually forced the resignation of a Director). Historians of Russian theater must therefore revise their understanding of the Directorate and its relationship with Russian theater culture during the Silver Age. Court administration of the St. Petersburg Imperial Theaters was often cited as a negative factor when discontent arose, but it did not seriously impede the theaters' artistic activity and neither did it completely ostracize them from wider innovations in Russian theater at the time.

Chapter 3

The Audience

The institutional identity of the St. Petersburg Imperial Theaters in the vibrant cultural world of pre-revolutionary Russia cannot fully be comprehended without consideration of the audiences that frequented their auditoria. The activity of theatergoing became increasingly widespread in the late nineteenth and early twentieth centuries, not only in Russia but throughout Europe. This was clearly evidenced by the rise and consolidation of a wide variety of popular commercial entertainment, such as operetta, music halls, cabaret, and the new drama theaters such as the Moscow Art Theater and the Suvorin Theater. Simultaneously, theatergoing became a more respectable middle-class pastime. In Russia this was reflected in the fact that commercial newspapers such as the widely-read *The New Times* and *The Stock Exchange Gazette* (*Birzhevyia vedomosti*), whose readership consisted of the "educated middle groups," all carried effusive theater columns and reviews.[1] Critics such as Alexander Kugel and Iurii Beliaev became prominent commentators on theater art, and a growing number of *intelligenty* with no practical connection with the stage, foremost among whom was Viacheslav Ivanov, engaged in polemical discourse about the function of theater. In other words, theater was no longer an exclusive recreation, and although cinema was increasingly popular in the 1900s, it had yet to displace the live performing arts as a popular source of entertainment in the manner it subsequently did. Theater had become a widely popular entertainment and a legitimate subject of intellectual debate amid contemporary discourse about art and culture in general. Never before had it been so fashionable to descant on the art of theater or, more significantly, to attend theatrical performances.

The question this chapter aims to consider is: Who attended the St. Petersburg Imperial Theaters, and why? Were the court theaters admitting a more democratic audience, as the general expansion of theatergoing might suggest? Or did they remain largely exclusive institutions, accessible only to the higher echelons of St. Petersburg politics and society? Moreover, what was the attraction of the Imperial Theaters to the Petersburgers who attended them? It goes without saying that audiences gathered to appreciate creative achievement, to marvel at, and be entertained by, the prominent "stars." Yet was there also a sense in which the St. Petersburg Imperial Theaters, as court theaters, constituted a cultural club for those connected to, or associated with, the centers of power in tsarist Russia? It will be argued that there is certainly some validity to this interpretation, that the St. Petersburg Imperial Theaters, unlike other more accessible theaters in Russia, did constitute a sort of club for the elite.* But at the same time it will be argued that the composition of the audience was increasingly less exclusive than it often appeared. While examination of the audience enhances and strengthens the impression of the St. Petersburg Imperial Theaters as institutions associated with privilege and power, it also indicates that they did not entirely exclude the wider theatergoing public.

Profile of the Audience

In the early 1900s, the St. Petersburg Imperial Theater audience largely comprised specific elite groups. This was ensured by the two chief factors governing access to the theaters: the subscriptions system and ticket prices, the latter held artificially high by illegal profiteering. The system of subscriptions (*abonementy*) enabled individuals to pay in advance for access to Imperial Theater performances for a whole season. Holders of subscriptions did not necessarily have access to all performances; sources indicate that there were too many *abonementy* in circulation to enable *all* subscribers to attend *all* performances (for instance, twenty thousand people had subscriptions to the opera, but the Mariinsky had a seating capacity of only 1,625—see below). Rather, subscriptions were available for certain nights of the week or certain cycles of performances. Alexander Benois recalled that his parents subscribed to Italian opera performances and that they had a box reserved for each Monday.[2] Patrons could buy a subscription for a cycle of Rimsky-Korsakov operas.[3] Of course, as one Western observer of the system noted, subscriptions were extremely valuable: "Abonnements passed jealously from hand to hand, and a seat was left in a man's will to his heir amongst the most cherished heirlooms."[4] A seat at the ballet and the title of "balletomane" were becoming an "hereditary dignity."[5] One critic commented that, "[f]or those who are not consecrated, in other words those who do not have subscriptions, it is almost impossible to penetrate into this sanctuary."[6] The same critic, in an article attacking the system, claimed that subscription performances, which

---

*"Elite" remains a provocative word. Here it is broadly used to signify those who were pre-eminent in their profession or social group. Thus, it refers broadly to those who dominated the court, politics, the army, business, and other institutions.

amounted to the majority of Imperial Theater performances, were "completely inaccessible for the public." Subscriptions were the "ancestral property of a small circle of Petersburg bureaucrats and plutocrats," of people from "influential spheres, who also wanted to display their *toilettes* at the opera." The consequence was that "the right to listen to the Imperial opera has become the privilege of a small official and rich circle of Petersburgers."[7]

It is fitting testimony to the exclusiveness of the subscriptions system that it was not seriously questioned until the 1917 revolution. The issue of access to opera performances at the Mariinsky was raised immediately after the February Revolution. A letter to the leader of the opera troupe, Tartakov, evidently from Telyakovsky, states that approximately twenty thousand people were served by the opera subscriptions system. This amounted to "less than one per cent" of the city's total population, and for several years those people had attended opera performances at the Mariinsky Theater almost without interruption. Four nights per week were devoted to opera and out of those four only Fridays and some Tuesdays were available for the non-subscription public. Therefore, ninety-nine per cent of the population of the imperial capital had no access, or only a limited possibility of access, to the opera. Fewer subscriptions were available for ballet at the Mariinsky, but only because ballet was presented twice per week, on Sundays and Wednesdays. Access to ballet performances was still dominated by the subscription public.[8] For instance, during the 1904-05 season, of the forty-eight ballet performances, access to thirty-four was by subscription. Of the remaining fourteen performances, seven were matinee shows, leaving only seven ballet evenings for the non-subscription public. The following season was more favorable to the non-subscription public, with only twenty-six of the forty-two ballet performances restricted to subscribers, but during 1906-07, the discriminatory figures returned, with forty-four of fifty-seven performances reserved for subscribers.[9] This continued to be the trend for the next few seasons, and no doubt beyond. There is no indication that subscriptions were as important at the Alexandrinsky as they were at the Mariinsky, probably because drama was less prestigious than opera or ballet and therefore drama *abonementy* were less highly valued. Nevertheless they were still used: For example, in October 1915 the Directorate announced the sale of subscriptions to a cycle of Ostrovsky plays.[10]

Telyakovsky defended the subscriptions system on the grounds that it was convenient for the public to be able to buy access to several performances with one purchase, and that it ensured the finances of the theater for the forthcoming season.[11] The Provisional Government took no decisive action against *abonementy*, and in September 1917 the *Journal de Pétrograd*, formerly the *Journal de St. Pétersbourg*, announced the sale of subscriptions for the 1917-18 season at the Mikhailovsky.[12] Yet within a year, the Bolshevik Revolution had caused the displacement of the old audience. The former Imperial Theaters were now inhabited by a new audience of workers, soldiers, and peasants, encouraged to some extent by a Soviet version of the *abonement*—ticket quotas for factories, barracks, and villages (see Chapter 8).

The more "democratic" element of the audience gained access via the few non-subscription tickets, or to non-subscription performances. Tickets were sold, officially, at theater box offices and were in high demand. People queued for hours to obtain the cheapest seats in the auditorium, particularly if a famous artist was scheduled to perform. According to Karsavina, "The [Mariinsky] box office opened at eight o'clock in the morning. Even in the bitterest cold the queue round the theater started overnight, though a ten hours' vigil by no means ensured a ticket."[13] According to Boris Almedingen, a young set designer who trained under Golovin, one night in the winter of 1908, as the audience left the Mariinsky, a group of students and workers, *"vsia galerka"*—all the gallery—gathered outside to begin an all-night wait to buy tickets for a Chaliapin performance.[14] The public would go to inordinate lengths to see such performances. In November 1903 a Chaliapin performance at the Mariinsky had attracted large numbers of enthusiasts without tickets who crowded into the corridors of the theater and the entrances to the boxes. An irate official from the St. Petersburg Office requested that, when such crowds invaded the theater in the future, the police be called to assist theater officials in removing them.[15] The popularity of the St. Petersburg Imperial Theaters in pre-revolutionary Russia was such that access to the theaters' box offices, particularly that of the Mariinsky, for the purchase of non-subscription tickets had to be regulated by a lottery scheme. This was designed to ensure the maintenance of order around the theaters.[16]

St. Petersburg Imperial Theater ticket prices were high enough to put them generally out of the reach of the city's working classes. At the Alexandrinsky in 1900 the most expensive seats, in the boxes, cost between six and twelve rubles. Armchairs in the stalls ranged in price from two to four rubles. Gallery prices ranged from forty to ninety kopeks, and the gods (lesser gallery, or *raёk*) from ten to twenty kopeks.[17] It has been estimated that the average annual wage of a St. Petersburg worker in 1900 was 314 rubles, or approximately twenty-four rubles per month, and that single male workers required twenty-one rubles per month for food, accommodation, and clothing.[18] However, the exclusion of those with low incomes was made certain by widespread ticket profiteering, a phenomenon referred to in pre-revolutionary Russia as *baryshnichestvo*. The problem of the *baryshniki* was long-standing. In 1882, one Alexandrinsky actor described them as an "evil" which even imperial commands (*Vysochaishee povelenie*) could not defeat.[19] The *baryshniki* plied their trade during the whole theater season, from the end of August until April or May, and were particularly successful when famous personalities performed. According to one observer, in 1904, when rumors abounded that Kshesinskaya was to retire, the *baryshniki* made "no less than the great stock brokers."[20]

In the late imperial period, the authorities in St. Petersburg fought unsuccessfully to outlaw the illegal activity of the speculators. In January 1906 Telyakovsky sent to the town governor a report that had been drawn up by a cashier of the Mariinsky box office and which spoke of the ticket-sale abuse perpetrated by the *baryshniki*.[21] The town governor took no action at that stage. A year later, prompted by a newspaper article about the *baryshniki* entitled "Flea-market on Theater Square," Telyakovsky contacted the Court Chancellery with a request that the problem of the profiteers be brought to the attention of the police. Evidently, the problem was too difficult for the theater authorities to solve on their own, and so the town governor was forced to convene a "consultation" that came up with two suggestions. Firstly, members of the audience who had purchased tickets but could not attend a performance should be allowed to return their tickets to the box office (*obratnyi priëm*). This would prevent speculators from obtaining more tickets because it would discourage the private disposal of tickets at low prices (which the *baryshniki* could exploit). Secondly, due to limited police numbers, the theater administration should appoint, at its own expense, two agents to monitor the *baryshniki* with a view to frustrating their activity.[22] However, two years later the problem had still not been solved, and in March 1909 another consultation was held under the auspices of the town governor's office. The only concrete proposal was to repeat the request to the Directorate to establish a system of *obratnyi priëm*. Telyakovsky, however, refused to approve this measure.[23] The next proposal to outlaw the *baryshniki* emanated from the Court Chancellery in March 1913. The report, drawn up by a certain Dobrovolskii, started with a realistic point: There were people who were quite willing to pay inflated prices for theater tickets. Two separate solutions were suggested. Firstly, profiteering with Imperial Theater tickets should be legalized. This would result in open competition to resell unwanted tickets and consequently would lower the prices of such tickets. The report pointed to the experience of the Moscow Art Theater as an example. It was not illegal to profit from reselling Moscow Art Theater tickets because it was a private institution, and consequently differentials between box office prices and speculators' prices were very small compared to those of the St. Petersburg Imperial Theaters. Paradoxically, legalisation of the *baryshniki* would help reduce their influence on ticket prices. The second proposal recommended that the theater box office turn profiteering to its own advantage. If there were people willing to pay double the price of a ticket, then let them pay—not to the *baryshniki*, but to the theater box office. For example, ten days in advance of a performance, the repertoire was announced and the few non-subscription tickets went on sale. On the first day of the sale, prices would be doubled. Those unable to pay would make way in queues for those able to pay. On the second day of ticket sales, remaining tickets would be priced at ten per cent off the doubled price, that is, ninety per cent above the original ticket price. This would continue until the day of the performance when remaining tickets would be sold at their "real" price. However, this proposal was rejected by the Director on the dubious grounds that there already existed at Imperial Theater box offices a system of sale of tickets by preliminary registration ("*po predvaritelnoi zapisi*").[24]

The persistence of the profiteers to 1917 and the high demand for tickets that sustained them testifies to the popularity of the St. Petersburg Imperial Theaters. It suggests that a considerable number of people were determined to attend the theaters and were willing to pay large sums of money to gain access; this also underlines the exclusive character of the audience in terms of financial background, although the presence of some students and workers in the ticket queues and theater galleries confirmed that some cheaper seats were obtainable.

A descriptive profile of the St. Petersburg Imperial Theater audience which confirms the general exclusiveness of those institutions can be reconstructed from memoirs written by witnesses to performances. Such impressionistic evidence confirms that the Imperial Theaters catered chiefly to the political and social elites of St. Petersburg, but that people outside of those groups were not entirely absent. One memoirist recalls that, apart from the occupants of the cheaper seats at the ceiling, the Mariinsky had a "brilliant audience" of "the upper and propertied classes."[25] The elite were particularly prominent in the auditoria during special occasions, such as the visits of foreign dignitaries. The *Yearbook of the Imperial Theaters* described the scene at the beginning of the gala performance for Emperor Francis Joseph at the Mariinsky in 1897: "At eight o'clock in the evening court ladies—and ladies with access to the court—the diplomatic corps, and the highest court, military and civilian ranks gathered in the parterre and boxes."[26]

Telyakovsky provides us with more precise information. According to him, in the last decades of tsarism, the aristocracy, which he equates with high society (*vysshoe obshchestvo*), was attending the Imperial Theaters less frequently than it had done previously. In fact, "the majority of the public visiting the Imperial Theaters in Moscow and Petersburg consisted of the nobility of average prosperity, the intelligentsia, officials, merchants and students. There were few ordinary people and workers in the theaters, even in the Alexandrinsky, never mind the others." Telyakovsky pointed out that he occasionally received letters from workers requesting tickets for seats in the lesser galleries, usually for non-subscription performances at the Mariinsky.[27] The audience categories listed by Telyakovsky, if not constituent parts of "high society," certainly included constituent parts of imperial Russia's elite.

Contemporary sketches and drawings provide some visual evidence of audience types. To some extent, they reinforce the image of the Imperial Theaters as elitist institutions, yet they also indicate that a reasonable variety of

Petersburg social groups were represented in the auditoria. One depicts two men conversing in an Imperial Theater parterre; insofar as attire provides clues to status in late tsarist Russia, their smart collars and ties suggest a clientele derived from the middle to upper sections of society. Another sketch, entitled *At the Interval* (*V antrakte*), depicts five gentlemen standing in front of the orchestra pit; three are wearing military uniform, two are wearing evening dress. Two drawings of queues at the Mariinsky box office portray more motley gatherings (the non-subscription public): a bespectacled intellectual, a society lady with parasol, people slumped against a wall trying to keep warm,

Two gentlemen of the Imperial Theater parterre. *Vos pominaniia* **(Moscow-Leningrad, 1965)**

students drinking from a bottle (see illustrations). It goes without saying that such evidence must be treated with caution; it says nothing conclusive about the collective identity of the audience. Yet it generally supports the view of an audience composed chiefly of St. Petersburg elites, with a "democratic" fringe looking on from the galleries. The word used by contemporaries to describe the highest seats in the lesser galleries, *raëk*, is instructive. In the nineteenth century a *raëk* was a fairground peep show that consisted of a popular *lubok* illustration in a box with a storyteller narrating the events of the picture.[28] The use of the word to describe the lesser galleries in theater auditoria suggests outsiders peering at a spectacle they were not fully admitted to, in marked contrast to the inhabitants of the parterre.

A comparison between the St. Petersburg Imperial Theaters and their Moscow counterparts further illuminates the general character of the audience. In Moscow, the Russian merchants tended to be prominent at performances. The writer Vladimir Giliarovskii observed the prominence of merchants at the Maly Theater in the 1880s although he noted that the parterre of the Bolshoi tended to be inhabited by members of an older generation who spent their time ruing the end of serfdom.[29] In St. Petersburg, on the other hand, foreign merchants and diplomats were more in evidence in the auditoria. Most likely this difference was a consequence of Moscow's turn-of-the-century status as a financial center, while St. Petersburg remained most obviously an administrative center, as far as the profile of its elite was concerned.[30]

"At the Interval." Etiquette demanded that soldiers who remained in the auditorium during intervals stand in order not to slight their superiors who might be moving around the theater or between boxes. *Teatr i iskusstro* no. 41, 1900.

Another distinctive feature of the Imperial Theater audiences which emerges from the available evidence is the generational and attitudinal difference between the stalls and the gallery. While the stalls were full of high-ranking notables and rich merchants, the galleries were full of students and young balletomanes. Karsavina recalled that "[t]he young generation [seated in the gallery] showed an exaggerated mistrust of the smart set of the stalls."[31] It was the younger members of the audience, such as "the high school student in his best clothes, twirling a non-existent moustache," "the new made intellectual, the son of some tradesman," and "the inevitable moustachioed figure in his beaver fur collar, puffing at cigarette after cigarette," who tended to gather at the stage door after a performance, hoping to catch another glimpse of their idols.[32] Therefore, while the St. Petersburg Imperial Theater audience was predominantly composed of members of the social and political elites of the imperial capital, it is important to bear in mind that the audience was not simply a uniform, homogeneous unit.

Moreover, it is possible to identify a difference between the character of the Mariinsky and Alexandrinsky audiences. The Mariinsky, without doubt, was the abode of the extremely wealthy, as the evidence above (and below) indicates. According to Slonim, "aristocrats" considered the Alexandrinsky a "theater for the people,"[33] and although that is an exaggeration—the Alexandrinsky was by no means a *narodnyi teatr*—the Alexandrinsky catered to merchant classes more than the Mariinsky and it was often referred to as the "merchants' [*kupecheskii*] theater."[34] Pleshcheev claimed that the Alexandrinsky audience was more "democratic" than that of the Mariinsky ballet audience. The Alexandrinsky auditorium was dominated by "journalists, dramatists, merchants, actors, bureaucrats and others." "High society" (*vysshii svet*) generally preferred French drama at the Mikhailovsky, he claimed.[35] But this distinction does not detract from the fact that the St. Petersburg Imperial Theater audience, as a collective, was composed of elites, although less exclusively of the old aristocracy.

While it is thus possible to identify individuals from various social and occupational backgrounds among the Imperial Theater audience, particularly with regard to the eclectic crowds in the lesser galleries, there remain certain prominent and general characteristics of the audience that allow us to distinguish it from audiences at other St. Petersburg theaters. To be sure, many patrons of the Imperial Theaters would have attended other theaters—indeed, given the demand for Imperial Theater tickets, it was not always possible for theatrophiles to attend performances and inevitably they would have patronized other venues. Yet even allowing for some fluidity in audience composition, the above profile of an elite audience, consistently attested to by the sources, contrasts with general audience profiles for other St. Petersburg theaters. The obvious contrast is with the popular workers theaters, such as the Vasileostrovsky. Other theaters, such as the Suvorin, the Nemetti, or the Komissarzhevskaya generally were associated with the "intelligentsia," an amorphous caste that is difficult to define accurately; but certainly such "intelligentsia theaters" did not have the elite parterres, crowded with imperial officialdom, of the court theaters. The exceptions were usually premieres at theaters which had become fashionable among the "middling" groups of civil society or the intelligentsia. The Suvorin Theater, for example, was very modish during the first years of its existence and attracted a diverse clientele that included members of "high society" normally associated with the Imperial Theaters. Notable events were the production of Alexei Tolstoy's *Tsar Fyodor Ioannovich* during the 1899-1900 season, and the production of Alexander Sukhovo-Kobylin's *The Death of Tarelkin* during the 1900-01 season. Similarly, the Nemetti Theater, accustomed to a more popular audience, attracted the attention of "high society" with its premiere of Ibsen's *Gengangere (Ghosts)*, the first Russian production of that play.[36] Yet the general distinction remained. The St. Petersburg Imperial Theater audience was by no means rigid or unchanging, but it did have a predominant characteristic that set it apart from the broad audience profiles of other theaters: a parterre clientele broadly associated with the loci of political and financial power in tsarist Russia.

The Auditorium as Stage: the Performance of the Audience

In 1836, Gogol quipped that theater and concerts gave "the classes of Petersburg society ... the opportunity to stare at one another to their heart's content."[37] This comment prompts three observations. First, the horseshoe

Top, bottom and opposite: Two contemporary sketches of Mariinsky box office queues, and one of the Mariinsky gallery during a performance. The sketches depict members of the non-subscription public and indicate that part of the Mariinsky auditorium was accessible to a much wider cross-section of St. Petersburg society than is suggested by the elite profile of the parterre. *Top: Vospominaniia* (Moscow-Leningrad, 1965) *Bottom: Teatr i iskusstro* no. 2, 1900 *Opposite: Vospominaniia* (Moscow-Leningrad, 1965)

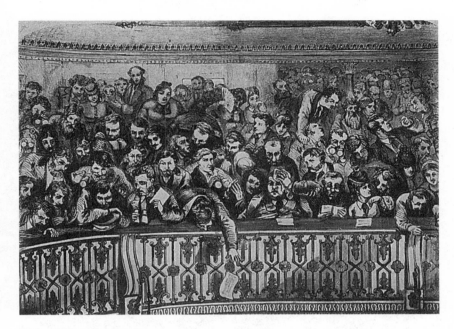

design of the auditoria certainly encouraged most theatergoers to observe other members of the audience as much as they observed the performance; indeed, many seats offered better views of an auditorium than a stage. Second, the comment, admittedly considered in isolation, implied that the stage was not the center of attention in Petersburg theater; this in turn suggested an associate, social function for theater. Third, it evoked a scenario in which representatives of different/similar social groups (or "classes") of the imperial capital, who did not ordinarily come together in such close proximity, had an opportunity to intermingle on a social level; one possible function of such interaction was the reinforcement of group identities. Taken together, these observations point to a wider social function for the St. Petersburg Imperial Theaters than the provision of drama, opera and ballet. The remainder of this chapter will explore this idea. Is there evidence that audiences were conscious of participating in a social occasion? Was it important to be seen at the Imperial Theaters, as well as to see? Did attendance constitute a social gathering beyond that minimum contact necessary to experience a live play, opera, or ballet? Were the St. Petersburg Imperial Theaters, as one historian observed for the eighteenth and early nineteenth centuries, places where the *beau monde* could engage in "tittle-tattle and society gossip"?[38]

Several examples provide evidence that the St. Petersburg Imperial Theaters were regarded by contemporaries as institutional spaces which performed the function of a sort of meeting place for society. Avseenko suggested that the public was more attracted by the auditorium than it was by what happened

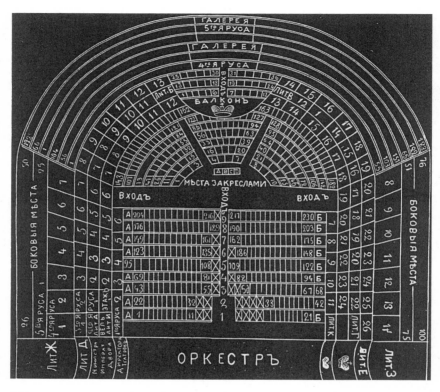

This page and opposite: Plans of the Alexandrinsky and Mariinsky auditoria. Crowns indicate the location of boxes reserved for use by the imperial family. To the left of the orchestra pit are boxes for the Minister of the Imperial Court and the Director of Imperial Theaters. *Ezhegodnik imperatorskikh teatror*

on stage.[39] Pleshcheev remarked that "Everyone in the [Mariinsky] auditorium knew one another," and that collective box subscriptions were arranged by organizations such as the Imperial Yacht Club and the English Club, as well as the Preobrazhenskii and Husar Regiments. Equally at the Alexandrinsky, everyone knew each other. Pleshcheev claimed that he could state, without any exaggeration, that the theater ushers knew most people by their patronymics.[40] In the late 1890s, the Directorate even organized masquerades in the Mariinsky, and although not always well attended, they did attract members of the public.[41] Such examples are not unusual in themselves, but collectively they support the view that the Imperial Theaters provided more than stage entertainment for their audiences.

This social function entailed the presence of behavioral rules and etiquette in the auditoria. One frequent member of the audience, Meriel Buchanan, daughter of the British ambassador to St. Petersburg, Sir George

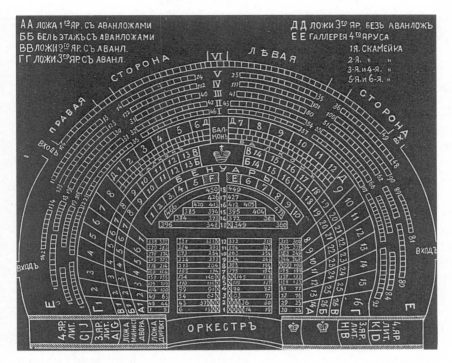

Buchanan, indicated in her memoirs a preoccupation with the social rules and conventions obtaining within the Mariinsky. For example, it was "considered highly unseemly to remain sitting in the box during the *entr'acte*, so, directly the curtain went down, everybody retired to the little ante-room at the back of each box where one could smoke and talk and receive the visits of young men who had been sitting in the stalls."[42] Fokin, too, recalled the etiquette of the interval, pointing out that men were required by convention to stand in the space between the stalls and the orchestra and to face the auditorium. According to Fokin, this originated with officers who were not allowed to sit while their superiors might be standing. For the non-military, the implication was that they would insult the royal family by turning their backs to the royal box.[43]

Dress codes were observed in the auditoria.* Telyakovsky remarked upon the contrast between the appearance of the Moscow and St. Petersburg Imperial Theater audiences. "It is not like in Moscow, where the public is in shawls and jackets. Here everyone is in evening dress, officers are with spurs and

*I have been unable to locate written regulations governing dress in the theaters; probably they did not exist, and patrons relied instead on an acquaintance with established social conventions. Here I have relied on contemporary impressionistic evidence gleaned from memoirs, novels, photographs, drawings and caricatures.

remarkable moustaches, ladies with bare, snow white bosoms—diamonds, perfume, lace...."[44] Isadora Duncan was struck by the Mariinsky audience during a visit in 1905: "In the entr'acte I looked about me, and saw the most beautiful women in the world, in marvellous décolleté gowns, covered with jewels, escorted by men in distinguished uniforms."[45] Tolstoy's central character in *Resurrection* dons his formal evening attire in order to meet an acquaintance at the Mikhailovsky Theater who seems interested only displaying herself to him, "in all the splendour of her evening dress."[46] A sketch of balletomanes from 1905 depicts them in evening dress: collar and tails.[47] Shkafer observed the Mariinsky ballet audience during an assignment from the Moscow Bolshoi opera: "The elegant dresses of the ladies, the tail-coats and dinner jackets, the uniforms of the tsar's guards constituted a picture of that so-called fashionable society, for which a ballet performance was a way of pleasantly spending one's time."[48]

Individual members of the audience appeared conscious of the need to perform in the presence of their peers. Telyakovsky suggested that women who attended the ballet were "elegantly dressed with diamonds" because they were more interested in the men in the auditorium than they were in ballet.[49] The Imperial Theater auditorium could also function as a forum for courting; in this respect, one is reminded of Oblomov, the eponymous anti-hero of Goncharov's novel, who knew that, if he wanted to meet his beloved away from the domestic milieu, he would almost certainly find her at the theater. A conspicuous "performer" in the audience was the male patron of ballet, the balletomane. Balletomania was a distinct cultural phenomenon in late imperial Russia. Balletomanes formed a distinctive group identity: They sat in the front rows of the stalls, repaired to the same restaurant, often the Cuba on Bolshaia Morskaia, after a performance, and were identified collectively.[50] Their love of ballet, in particular ballet dancers, verged on the obsessive. According to one critic, during the time when Marie Taglioni was appearing in St. Petersburg (1837–42), a pair of her ballet shoes were "purchased for 200 rubles, drawn in a lottery, and eaten with sauce by admirers."[51] Even if the story is apocryphal, it symbolizes the extent of the obsession.

We are indebted to Telyakovsky for bequeathing a short descriptive essay on the St. Petersburg balletomanes in the early 1900s. A balletomane could not be described as a lover of ballet in the way that a melomaniac could be described as a lover of music, claims Telyakovsky. Not all lovers of ballet could be considered balletomanes, and not all balletomanes could be considered lovers of choreographic art.[52] The corpus of balletomanes included many types, as listed by Telyakovsky: people from the tsar's retinue; courtiers; generals and admirals; directors of departments; former governors and governors-general; people from the financial world; editors and journalists (*sotrudniki gazet*); students and the "golden youth"; *rentiers*. They were always male, usually of high rank, and with close connections to the imperial court.

They were in love with a particular female dancer, and during the intervals they enjoyed the privilege of smoking in the Police Master's office in the theater. "In general," says Telyakovsky, "balletomanes were people with resources, or people skilled in showing that they have resources.... By character and persuasion [they] were monarchists, adherents of olden times, of fictitious traditions—essentially, of routines."[53]

Balletomanes were extremely conspicuous in the theater. "They entered the auditorium with a special confidence, exchanging a few words of greeting between themselves, and with representatives of the theater administration; the ushers bowed particularly low for them, to which the balletomanes answered with an imperceptible upwards nod of the head, the way they usually greeted important people."[54] Words were also exchanged with members of the orchestra. According to Telyakovsky, the balletomane attached great significance to the fact that during performances he had a specific place in the auditorium which he considered his personal property. In newspaper articles, balletomanes were often referred to simply by the number of their seat, which would not change during a season because it was, most certainly, a subscription seat.[55]

Besides specific individuals in the auditorium, the audience could be considered a single, unified entity, the sum of its parts, itself an individual. As such, it could behave as a social animal independent of what was happening on stage. For example, dramatic and subversive instances of the audience "performing" occurred during the revolution of 1905 (see Chapter 6). On February 21, 1913, a gala performance was held in the Mariinsky to celebrate the three hundredth anniversary of the Romanov dynasty. The tsar and tsarina were present, but the empress did not stay in the royal box for long. Meriel Buchanan records that "a little wave of resentment rippled over the theater, women glanced at each other and raised their shoulders expressively, men muttered despairingly below their breath,"[56] a public expression of the popular disapprobation of Alexandra's well-known scorn for Petersburg society. During the First World War, the Imperial Theaters were used for collective public demonstrations of Russian solidarity with the Allies, in the presence of foreign ambassadors. Allied national anthems were played by the orchestra: *God Save the Tsar*, the *Marseillaise*, and *Rule Britannia* (*God Save the King* was avoided because it was the same as the Prussian anthem).[57]

The Ritual of Attendance

The St. Petersburg Imperial Theaters clearly performed a wider social function beyond the mere provision of stage entertainment. They functioned as public arenas where a specific elite group could indulge its thirst for display and its preoccupation with etiquette. Attendance could even be described as a ritual, reinforcing the impression of a wider social, group-integrative function. It seems to the present writer that three essential elements must ultimately be present for an activity to be described as a ritual: repetition, hierarchy, and symbolism. According to such criteria, the laying of poppy wreaths at the London Cenotaph in commemoration of the war dead might be described as a ritual. It is repeated on an annual basis, on Armistice Day; it clearly invokes the formal hierarchies of the British state (the Queen lays the first wreath, followed by other members of the royal family, down to senior politicians and heads of the armed forces); and the ceremony is replete with symbols, most obviously the Cenotaph itself, which symbolizes the war dead. These three elements, in combination, seem to be the distinctive features of what we term "ritual," an act associated with established practice which invokes an accepted order of authority, reified by recognizable images and signs.

The St. Petersburg Imperial Theater audience conforms to the first condition. As we have seen, the audience was restricted to a specific number of people who either held subscriptions or could afford non-subscription tickets at speculators' prices. The theaters' repertoire was relatively static, too. As one critic stated: "The repertoire is almost unchanging. New plays, and in particular operas, are put on two to three times a year, sometimes even more infrequently. The production of a new ballet is an event. Even so, operas are always fully attended."[58] If both audience and repertoire were relatively static, then it follows that a considerable proportion of Imperial Theater patrons must have seen the same production several times. This was pointed out by the ballet critic Valerian Svetlov, who remarked that "laymen often confuse balletomanes" by asking them such questions as: "How is it that you can watch 'The Pharaoh's Daughter' for the 146th time?"[59] Fokin reminisced in his memoirs about a balletomane who had a permanent seat in the balcony and who would "watch the performances of the same ballet innumerable times."[60]

The second component of ritual is hierarchy. Rituals are strongly associated with liturgy in which there is a clearly defined hierarchy extending from God, through His mediator, the priest, to the lowly worshipper. Similar hierarchies characterize other forms of deification. Throughout history, theater has provided a public forum for the display of formal hierarchies. For example, in English Elizabethan court theater, proximity to the monarch served as an indicator of status or favor. As one historian affirms, "James I found that an easy way to insult the Venetians was to seat them farther than the Spaniards from the royal box. The theater thus became, in the most direct way, a political entity as well."[61] A similar hierarchy was evident in the St. Petersburg Imperial Theaters, as we saw in Chapter 1. At the summit of the state theater organization was the tsar, proprietor of the "Emperor's Theaters." They were run on the tsar's behalf by his Minister of the Imperial Court, who delegated responsibilities to a Director of Imperial Theaters. Employees of the state theaters were in the service of the tsar, part of his expansive retinue. When artists took their stage bows, they were required by law to bow first to the tsar's box—even if he was not there, a member of the family was likely to be in attendance—then to the Director's box, and only then to the audience.[62] In this way, formal hierarchies were publicly acknowledged and reinforced. The place where someone sat in the auditorium indicated the person's status. While status in the Elizabethan auditorium was indicated by proximity to the monarch, in the St. Petersburg Imperial Theaters it was indicated by how good a view was had of the stage. The tsar and his retinue occupied the best seats, in the middle of the central balcony, just above stage level. Those with high status, and who were generally affluent, usually occupied the boxes and stalls. Those in the cheaper seats in the galleries and lesser galleries were less affluent. The constant reference in memoirs to the uniformed gentlemen in the stalls suggests that officers enjoyed displaying their status through dress. Fashionable ladies wore elaborate hats to indicate their importance.[63]

The third essential component of ritual is symbolism. Symbols are intertwined with the hierarchy. They help to define it and to reinforce it. The St. Petersburg Imperial Theaters were monumental symbols of the tsarist order, and one might reasonably refer to them as "power symbols." They did not constitute an illusion of that power, but an extension (or incarnation) of it because they originated as theaters at the Russian court and were financed by the state until 1917. The symbolic connections with tsarist power were inherent, as noted in Chapter 1, in the very names of the theaters and in their architecture. One historian even suggested that the architecture of the Imperial Theaters was part of a deliberate strategy adopted during the reign of Nicholas I to "[blind] the eyes of the contemporaries by a pretended magnificence of the regime as a whole and that of its Capital City in particular."[64]

It is difficult for historians to assess adequately the impact of symbolism, but there is evidence to suggest that patrons of the St. Petersburg Imperial Theaters were impressed by their architectural environment. For one enthusiast of the Alexandrinsky, the surroundings clearly were significant:

> As solemn, steadfast and imperturbable as the Senate and Synod or Isaac's buildings stands the building of the Alexandrinsky Theater, painted in the Alexandrovsky colors of yellow and white, surrounded by the unending extensions of its Directorate and schools, and having on its pediment an immovable triumphal chariot, surrounded by great shadows. You enter as to an enchanted reign of sleeping queens. The vestibule with massive columns, the collections of corridors, the clean-shaven, condescendingly important ushers, the cosy boxes—all this takes you back, not to childhood, but to somewhere farther, to that era when dandies in tight blue pantaloons crowded at the orchestra barrier....[65]

After a summer recess, the same writer became even more ecstatic about the Alexandrinsky: "After a three-month abstinence, when you enter this beautiful theater, the auditorium familiar to you since childhood, you are enveloped by an atmosphere of another, true, dream-like [*mechtaemyi*] theater, a theater that is not ours, but is of past and future days."[66] Paléologue wrote of the Mariinsky's "sumptuous hall, with its blue and gold hangings."[67] Benois recalled his first visits to the Mariinsky:

> It was somehow especially awe-inspiring and charming to experience one-self in it, in this circular auditorium with five tiers with rows of boxes in each one. Above the blue curtains of the tsars' boxes fat white cupids supported golden crowns and coats of arms with eagles, and from the circular ceiling, on which were depicted dancing maids, a huge, burning chandelier sparkled with innumerable lights.[68]

Gnedich recalled D. V. Grigorovich, chairman of the St. Petersburg Theater-Literary Committee in the 1890s, waxing lyrical about Rossi, architect of the Alexandrinsky and Theater Street: "What proportions! What walls! How monumental!"[69] Petrov, after having signed his first contract with the Directorate in the offices at Theater Street, stood outside and admired the Alexandrinsky, overwhelmed by its physical presence:

> For a long time I stood admiring the architectural harmony of the Alexandrinsky Theater. I went round it twice, looking from all sides. Probably for the first time in my life I felt, precisely felt, but did not understand, the beauty, strength and power of an architectural structure. The power of the harmony of the building's separate parts, and its sublimity as a whole.[70]

Such qualities of the St. Petersburg Imperial Theater buildings were contrasted to those of London theaters by members of the ballet troupe which toured with Diaghilev in 1911. "What amazed us above all," wrote Sergei Grigorev, "was the Theatre Royal in Covent Garden itself":

> It stood in the midst of a vegetable market and was closely hemmed in by greengrocers' warehouses and vast mountains of cabbages, potatoes, carrots and all manner of fruit. Being accustomed in Russia to theatres erected in large open spaces, where they might be seen and admired from all sides, we could not understand why the chief theatre in London should be situated in a market of all places, where it was impossible even to obtain a view of the façade.[71]

All this suggests that the St. Petersburg Imperial Theaters were important to contemporaries as physical structures; hence, one might reasonably conjecture that their symbolic qualities, to some degree, were transmitted to their clientele. The problem is that there is no reliable means of measuring the nature and extent of that transmission. In the end, two points need to be emphasized. First, although the buildings and auditoria symbolized the grandeur of the court, there is no evidence that audiences consciously acknowledged the fact that the surroundings with which they were enamored were *court* institutions. That is to say, court status was incidental to the immediate impact the auditoria had on audiences. On the other hand, court status, and the resources it conferred, explains why the Imperial Theaters were more elaborate and opulent than other theaters in the capital, which in general had a more spartan character and modest decor.

* * * *

In conclusion, the profile of the St. Petersburg Imperial Theater audience portrays auditoria dominated by privileged and wealthy patrons whose attendance was a high-profile social occasion. The audience itself "performed." Dress codes and behavioral conventions were much in evidence, and the opulent display of the promenading audience arguably was as central to the event as the spectacle enacted on stage. The Imperial Theaters thus constituted a cultural club for the St. Petersburg elite, an arena where they might identify themselves as members of an exclusive circle. Furthermore, many patrons were closely associated with the imperial court and other loci of state power: military officials, bureaucrats, Grand Dukes, and so on. The audience profile and its ritual of attendance therefore enhances the image of cultural institutions closely associated with power in imperial Russia (though not exclusively with the court).

There is no direct evidence that this *pridvornyi* association was a key reason why audiences were attracted to the Imperial Theaters, or that audiences were there *because* it was an elite club that it was fashionable to be seen in. It could be argued that the fact that so many elements of the tsarist elite appreciated theater art rendered the Imperial Theaters elite clubs anyway. It is difficult to disentangle these two reasons for the attraction of the Imperial Theaters and to establish one (elite club or artistic appreciation) as the more important, but it seems clear that the Imperial Theaters were regarded as "a place to be seen." This aspect of the St. Petersburg Imperial Theaters arguably became more significant for the privileged coteries of high society in the years after 1900. The famous court balls, where members of the imperial Russian establishment traditionally displayed themselves, were in abeyance during that period. This was attributed by one anonymous observer in 1917 to the tsarina's dislike for such functions, and so "for ten years there have been no balls or receptions at Court" with the result that St. Petersburg lacked a "social center of gaiety and pleasure."[72] The anonymous observer did not refer to the Imperial Theaters as alternative venues for "gaiety and pleasure," but there is plentiful evidence to suggest that they performed a social function which transcended the mere provision of stage entertainment for audiences.

The St. Petersburg Imperial Theaters were broadly exclusive institutions whose audiences represented the city's elites and reinforced the Imperial Theaters' status as institutions for the privileged. Yet the nature of the audience was not entirely static. Representatives of the lower orders were present in the lesser galleries, the high aristocracy was less in evidence, and so the audience profile was not immune to wider social changes. In other words, the history of the audience indicates that the state/power association was still important in defining the cultural status of the Imperial Theaters; but this was waning. The demand for tickets, and the preoccupation with etiquette and display cannot be explained exclusively in terms of the Imperial Theaters' court status.

Chapter 4

The Alexandrinsky Repertoire, 1900–1917

As an institutional history broadly concerned with the significance of the St. Petersburg Imperial Theaters' court status to their identity in the late tsarist period, the central question this study must ask of the repertoire is not so much what was performed, but what was its contemporary meaning. In particular, did the content of the repertoire serve to identify the St. Petersburg Imperial Theaters as tsarist court institutions, or was it essentially autonomous? There are two dimensions to this question that must be considered in turn. First, did the Russian government have guidelines on the repertoire; in other words how important, and in what ways, was theatrical censorship in determining the repertoire? Second, was the repertoire, as approved by the censor, "political" in any respect—at the crudest level, did it uphold the values and interests of the tsarist state; or was it part of what might be termed the "critical repertoire" that was evolving in Russian theater through the works of contemporary dramatists such as Chekhov and Gorky? That is to say, did the cultural product of the St. Petersburg Imperial Theaters reflect the concerns and interests of state or society in late tsarist Russia? Alternatively, was it thematically autonomous and best understood in terms of "art for art's sake" rather than as part of a wider political and social discourse?

Censorship and the St. Petersburg Imperial Theaters

One of the Russian intelligentsia's principal grievances against the tsarist autocracy was censorship of the written and spoken word undertaken by the Chief Administration for Press Affairs in the Ministry of Internal Affairs.[1] Although there was a limited progressive reform of censorship laws relating to the press and other publications in the wake of the 1905 Revolution, theatrical censorship, despite calls for its abolition from private theater leaders,[2] remained unaltered until the February Revolution of 1917. Theater was regarded as a separate censorship category by the authorities, who continued to view the spoken word and public performance as potentially more subversive than the printed word.

All Russian theaters were subject to the censorship of the Chief Administration for Press Affairs. However, the Chief Administration did not apply its decisions uniformly. It distinguished between the Imperial Theaters, certain private theaters, and popular (*narodnyi*) theaters. Censorship was less onerous for the Imperial Theaters, a privileged status implicit in the government's approach to censorship in the new popular theaters. With the growth of popular theater in the 1880s, the tsarist government became increasingly concerned about the potential impact such entertainment might have upon the Russian people. The benefits of theatrical entertainment in terms of promoting temperance and providing an alternative to political radicalism or criminal activity were acknowledged, but there was concern that popular theater might prove subversive if "inappropriate" material was performed. The direct result of this concern was that, in January 1888, Minister of Internal Affairs Count Dmitry Tolstoy promulgated a special censorship regulation for popular theaters. From then on, the censor was required to consider not only the content of a drama or libretto, but also the category of theater it was intended for. Works proposed for performance on the popular stage had to be selected from the list of works already approved by the Chief Administration for performance elsewhere; they then had to be considered separately for the popular stage. This resulted in a situation where certain works were approved for the Imperial and private stages, but not for the popular stage.

To determine what was or was not a popular theater, the government was guided by ticket prices: the lower the price, the more "simple" (*prostoi*) and therefore more impressionable the audience. The assumption was that low income signified little education. In other words, the government believed that Russian theatergoers could be differentiated according to education. It was considered more dangerous for poorly educated audiences to be exposed to works that contained implicit criticism of autocracy, the administration, or the nobility than it was for educated strata to be exposed to them. Count Tolstoy's 1888 memorandum on censorship for the popular theaters stated that:

> The censorship, in considering plays, has in mind a more or less educated theatergoing public, though not exclusively one class of society; in the level of his intellectual development, views and understanding, the ordinary person [*prostoliudin*] is often capable of interpreting in a completely false way

that which does not present any temptation to an educated person, and therefore a play that contains nothing reprehensible from a general point of view might turn out for him [the *prostoliudin*] to be unsuitable and even harmful.[3]

In addition to the regulation of 1888, posts were created in 1901 in St. Petersburg and Moscow to ensure that plays already approved for performance in private theaters were not being reinterpreted on stage during actual performances.[4]

Although there were no specific guidelines on what should be prohibited, a pattern of forbidden categories emerged which one historian lists as: depictions of rulers and clergy, historical works depicting rebellion or oppression, plays satirizing government and officialdom/authority, works inciting class envy, and works depicting crime or sex.[5] Plays considered progressive or radical which were prohibited from the popular theaters but were performed at the St. Petersburg Imperial Theaters included Tolstoy's *The Power of Darkness*, a play dealing with adultery and infanticide, of which the censor, when considering the work for translation into Latvian in 1899, wrote:

> If the stage performance of such vile crimes creates, and it must create, disagreeable feelings for educated theater audiences, then especially for uneducated audiences the impression of such a scene must create a really debauched image for the disposition of ordinary folk, who comprise, in the majority of cases, the masses of Latvian theater audiences.

Also prohibited for the popular, but not the Imperial, stage was Beaumarchais's *Le Nozze di Figaro*, banned from the popular theaters in 1896 because it was "spotted with witty escapades against the nobility."[6] In general, monarchs could not be portrayed on the popular stage, but they could be, and were, on the Imperial stage, for example in Tolstoy's *The Death of Ivan the Terrible* and *Tsar Fyodor Ioannovich*. The implication was that these plays were not dangerous for Imperial Theater audiences but might give popular audiences "subversive" ideas if certain scenes depicted monarchical weakness or cruelty.

There were no special rules for the Imperial Theaters, but in practice they were specially treated. As long as a play or libretto had been approved for performance by the censor, the Directorate was entitled to produce it. In other words, the Imperial Theaters were not singled out by the dramatic censorship. This perhaps explains why censorship was never a major issue for Imperial Theater artists, for instance in 1905, when calls for the abolition of the censorship were led by leaders of the private theaters. The extent to which censorship was not a recurrent issue in the Imperial Theaters is underlined by the fact that only on occasion did the issue arise when works were censored or banned for specific reasons. For example, Gorky's *The Lower Depths* was banned from both the popular and Imperial stage, but not from the private stage. In 1902, Telyakovsky decided that the play should be produced at the Alexandrinsky as it recently had been a success at the Moscow Art Theater and might breathe some life into the St. Petersburg repertoire. By January 1903, the Minister of Internal Affairs, Viacheslav von Plehve, had learned of this decision. He expressed disapproval. According to Telyakovsky, Plehve admitted that "the censor had passed the play, but this applied, of course, to private theaters—as regards the Imperial Theaters, this is the competence of the Minister of the Court." Plehve appeared to suggest that even though a play had been approved for performance in private theaters it was not, *ipso facto*, approved for the Imperial Theaters, although in statutory terms, the Directorate was not required to obtain separate permission to perform works which had been approved by the Chief Administration for Press Affairs. The following day (January 25, 1903) Telyakovsky had another audience with Plehve during which the Minister reiterated his objections to the proposal to stage *The Lower Depths* at the Alexandrinsky, stating that he considered Gorky to be a dangerous revolutionary and that if he had a good excuse he would send him immediately to Siberia. Plehve then added that "I cannot ban the play *The Lower Depths* from the Imperial Theaters, but if it is produced I will protest." As Plehve had already conceded, it was the competence of the Minister of the Imperial Court to adjudicate in such matters. Telyakovsky, however, recognized that the Minister of the Imperial Court never contradicted the Minister of Internal Affairs, and so he abandoned the idea of repeating the Moscow Art Theater's success with Gorky. But the Director was perplexed by the ban. "Why private theaters can perform Gorky, but the state theaters cannot, is quite incomprehensible." Indeed, he continued, "if these plays really are dangerous, then they are dangerous to all theaters."

Further reasons for the hostility to Telyakovsky's proposal emerged when he met Fredericks the day after his audience with Plehve. According to Fredericks, the tsar had been consulted on the issue and had expressed his desire that a distance be maintained between the Imperial Theaters and revolutionaries. The tsar is alleged to have remarked that, "once Gorky has been placed under police surveillance, his surname has no place on an Imperial Theater poster." On February 6, 1903, Telyakovsky spoke with Nicholas II during a performance at the Mikhailovsky. The subject of Gorky arose and the tsar repeated to Telyakovsky the sentiments he had already expressed to Fredericks, adding that "it is necessary that the public visiting the Imperial Theaters do not derive from what they have seen and heard that oppressive impression which is particularly difficult for people who are discontented with life to bear."[7]

This incident highlights the fact that occasionally the tsar exercised influence over the repertoire of his theaters, and that there was an implicit understanding amid governing circles that only certain types of material should be performed. Its rarity also emphasizes the fact that censorship in the Imperial Theaters was carried out on an *ad hoc* basis, as Telyakovsky indicated:

> The decisions of the censor were sometimes exposed to the criticism not only of the Grand Dukes and ministers, but also of the tsar himself. This was particularly the case with regard to the French repertoire of the Mikhailovsky Theater. Once there was even a case when the Sovereign, attending a French production at the Mikhailovsky Theater, asked me why he had not heard the well-known phrases that the Grand Duke Vladimir Alexandrovich had told him about (these phrases concerned one of the French ministers) and which were so funny and witty. I reported that these phrases had been changed by the censorship—then the Sovereign said: "Oh, this censorship, always it is zealous where it's just not necessary." When I suggested that these phrases be restored for future performances, he agreed and the phrases were restored to general amusement.[8]

On balance, the government's explicit concern with the popular theater repertoire betrayed an implicit respect for the Imperial Theater audience and, by extension, the material it could be exposed to. This meant that the Directorate of Imperial Theaters enjoyed practically a free hand in selecting the repertoire from the hundreds of plays and libretti approved annually by the Chief Administration for Press Affairs. Further, the general absence of the issue of censorship from the St. Petersburg Imperial Theaters suggests that the Directorate produced what it wanted to produce. Of course, this did not mean that the Directorate did not insist on alterations to works it had selected for production. The fate of Rimsky-Korsakov's operas was an obvious case in point: For instance, even after the censor had stipulated certain alterations to the libretto of *The Golden Cockerel*—produced at the Moscow Imperial Bolshoi Theater in 1909—to address areas where it was perceived to mock tsarism, the Directorate in St. Petersburg kept delaying the premiere because it continued to discover aspects of the opera that were "impermissible" on the Imperial stage.[9]

The Directorate did not employ specific criteria for selecting the repertoire, and the wide range of material produced at the St. Petersburg Imperial Theaters renders it difficult to ascertain a particular tendency in the repertoire. Some people accused Telyakovsky of ignoring the classics and of making the repertoire almost too "German"; but these accusations are not justified when the repertoire is considered as a whole. It is true that Telyakovsky encouraged new drama (as in the case of his unsuccessful attempt to stage *The Lower Depths*), and that Wagner's operas became popular at the Mariinsky during his Directorship, but the repertoire remained predominantly Russian. And the classics remained prominent, as we will see, as we now turn to consider the second and third questions posed by this chapter: Was the Alexandrinsky Theater repertoire "political," and in what other ways—if any—did it reflect its epoch? An essential preliminary consideration, however, is the methodology used to interpret the repertoire.

Methodology

During the nineteenth and early twentieth centuries, Russian artists made a significant and outstanding contribution to world drama, music, and dance. These developments are well-known and this study is not concerned with them *per se*, but rather with what might be termed the "politics of the repertoire": What did the repertoire contribute to the contemporary institutional identity of the St. Petersburg Imperial Theaters in the context of their relationship to the state? The chief way historians can address this question with any accuracy is to consider how audiences viewed the repertoire. Only an understanding of audience reception will provide an historical picture of what the repertoire signified to audiences and, therefore, how the repertoire contributed to the identity of the St Petersburg Imperial Theaters. For example, historians argue that Gogol's dramatic masterpiece, *The Government Inspector*, constituted a satirical attack on the Russian bureaucracy of the nineteenth century, and there exists plentiful evidence to support this. Yet it does not necessarily follow that when *The Government Inspector* was *performed* at the St. Petersburg Imperial Theaters in the early twentieth-century audiences viewed it as primarily an attack on the administration. Perhaps it was popular to St. Petersburg audiences simply because it was amusing, or because it depicted provincial rather than metropolitan corruption.

In other words, writing the history of the repertoire beyond simply listing what was performed is a problematic task. It raises a methodological problem: How can historians decipher what the repertoire signified to contemporary audiences? It is not entirely sufficient for the historian to endeavor to interpret the texts of the works which were performed. That would result in literary criticism, not history, although the text and the story obviously contain useful clues. Nor is it acceptable to be guided by authorial intentions because often they did not correspond to the theatrical production or the artists' interpretation. Most notably, Chekhov was dismayed by the Moscow Art Theater's interpretations of his plays. The writer described *The Cherry Orchard* as a comedy, but the imperious Stanislavsky adjudged the play a tragedy.[10] Judging by the correspondence between Turgenev and Savina, historians would learn very little, or nothing, about the contemporary meaning of *A Month in the Country* simply by reading its text. When she first acted in *A Month in the Country* for her benefit performance in January 1879, Savina played the part of Verochka. Turgenev considered this character to be too minor for Savina and felt that, as a leading actress, she ought to have played Natalya Petrovna, the play's principal character. "True, you are too young for the part of Natalya Petrovna, but Verotchka ... what is there to play?" asked Turgenev. Savina, of course, could defend her decision with ease:

> The play was produced, and it created a sensation. I had great success in my role as Verotchka, which became my favourite part—my "creation." I gave

myself up entirely to the role. I did not *play* Verotchka—I performed a sacred rite—I walked in the clouds. That night, there was an electric current between myself and the audience. I felt that they loved me, loved Verotchka for my complete identification with her.[11]

In other words, Savina, the actress, had transformed Verochka successfully into the play's principal character, and it was not until 1903 that she decided to play the "main" role of Natalya Petrovna.

Furthermore, the late nineteenth and early twentieth centuries witnessed the rise of the *régisseur*, who began to replace both authors and individual stars as the dominant interpreter of a theatrical production. "The director [*régisseur*] is now the autocrat of the theatre," announced Andrei Bely.[12] The obvious example of this development is the Moscow Art Theater, where considerable emphasis was placed on the overarching role of the *régisseur*.[13] The St. Petersburg Imperial Theaters were not isolated from this trend and were beginning to employ individuals such as Sanin and Meyerhold, whose chief role was to direct performances. In other words, the centrality of the author and his interpretation of a play was being challenged by the *régisseur* and his interpretation. This was certainly the case with regard to the relationship between the dramatist and the theater. It might also be argued that this was equally the case with regard to the relationship between the stage—in other words, the performance—and the audience. That is to say, an understanding of the *artists'* interpretations of performances does not necessarily entail an understanding of audiences' interpretations. There are multiple components, signs, and messages contained within a single theatrical performance and it is impossible to ascertain which ones communicated themselves most forcefully to audiences.[14] Individual members of an audience are inspired, entranced, or moved by different aspects of a production and arrive at different conclusions about it.

Given these problems, how do we approach the history of repertoire? The contemporary meaning of a theater's repertoire is constructed by audience reception, and it is that which must be deciphered. Of course, audiences are composed of individuals who necessarily have individual perspectives on performances. Yet theater audiences are not completely heterogeneous. As the previous chapter indicated, although St. Petersburg Imperial Theater audiences were not entirely static, they also had homogeneous characteristics. The audience was not an entirely uniform or completely exclusive caste, but it did have a meaningful collective identity. This fact makes it easier for the historian to decipher the contemporary meaning of the repertoire. We can assume a sufficient level of conformity between the repertoire's themes and the general tastes and inclinations of the audience. Even the St. Petersburg Imperial Theaters could not afford to ignore the wishes of their patrons. As noted in Chapter 1, court and State Exchequer subsidies did not ensure financial stability, and the government theaters were ill-advised to overlook the wishes of the audience. As Samuel Johnson put it in 1765, "The Drama's laws the Drama's patrons give / For we that live to please must please to live." Ultimately, as a consequence of Dr. Johnson's dictum, serious financial problems did not emanate from the vicissitudes of box-office revenues. Artists thrived on applause and critical acclaim and did not persist with productions which made them unpopular.

It is a matter of quantification to establish what were the most popular and representative works of the repertoire, and what represented the types of material contemporaries wanted to see. As there are no known contemporary surveys which set out systematically to ask audiences how they responded to Imperial Theater performances, evaluation of the significance of the popular and representative productions can best be achieved by analyzing critics' reviews of performances. Though a small group, critics often remarked on the general reception of a performance and so the pursuit of answers need not be abandoned. Certain broad conclusions can be established by examining the predominant themes which critics perceived in the most popular works of the repertoire. This is the closest historians can come to an understanding of *what the repertoire meant to contemporaries.*

Alexandrinsky Drama

Between 1900 and 1917, the Alexandrinsky Theater produced a total of 394 plays.[15] This was an exceedingly large output compared with that of other Russian drama theaters. For instance, according to a recent history, the Moscow Art Theater staged "around seventy" productions between 1898 and 1917, about one-fifth of the Alexandrinsky's output.[16] The average number of times a play was performed at the Alexandrinsky during the period was 13.5. Many works were performed only a few times, then never resurrected, while others were notable successes during a particular season and then were performed infrequently. Others were performed regularly throughout the whole period. It can be assumed that plays performed with more than average frequency were popular with audiences—but not necessarily with critics. Attention will be focused on the corpus of twenty-four plays which were performed forty times or more during the period. When they are removed from the equation, the average number of performances of a play is 10.7. Therefore, the twenty-four most popular plays were responsible for boosting the average number of performances by almost three, a clear sign of their dominant position in the repertoire during the years from 1900 to 1917.

Only two plays were performed more than one hundred times at the Alexandrinsky during the period, Gogol's *The Government Inspector* (120 performances) and Sukhovo-Kobylin's *Krechinsky's Wedding* (116 performances). The other popular works, in descending order, were Alexander Ostrovsky's

Enough Stupidity in Every Wise Man (eighty-five performances); Lev Tolstoy's *The Fruits of Enlightenment* (seventy-seven performances); Alexander Griboedov's *Woe from Wit* (sixty-eight performances); Ostrovsky's *The Forest* (sixty-six performances); and Ostrovsky's *A Passionate Heart* (sixty-one performances). The remaining eighteen plays had performance figures in the forties and fifties. Thirteen of them were by Russian dramatists: Chekhov's *The Cherry Orchard*,[17] Denis Fonvizin's *The Minor*, Gnedich's *The Assembly* and *Slaves*, Viktor Ryshkov's *Philistines* and *The Passers-By*, Tatyana Shchepkina-Kupernik's *The Wings*, Sumbatov-Yuzhin's *The Old School*, Vladimir Tikhonov's *The Great Secret*, Lev Tolstoy's *The Living Corpse*, and Turgenev's *A Month in the Country* and *Breakfast with the Marshal of Nobility*. The remaining five plays were by non-Russian dramatists: Albert Guinon's *Décadence*, Wilhelm Meyer-Förster's *Alt Heidelberg*, Molière's *Don Juan*, Shakespeare's *The Merchant of Venice*, and Zuderman's *Johannisfeuer*. Our discussion of the reception of the repertoire will draw upon this corpus of plays, yet without providing a detailed analysis of each single production.

The repertoire profile must be qualified in one significant respect. Three of the popular plays, *The Government Inspector*, *Woe from Wit*, and *The Minor*, were given principally as matinee performances. Of the 120 performances of *The Government Inspector*, sixty-seven were matinee performances; of the sixty-eight performances of *Woe from Wit*, forty-seven were matinee performances; and of the fifty-four performances of *The Minor*, forty-eight were matinee performances. Performance figures for other plays contain within them occasional matinee performances but were chiefly given in the evening. Matinee performances tended to be staged for charitable causes or for children. For the purposes of this study, performances are evening performances, when the audience consisted of the conventional evening clientele delineated in the previous chapter.[18] This is significant because it reduces the contemporary profile of two of the potentially most political dramas in the repertoire, *The Government Inspector* and *Woe from Wit*. Although after taking into account the number of matinee performances *The Government Inspector* was still presented at the Alexandrinsky fifty-three times during the period 1900–17 and therefore remained one of the most popular plays in the repertoire, *Woe from Wit* and *The Minor* become much less prominent in the repertoire profile, and the most popular play becomes *Krechinsky's Wedding*.

An examination of performance reviews indicates that three key ingredients ensured success for a production. The first was the depiction of a rich and comfortable lifestyle which audiences found pleasing to the eye, a world which they might dream of inhabiting, or perhaps already did inhabit. The second ingredient was love intrigue. The third was humor. Of course, the three key ingredients, or essential themes, of successful productions often were found in combination. If one theme united them, and at times appeared to supersede them in importance, it was familiarity. Audiences did not want to be exposed to ideas or scenarios which challenged their prejudices. They reveled in the familiar and the safe. The critic Alexander Kugel' remarked in 1897 that "the weakest aspect of contemporary Russian drama is poverty of analysis. We are quite unable to write plays à la thèse."[19] The familiar worlds conveyed to the audience were those of court society and the landed nobility in particular. Derzhavin attributed this to political reaction between 1907 and 1917, most evident, he observed, in a series of productions "belonging to the 'court' type of plays and idealizing the court life of epochs long ago elapsed and marked by the happy florescence of Russian aristocracy."[20] At the same time, however, the repertoire reflected the rise of the merchantry (a growing presence in the audience itself) in several plays which included entrepreneurs among their principal characters. Thus, although the predominant environment depicted by the repertoire tends to reinforce the court identity of the Alexandrinsky, the wider changes occurring in Russian society were making their impact on it, forging a more complex image. Indeed, the fact that the Alexandrinsky, a court institution, was often referred to as a merchant's theater (see Chapter 3) is indicative of the growing ambivalence of its identity. Moreover, several of the popular Alexandrinsky productions alluded to issues that were increasingly the subject of debate by the nascent civil society, such as the "woman question" (*zhenskii vopros*).

Sukhovo-Kobylin's *Krechinsky's Wedding* was one of the most popular Russian plays. It was "enormous," according to the critic "Lvoff."[21] This three-act comedy tells the tale of Krechinsky, a leading light of the Moscow *beau monde*, who arranges to marry Lidochka, the daughter of a wealthy landowner, Muromsky, in order to obtain money to settle his gambling debts. Krechinsky becomes so desperate that he steals back the diamond pin which he had presented to his fiancée in order to pawn it. But at the pawnbroker's, while he shows the money lender the real diamond pin, he hands over to him an identical, but worthless, substitute. That way, he can return the real pin to his future wife. However, his deceit is revealed at the end of the play, and the Muromsky family flee the stage to avoid the disgrace of being associated with this event. For Derzhavin, *Krechinsky's Wedding* "reveals the utter depression and decay of Russian Aristocracy and of the contingent of Russian land-owners."[22] Yet there is no evidence to suggest that contemporary audiences viewed the play that way. Rather, it was the comic aspect of *Krechinsky's Wedding* which held the key to its popularity. Of Raspliuev, Krechinsky's associate, the critic Dolgov writes: "In our repertoire, there are no roles which are more colorful and richer in humor."[23] Petrov suggests in his memoirs that *Krechinsky's Wedding* was the play which made the greatest impression on him, and it is the comic scenes which he recalls. In particular, Petrov was enamored of the "pause," when Raspliuev (played by Davydov) and Muromsky (played by Varlamov) both insist that the other be the first to sit down on the divan in the center of the stage. They stand at opposite ends of the divan, motioning

View of the Alexandrinsky from the Nevsky Prospect, with a statue of Catherine the Great in the foreground. Author's collection

each other with one hand to sit. Then Raspliuev approaches the middle of the divan, and with his back to the audience motions with *both* hands for Muromsky to sit. Muromsky then does the same. In the end, they look at each other, smile, and sit down simultaneously—and all this was accompanied by growing laughter from the audience.[24]

Familiarity is a further theme in the reviews. When the curtain goes up, the audience sees the drawing room in Muromsky's house, "an ordinary room."[25] The room was "ordinary" to a particular group of people: the Alexandrinsky audience. While to an outside observer (Derzhavin) this may have conveyed the impression of "depression and decay," to contemporaries who witnessed the performance, the inside, or *real*, observers, an altogether different impression was conveyed, and one which did not excite hostility.

Turgenev's *A Month in the Country* is conventionally regarded as a play replete with criticism of the Russian social system. Isaiah Berlin detected in it "a strong undercurrent of social criticism" and claimed that "to ignore this aspect of the drama is to fail in understanding." He went so far as to say that there is in the play "a bitter indictment of a social system which no reader, no member of a theatrical audience in Russia in the nineteenth century, could have missed."[26] No reader, perhaps, but the evidence again indicates that, in general, Alexandrinsky audiences did not detect in this play any devastating social criticism which Turgenev might have intended, and which readers of the text have discerned. The main attraction of this play was the lifestyle it depicted and the sentimentality it evoked. While Kugel does refer to the "unconscious brutality" (serfdom) of the mid-nineteenth century, when *A Month in the Country* was written and which period it depicts, his overwhelming impression is captured in the quote from George Sand which he repeats in his discussion of this play: "Ah, que j'aime cette vie, si calme et douce."[27] The critic Iurii Beliaev was rhapsodic about the setting of the play, commencing his review in the following way: "I was in an old landowner's estate, in a spacious and cool gentleman's residence, with a shady garden, with picturesque surroundings, with a rich, semi-destroyed conservatory..." (Beliaev's ellipsis). Again the theme of familiarity stands out. There is a "familiar, typical room." "You know Rakitin from the great number of daguerreotypes," as you do Natalya Petrovna. Beliaev does not criticize the lifestyle he sees portrayed. Rather, he sentimentalizes it: "O, sweet bygone era."[28] Had the critics failed to understand the drama? Or were they simply moving in circles whose members perceived something other than social criticism in the play? The latter is the more probable answer. Berlin himself stated that the view of *A Month in the Country* as an indictment of a declining social system is the *Soviet* view (the view of Derzhavin), and not that of pre-revolutionary Russian or Western criticism.[29] The more plausible interpretation of what Turgenev's play *signified to the Alexandrinsky audience* in the early years of the twentieth century can be gleaned from critics who actually witnessed the production.

The reception of Gnedich's *The Assembly*, which enjoyed a successful premiere and run of performances, further refutes the notion of an overtly political repertoire. Kugel regretted that its portrayal of Peter the Great meant that it was permitted for performance only on the Imperial Theater stage and implied that the play was suitable for all theaters because Gnedich "conceals the cruel features of Peter's character," and depicts instead the "sublime features"—Peter the seafarer and carpenter. In other words, the tsar was painted in a positive light. Kugel attributed the success of *The Assembly* not to its "psychological truth," its "historical interest," or its "technical perfection." Rather, its popularity was explained by its "pleasantness," which "all the time provides a feeling of complete happiness."[30] Another reviewer found it difficult to locate an "idea" in this play of "manners during the reign of Peter I." "If an idea is to be found in the play, then it is this: down with the corrupt, and long live honorable people."[31] The reviewer does not specify who the honorable people are.

Zuderman's popular play, *Johannisfeuer*, of following Beliaev's description of the Alexandrinsky production, is a love story which takes place within the familiar context of a prosperous landowning family, this time in Prussian Lithuania. Fogelreiger, the landowner, his wife and their daughter, Truda, have living with them Fogelreiger's nephew, Georg, who is also Truda's fiancé.

There also resides in the house the adopted child Marikka, daughter of a Lithuanian beggar. At one time, Georg was in love with Marikka and had written her clandestine love poetry, which she eventually discovers. Georg is thus torn between two women, and although he and Marikka display much sympathy for each other, in the end he insists that his marriage to Truda goes ahead.[32] *Johannisfeuer* contained the classic ingredients of the Alexandrinsky repertoire and was devoid of any explicit political content. Certainly, it does not appear to have had any "political" impact.

Ryshkov's *The Passers-By* devotes itself to relations between the sexes, even though it has been described as having "no definite plot." It is, of course, set in a landowner's house. Its general theme is that men treat women badly. According to one reviewer, if the play has a moral, it is that "it is sinful and shameful to hurt a woman."[33] According to the critic "Impr.," the tone of the play leads it to be classified not as a drama, but a comedy. The "passers-by" refers to "those men who, like butterflies flitting from one flower to another (if women in general ought to be considered as flowers!), imbibe the scent of the flower and then egotistically fly away in search of fresher and more over-powering petals." Oddly enough, this struck the critic as unusual, because in most plays the man is the "suffering character," who has to cope with female "coquetry," "perfidy" and "vengeance," which ultimately leaves the male "at the end of his tether."[34] Taking into consideration the twenty-four most popular Alexandrinsky productions, this assessment appears much mistaken because in most of those plays it is women who suffer the caprices of men. Ryshkov's comedy *Philistines* dealt with a similar theme, and both plays, taken together, alluded to the contemporary "woman question" (*zhenskii vopros*), an issue that was increasingly the concern of civil society.

The Alexandrinsky production of *Alt Heidelberg*, like the text of Meyer-Förster's play itself, was characterized most of all by sentimentality. The play tells the story of Karl Heinrich, the Hereditary Prince of Saxon-Karlsburg, who gains entry to the University of Heidelberg. Breaking free from the secluded life of his castle, the young Prince falls in love with the revelry of student life and with Käthie, who is unfortunately betrothed to someone else. Nevertheless, the love is mutual. When the Prince hears that he must return to Karlsbad to take over the reins of government, he resists, but is then persuaded to return. "You must live in the memory of a happy past," the Minister of State advises him. Two years elapse, but the Prince cannot elude his fond memories of Heidelberg, which are making him uninterested in the governance of his principality. He decides to pay a return visit to Heidelberg, where he learns from Käthie that she is soon to be married. The Prince tells her that he too is to be married, but that Käthie is "the only creature in the world whom I have ever loved!" At this, Käthie sobs, and the play ends. The critics were keen to point out that this was "German sentimentality," which nevertheless went down well in Russia. "If there is anything pleasant in this ponderous drama of a good sentimental German, it is the infectious joy of living of the students."[35] Certainly, in no conceivable manner can political interpretations be drawn from the story. The success of *Alt Heidelberg* rather derived from a combination of the princely life it depicted, from the context— upper-class society—rather than from the plot, though its sentimentalism was clearly an important factor in its popularity. The themes of this play, therefore, were apolitical and universal. In his preface to the 1903 English translation of the play, J. T. Grein argued that *Alt Heidelberg* was successful in general "because it was German, but it also succeeded because, at any rate in its foundations, it is thoroughly human." Moreover, according to Grein, "[a]ll the world must be charmed [by this play] because all the world has had its day of youth, when the azure of women, wine, and song obscured the clouds of sorrow, and of the struggle of life."[36]

Décadence, again following Beliaev's description of the Alexandrinsky production, relates the tale of the families of the duke Barflet and the Jewish banker Shtroman. The duke has been financially ruined, but continues to lead the life of a wealthy notable. For example, he maintains a very expensive "kept-woman," whom his daughter, Zhanina, hears about. Meantime, Natan Shtroman, the son of the banker, is in love with Zhanina. Shtroman buys a promissory note from the duke, enabling the duke to continue leading his profligate lifestyle. The condition is that Zhanina must marry Natan, whom she does not love. Yet she agrees to go ahead with the scheme in order to protect her family. Needless to say, the newlyweds do not get on: "A witty altercation of society people occupies the whole of the second act." Meantime, it emerges that Zhanina and a fellow named Sheranse love each other. This is a long-standing love which both precedes and succeeds Zhanina's marriage to Natan. Zhanina leaves Natan for Sheranse, but with the threat of ruin hanging over her family, she is persuaded to return to the banker's son.

Beliaev asked whether Guinon was criticizing the aristocracy or Jews, and concluded that both were being attacked. Yet such political themes did not hold a central place in the reception of the play. Beliaev proceeded to argue that, for a Russian audience, there were no political, social or personal parodies in *Décadence*. "It can be watched, with pleasure, as a witty, light and adroit comedy. In the fashionable [*velikosvetskii*] society, I completely lost myself; here were so many 'counts and princes.'"[37] Once again, it was simply entertainment, escape to the life of the *beau monde*, that was extracted from the repertoire.

The Merchant of Venice was the most popular Shakespeare play at the Alexandrinsky. The title used for the production was in fact *Shylock*, reflecting the fact that the chief interest of the play for the audience was the eponymous character. Kugel regarded Shakespeare's tragedy as a comedy because, he implies, a Jew cannot have a tragic role (Kugel was himself a Jew).[38]

Beliaev argued that what he regarded as the traditional theme of *The Merchant of Venice*, the only problem raised in the play (should a Jew be baptized), once appealed to antisemitic audiences, but he perceived that audiences now had a greater demand which transcended such issues and which Shakespeare's play fully satisfied, at least in the Alexandrinsky's production: the demand for "enchantment, court life, love intrigues, flavored with lard [*salo*]."[39] Another reviewer simply described the production as "pleasant and worthy," offering no comment about its political aspects.[40]

Thwarted or frustrated love was a common theme in the Alexandrinsky repertoire. The story of *The Wings* revolves around an actress, Lesnovskaia, who is besotted with an advocate. When he abandons her for a "girl with violets," Lesnovskaia gains revenge by persuading the "girl with violets" to elope with an entrepreneur. The advocate returns to Lesnovskaia, who now decides that she no longer loves him. The sub-plot of Shchepkina-Kupernik's tale concerns the manner in which personal tribulations affect Lesnovskaia's stage work, which begins to deteriorate, until the desire for vengeance enables her to "raise her performance." In the end, when she has rejected the advocate's renewed advances, as Kugel describes it, "The impulse for the stage again envelops her." Kugel felt that the production lacked something. "Undoubtedly, the author knows theater life and the backstage atmosphere well. But it often happens that, for things with which we are very familiar and to which we are very close, there is a loss of liveliness and pungency."[41] *The Wings* was an introspective, incestuous story which declined to raise any direct political point, although again its theme alluded to the "woman question." It was a standard, formulaic tale of broken love, and its setting, the theater, arguably underlined the limited horizons of all involved—playwright, actors, and audience. To Beliaev, it was nevertheless an "elegant comedy … light, observant, witty."[42]

Of the twenty-four most popular Alexandrinsky productions, Lev Tolstoy's *The Living Corpse* arguably contained the most overt instances of social criticism. The play tells the story of Fedia Protasov, a spendthrift and drunkard who cavorts with gypsies. Protasov abandons his wife, Lisa, who then agrees to marry Karenin, the man who truly loves her. Yet for this marriage to take place Lisa must be divorced from Protasov. It was difficult to obtain a divorce in imperial Russia because incontestable evidence of adultery was required; hence, people resorted to bribery. However, because Protasov cannot afford bribery, he fakes his own suicide, thus "freeing" Lisa to marry Karenin. Unfortunately, the "living corpse" is betrayed to the police and Protasov, Lisa, and Karenin are brought before an Examining Magistrate to answer charges of bigamy. Protasov laments that he is being tried for *not* having committed suicide. In the end, realizing that his options are either exile to Siberia or reunion with Lisa, and hence the destruction of her happiness, Protasov shoots himself. The fundamental criticism made by *The Living*

Corpse was that the law did not allow people to be happy without either lying (in order to obtain a divorce) or breaking the law (bigamy or suicide). Yet Tolstoy arguably offered an even wider critique of Russian society in the person of Protasov. While Protasov is not indifferent to his life, he feels alienated from the world beyond the tavern. In act five, he tells his drinking companion that there are three options in life: You can become part of the establishment, that is, the civil or military service, but he finds that idea repulsive; alternatively, you can destroy that establishment, but that task requires a hero, which Protasov claims he is not; or you can forget about this problem altogether by drinking and singing. Derzhavin states that the reason *The Living Corpse* was performed forty-five times during the 1911-12 season was that the "Protasovshchina" suited the "suffering mood" of what he terms the bourgeois intelligentsia.[43] However, he provides no evidence to support this view. In fact, so far as can be deduced from contemporary reviews, the performance of *The Living Corpse* at the Alexandrinsky provoked no political discussion. Rather, debate centered around whether it could be viewed as a play at all. One reviewer suggested that it was not a play, but the "draft" of a drama, and complained that the Alexandrinsky troupe performed it "without enthusiasm."[44] Beliaev argued that, while it was a "remarkable work," *The Living Corpse* was not a play, but rather a stage in the development of a play (*stadium p'esy*). The remainder of his review was devoted to the style of production, and to the question of Tolstoy's indebtedness to Chekhov.[45] Lev Tolstoy's other popular play at the Alexandrinsky, *The Fruits of Enlightenment*, likewise produced little "political" response. Kugel had little to say about its production except that it was "bad, sluggish, and vague."[46]

One play which the critics did believe portrayed the Russian political and social system in a negative light was Gnedich's *Slaves*. An anonymous reviewer suggested that Gnedich had found a "very successful theme" in serfdom during the reign of Emperor Paul, as the prominence of *Slaves* in the Alexandrinsky repertoire implied. Yet the critic was disappointed with the end result. The epoch was well observed, but the play lacked an engaging plot, having no "clear stage break" or "unexpected tempest" which might have "raised the mood" of the play.[47] The reviewer claimed that this induced boredom in the audience. Another critic complained that "The epoch has been painted in too much of a monotone and too somber a color." The play contained few positive features for the reviewer, and he provided a rare instance of a critic discerning unsavory traits in a play which the likes of Derzhavin would be quick to perceive in retrospect: "Among the grandees, among the officials, among the serf cattle, nothing is depicted except servitude, venality, corruption, rudeness, ignorance, petty despotism, and shameful mediocrity."[48] Yet *Slaves* must have held some appeal for the general audience otherwise it would not have enjoyed so many performances. Moreover, the tepid response of the critics was an exception which proved the rule: They did not enjoy witnessing "monotone" or "shameful mediocrity" depicted as the norm in Russian society.

Many reviews simply commented on the production style and artistic technique of a performance, rather than its content. Kugel described Ostrovsky's *A Passionate Heart* as an "excellent play," arguing that it was best not to view it as a farce, as most critics had done since the play was first produced in 1869, but as a work which "expressed the spirit of Ostrovsky" in a way that few of his other plays did.[49] *Don Juan* attracted attention for the novelty of its production style (Meyerhold removed the footlights, the prompter's box, and the curtain, limited most of the action to the forestage, and kept the auditorium lights on during the performance), and that is what critics focused on, in addition to praising the acting.[50] As far as the content of Molière's classic was concerned, it was simply a great comedy, not a political diatribe.

The Alexandrinsky repertoire, therefore, appears innocuous to the impartial observer. Judging by the reviews, there is no sense in which it overtly sought to uphold or undermine the values and interests of the tsarist state (although some of the popular plays certainly had that potential). Moreover, this does not appear to have been a function of press censorship because there is no discernible change in the nature of reviews after 1905; they remain essentially "apolitical," despite the new opportunity afforded by changes to the censorship regulations for more direct engagement with contemporary political issues. This interpretation is enhanced if we compare the contemporary reception of the Alexandrinsky repertoire with the definition of the political play espoused by the great Russian theater historian, Konstantin Rudnitsky, who described Mayakovsky's *Mystery-Bouffe* (produced in 1918 by Meyerhold for the first anniversary of the Bolshevik Revolution) as "the first fully and thoroughly political play in the history of Russian theater." This play, in which the "Unclean" oppressed initiate a revolution which overthrows the "Clean" oppressors and leads to the construction of paradise on earth, was, according to Rudnitsky, "a play without love, without psychology, without plot in the previous, traditional sense. Its actual subject was contemporary political life."[51] In fact, *Mystery-Bouffe* was a crude propaganda play which preached the righteousness of the Bolshevik Revolution and sought to assure its audiences that the revolution marked the beginning of a new order bereft of exploitation.

By contrast, the Alexandrinsky repertoire had offered a mild form of escapism which did not engage its audience in critical social or political discourse. This is evident from what was *absent* from the government stage, as well as from what was permitted for performance. Arguably, the two leading dramatists of the age whose works were "political" were Chekhov and Gorky, yet the dramaturgy of Chekhov was not entirely successful at the Imperial Theaters, and that of Gorky was prohibited, as noted above. Chekhov described some of his major plays as comedies, yet many contemporaries regarded them as serious, critical chronicles of the age, attacks on the idleness and arrogance of the landed gentry. His plays were very successful at the Moscow Art Theater, but less so at the Imperial Theaters. Why was this so? It was not because Chekhov was too "political" for the government theaters or that he ridiculed the type of individual who patronized the Imperial Theaters. The play which established Chekhov's reputation as a dramatist, and the Moscow Art Theater's reputation as the leading realist theater in Russia, was *The Seagull*. This was first performed at the Alexandrinsky in November 1896, and its "failure" there is almost as famous as its resounding success at the Moscow Art Theater a few years later. The play survived only six performances. One observer implies that Chekhov's play was too modern for the Alexandrinsky. "The repertoire of this theatre consisted of plays which were highly conservative as regards their dramatic form and structure. It is because of this that *The Seagull* was a complete failure, its first performance being, indeed, generally considered as a shocking dramatic and literary *faux pas*."[52] The reasons for the relative failure of *The Seagull* at the Alexandrinsky were noted in the Introduction to the present study. The general reason why Chekhov was not popular at the Imperial Theaters is most likely explained by the incompatibility of the Imperial Theater star system and the ensemble method required to make Chekhov's plays work. Nevertheless, the Imperial Theaters did not ignore Chekhov's corpus, and *The Cherry Orchard* was performed regularly during our period at the Mikhailovsky by members of the Alexandrinsky troupe.

Of course, the above survey of the Alexandrinsky repertoire only demonstrates that it was not overtly political according to a crude, somewhat reductionist analytical formula (was the repertoire reinforcing or undermining the regnant values and interests of the tsarist state). To the extent that such an approach is reductionist, it nevertheless serves the function (in the context of the theme of this study) of determining the extent to which the repertoire was broadly supportive of the state that subsidized it. In that basic sense, the repertoire was simply apolitical. Yet that fact, perhaps somewhat paradoxically, is itself of political significance. The fact that the repertoire largely offered gentle confirmation of what probably were already the audience's preconceptions of what was "correct" in terms of politics, the social order, and comfortable living, and did not challenge their prejudices, needs to be emphasized. It implies that politics was not an urgent issue for this audience, or at least was not considered appropriate for the court theater. The repertoire did not overtly seek to support or denounce tsarism—but then it should not be assumed that audiences believed that tsarism was under immediate threat and therefore *required* support or propagation. In other words, the "apolitical" repertoire might suggest political complacency. It also removes the Imperial Theaters from political discourse conducted via dramatic art. It was elsewhere that the drama repertoire acquired political credentials, in particular at the "intelligentsia theater" of Vera Komissarzhevskaya, which was associated with Gorky's progressive publishing group *Znanie* and premiered his plays *Summerfolk* and *Children of the Sun*. The Alexandrinsky audience wanted sumptuous environments, love stories, and humor.

Of course, drama can be political in covert or subtle ways. It has the ability to convey ambiguity, intimation, and nuance, and the historian must consider alternative readings of the repertoire as received by contemporaries. The manner in which art reflects contemporaneity is extremely complex. It reflects different facets of politics and society in multiple ways, and it is "read" differently by different groups. That is to say, there are multiple ways in which art is connected to its epoch: We cannot describe an epoch as having only one characteristic ("progressive," "reactionary," etc.). To some extent, the repertoire touched on issues arising from the steady emergence of civil society in Russia (such as the *zhenskii vopros*), and many of the popular plays depicting entrepreneurs and bourgeois life must have reinforced the beliefs of many in the audience about fashionable and desirable lifestyles and so forth. As noted in Chapter 3, the Alexandrinsky was considered by many to be a "merchant's theater"; given the fact that much of the repertoire depicted aspects of merchant life, there was certainly a degree of congruence between stage and auditorium. The fact that the reviews generally did not discuss such issues does not preclude the historical observation of their presence. Audiences were exposed to them, if indirectly and subliminally. What is less certain is the impact or the significance attached to them. It is also important not to exaggerate this feature of the repertoire, for most of the plays remained dominated by depictions of the landed-aristocratic lifestyle.

Ultimately, Alexandrinsky audiences wanted to be entertained. It is difficult to disagree with the description of the audience bequeathed by Kugel, who confessed that, when in the theater, "I study the public more than the play." In his review of *The Assembly*, he wrote:

> Everyone knows that, to a high degree, the theater audience is conservative. Only infinite conservatism, along with some sacred dullness of this audience, can explain that, not only in France, but here, on a daily basis hundreds of thousands of people watch and listen to the same unending combination of three characters—the lover, or mistress, and the husband and wife—and find yet more and more novel amusement in the fact that today one climbs under a table, but tomorrow under a bed, and today lies like this, but tomorrow like that.

For Kugel, what satisfied audiences was the "familiar situation." In this way, the audience was not challenged intellectually, but merely entertained. "The audience first and foremost does not want to think. It goes to the theater not to think."[53] It might be argued that what the audience expected most from the repertoire was the opportunity to laugh. Indeed, sixteen of the twenty-four most popular Alexandrinsky productions were officially classed as comedies. Four were classed as dramas, one as a play, and one as a tragedy (*The Merchant of Venice*, which Kugel preferred to regard as a comedy). Of the remaining two, one was described as an "étude in one act," while the other was subtitled "scenes from a family chronicle." Moreover, it is noteworthy that the most prominent Alexandrinsky artist, Savina, was most successful as a comic, rather than as a tragic, actress.[54]

If the principal attraction of the Alexandrinsky repertoire to the audience of merchants, officials, bureaucrats, and assorted *intelligenty* was its entertainment quality, did it nevertheless advance an institutional identity for the theater? With many plays that depicted court life and landowners that were gazed at by the critics with general approbation, it certainly helped to identify the Alexandrinsky as a sort of establishment theater. Yet the repertoire represented a much wider reality, depicting the life not only of the landed classes, but of the merchant classes, and implicitly dealing with many of the issues they considered important. Therefore, the institutional identity of the St. Petersburg Imperial Theaters as conveyed by the drama repertoire was not narrowly "*pridvornyi*," but had a much wider social and cultural significance.

Chapter 5

The Mariinsky Repertoire, 1900–1917

This chapter examines whether the nature of the Mariinsky repertoire might be understood in terms of the court status of the St. Petersburg Imperial Theaters. The first point which requires emphasis is that, in practice, the associations between the Mariinsky and the formal loci of state power in tsarist Russia were more pronounced than they were in the Alexandrinsky or Mikhailovsky Theaters. This was evident in three ways. First, as noted in Chapter 1, the St. Petersburg Imperial Theaters were paraded by the court as showpieces of Russian culture for foreign dignitaries visiting the capital, and almost invariably the Mariinsky was the location for such events; usually a ballet performance was staged. Second, whenever the tsar attended the theater, it was the Mariinsky rather than the Alexandrinsky that he and his retinue went to (although on occasion he attended performances of French drama at the Mikhailovsky); and in general, the presence of the Russian courtiers and officials was more pronounced at the Mariinsky than elsewhere. Even Savina's benefit performance in January 1900 was staged at the Mariinsky in order that Nicholas II, Alexandra, and other members of the Romanov family might attend.[1] The association between the tsarist state and the Mariinsky was even symbolized at the personal level by the infamous relationship between Nicholas II and the *prima ballerina assoluta* Kshesinskaya; it was fashionable to dote upon a ballerina, less so a mere character actress, and it appears there were no similar *amours* between members of the ruling family and artists from the drama theaters. Third, as noted in Chapter 3, the Mariinsky audience generally was more "aristocratic" than that of the "merchant" Alexandrinsky. These three factors helped to give the Mariinsky a more prestigious image than the Alexandrinsky, or any other theater in Russian for that matter.

However, the Mariinsky's prestige derived not so much from its court status and its close associations with state power, but rather from the brilliant repertoire it produced. The Mariinsky remains legendary throughout the world today, not because it was once a court theater, but because it produced some of the most refined and accomplished theatrical art of the early twentieth century, particularly in the area of ballet. That is to say, the artistic history of the Mariinsky is of more durable significance than its institutional history. During the period under investigation, it attracted audiences by virtue of its stage achievements, and in particular by the growing fashion for ballet. The splendor and reputation of its art made the Mariinsky a place to be seen and reinforced its wider social function, which was highlighted in Chapter 3.

This is confirmed by the nature of the Mariinsky repertoire and its critical reception as recorded in reviews, which both underlined two things: that the repertoire was essentially "apolitical" in the sense posited in the previous chapter (it neither explicitly upheld nor undermined the values and interests of the tsarist state), and that the principal attraction of the repertoire was its artistic merit. The Mariinsky repertoire, therefore, cannot broadly be understood in terms of the theater's court status, or any other political or institutional framework that historians might deploy as an analytical tool, but only in terms of the history of opera and ballet.

In one sense, this is not surprising. The intrinsic differences between drama and opera and ballet as artistic forms precluded—with rare exceptions that will be noted—an overtly political opera or ballet that might serve to distinguish the Mariinsky as a court theater as opposed to a private theater. By its very nature, drama is invested with great potential to convey ideas (political or otherwise) to audiences: the spoken word can be direct and unambiguous. Opera and ballet, on the other hand, while still a form of theater, constitute an altogether different medium because they are dominated by artistic formulae which cannot easily convey a *particular* message because they are more likely to stimulate the emotions than the intellect. The two most popular operas at the Mariinsky during the period under consideration were Tchaikovsky's *Eugene Onegin* and *The Queen of Spades*. One critic claimed to have discovered the key to the success they enjoyed: "Not only the artistic beauty of the music of both operas and the apt choice of subject brought about their success, but—and this is the chief thing—*Russian listeners see in them the musical embodiment of their thought, their feelings, their whole life....*"[2] As Arnold Haskell put it for the ballet: "Words have a definite meaning, music and movement have not."[3] Hence the almost universal practice of including plot summaries in ballet programs.

There is evidence that the censor was cognizant of such a distinction between drama and opera in late imperial Russia. In 1911, Viktor Burenin's comedy play about a princess, *Zabava Putiatishna*, was banned from the popular theaters, but was granted permission to be performed as an opera.[4] The implication was that an operatic version of the work would have less impact because the content of the story would be marginalized by the music, or in the case of ballet, the dance. Even when there is an entertaining libretto it is the music that dominates. This is reflected in the fact that opera and ballet reviews tend to focus on music and choreography, not on political or social ideas, or even on the story of the opera or ballet. Nevertheless, it is worth while briefly considering the popular Mariinsky operas and ballets in order to ascertain whether any of them contained the *potential* to convey political or social ideas. As we will see, there were notable exceptions that proved the rule.

Opera at the Mariinsky

Between 1900 and 1911, the total number of operas produced at the Mariinsky was sixty-six and the average number of times an opera was performed was twenty-four. The most popular operas were those which were performed more than fifty times between 1900 and 1911. When they are removed from the equation, the average number of performances for an opera drops to fourteen. In other words, the popular operas were responsible for boosting the average number of performances by ten.* The twelve operas which were performed more than fifty times were, in descending order of popularity, Tchaikovsky's *Eugene Onegin* (108 performances) and *The Queen of Spades* (101 performances), Gounod's *Faust* (seventy-three performances), Glinka's *A Life For the Tsar* (seventy-two performances), Bizet's *Carmen* (sixty-seven performances), Glinka's *Ruslan and Liudmila* (sixty-three performances), Meyerbeer's *Les Huguenots* (fifty-nine performances), Wagner's *Die Walküre* (fifty-eight performances), Napravnik's *Dubrovskii* (fifty-seven performances), Verdi's *Aida* (fifty-six performances), Rubinstein's *The Demon* (fifty-five performances), and Wagner's *Tannhäuser* (fifty-four performances).

The majority of the twelve most popular operas had universal themes, rather than specific themes unique to late tsarist Russia. That is why they are still widely popular throughout the world today (as many of them were before the 1900-20 period). If there is one unifying theme, it is that of thwarted love, as a brief but necessary reiteration of the operatic narratives demonstrates. The most popular opera, *Eugene Onegin*, is a classic tale of rejection. Tatyana falls in love with Onegin, a friend of her sister's betrothed, Lensky, but Onegin coldly dismisses Tatyana's love. Years later, after Onegin has killed Lensky

---

These calculations are based on the annual repertoire lists published in the Ezhegodniki imperatorskikh teatrov. *The lists were discontinued after the 1910-11 season, but there is no reason to suspect that any subsequent changes to the repertoire render present calculations unrepresentative of the period 1900 to 1917 as a whole.*

in a duel, he meets Tatyana at a ball. She is now married, but still cares for him. Onegin now feels close to Tatyana and they confess their mutual passion, but Tatyana will not leave her husband and so true love is thwarted. In *The Queen of Spades*, Herman has fallen in love with Lisa, who is already engaged to be married. Eventually, she comes to love Herman, but Herman's addiction to gambling ruins their prospects because he ends up squandering his fortune after being tricked by the ghost of Lisa's grandmother, whose death Herman was responsible for.

In *Faust*, the overarching theme is good versus evil but the conflict is played out as a love scenario. Doctor Faust and Marguerite fall in love with each other with the aid of Mephistopheles (the devil). Meanwhile, Siebel, a village youth, is in love with Marguerite. When Faust and Marguerite have a child, Faust abandons mother and child. Marguerite ends up in prison, having murdered her child in a fit of madness. Mephistopheles is pleased because he believes she is damned but in the end she is saved by angels and Mephistopheles is defeated. The ultimate consequence of this tale is not the ruin of the state, but vanquished love. The theme of *Carmen* is seduction and unrequited love. The corporal Don José is in love with the peasant girl Micaela, and vice-versa. The gypsy Carmen manages to seduce José, who ends up leaving the army for a freer life with her, but they soon become bored with each other. When Micaela arrives to inform José that his mother is dying, he reluctantly goes with her, leaving Carmen to become involved with the toreador Escamillo. José continues to ask for Carmen's love, but she claims their love is over. José thereupon stabs Carmen.

In *Ruslan and Liudmila*, the daughter of the Grand Prince of Kiev is abducted by an evil dwarf. The Grand Prince offers his daughter's hand in marriage to whomsoever saves her, and, of course, it is Ruslan who comes to the rescue. The theme of Glinka's opera is good versus evil, but again the story is centered on a tale of love. Similarly, while *Les Huguenots* takes as its theme the conflict between French Catholics and Protestants in the sixteenth century and is set at the time of the St. Bartholomew's Day massacre in Paris, August 1572, the story concerns love: Valentine loves Raoul, but unfortunately she is married to Nevers. *Die Walküre*, part two of *Der Ring des Nibelungen*, is a legendary tale of impossible love. The principal character Siegmund is in love with his enemy's wife, Sieglinde, who also happens to be his sister. They become lovers and Siegmund's father, Wotan, ruler of the gods, agrees with his wife, Fricka, that such adultery and incest cannot be condoned and that Siegmund must die. Hunding, Sieglinde's husband, kills him and the opera ends with Wotan punishing another of his daughters, Brünnhilde, who had tried to defend Siegmund against her father's wishes. Wotan encircles her with a ring of fire which only a hero can penetrate.

Dubrovskii, Napravnik's popular opera based on Pushkin's story, is a tale of thwarted love in which the eponymous hero is besotted with his enemy's daughter, Masha. Despite the impressive backdrop of war between the Egyptians and the Ethiopians, the essential theme of *Aida* is how the mutual love of the eponymous heroine and the soldier Radames is hindered by the love of the Egyptian king's daughter, Amneris, for Radames. In *The Demon*, the Demon has killed the bridegroom of Tamara, a princess, and now pursues Tamara, whom he loves. The Demon ends up killing the princess, who gains redemption; needless to say, the Demon does not. Redemption is the underlying theme of *Tannhäuser*, but again the theme is explored through the issue of love.

The worlds and characters portrayed to the Mariinsky audience by the operatic repertoire were privileged and fantastical, the lives of princes and princesses, of the nobility and spectral demons. It might be argued that therein was an implicit conflation of the worlds of the repertoire and the world of the elite audience: "High society" in the auditorium observed only the lives and tribulations of "high society" on stage; and, therefore, that the operatic repertoire *did* underline the *pridvornyi* status and associations of the Mariinsky. The difficulty with that argument is two-fold. First, the enduring popularity of most of the above-mentioned operas points to an artistic appeal that transcends time and place, and more often than not, the appeal is the superlative music, not the dramatic message. Second, the opera repertoire was much smaller than the drama repertoire, which raises the question of alternatives: If we are searching for evidence that the opera repertoire helped to distinguish the Mariinsky as a court theater, what sort of opera repertoire in the early 1900s would *not* perform that function? At the most obvious level, there were no significant radical or revolutionary operas that, if performed, might have suggested an institutional empathy with the intelligentsia. These considerations merely emphasize the fact that the opera repertoire cannot be squeezed into a contemporary sociopolitical framework. In that sense, it was essentially autonomous, and not irretrievably bound up with any specific epoch or institution. (Of course, this is the case with all great art.)

Reviews of Mariinsky opera productions highlighted their artistic interest more than anything else. Typical concerns of the critics included whether an artist was performing well in a particular role, and whether the sets were appropriate for the performance. To cite a few examples by way of illustration, a review of *Ruslan and Liudmila* from *The New Times* focused on the sets:

> A dress rehearsal of "Ruslan" on the Mariinsky stage. Beautiful scenery in the first act and unusually picturesque costumes. Costumes not from ready-made cloth and brocade, but all drawn on canvas. This makes for a very diverse scene, and groups appear picturesquely. The costumes in Chernomor's castle are also sumptuous. But the decor of the castle, done in soft, watercolor tones, is not effective and not fantastical.[5]

A review of *Carmen* in *The Stock Exchange Gazette* concentrated on the demands of the lead part and the talents of the artist playing the eponymous character:

"Carmen" belongs to those operas where an exceptional artist is required for the lead part. This has precluded frequent performances of the opera, since to see a crude gypsy in an elegant French frame is the same as pouring Russian kvass into a Sèvres vase. On the other hand, the part of Carmen is so central, and the famous singers here have made so many changes, that the part was sung by (has been sung by) soprano, mezzo-soprano, and alto.

Yesterday she was played by the contralto, Zakharova, whose voice (and even appearance) was reminiscent of the famous Maria Gai, one of the most brilliant incarnations of Carmen. It may be that this higher type of alto, inclining towards passionately languorous low tones, is better for the part.

Zakharova is a young artist who has recently been on the rise, particularly in Serov's "Rogneda." Apparently her abilities tend exclusively towards everyday [*bytovoi*] Russian parts. Yesterday's performance demonstrated that her talent is far wider. True, her Carmen is still far from perfection: the artist's mimicry is still constrained by stereotypical devices. It is without doubt, however, that through this conventionality appears something independent and individual. [...][6]

With the obvious exception that these reviews referred to the Mariinsky Theater and Russian artists, quite conceivably they could have been written about opera productions anywhere in Europe at that time. In other words, the Mariinsky opera repertoire was not something that identified the theater specifically with the Russian imperial court, but rather with the European artistic-cultural world as a whole.

However, there were exceptions and instructive developments that, while not refuting the above argument in general, do suggest certain specificities in the Mariinsky opera repertoire that betrayed the Imperial Theater's *pridvornyi* associations. The obvious exception was *A Life for the Tsar*, Glinka's nationalistic opera which relates the legend of the peasant Ivan Susanin, who saves the new tsar, Mikhail Romanov, in 1613 from invading Poles. Susanin pays with his life, the "life for the tsar," by leading the Poles astray in order that a message can be sent to the tsar in time to allow him to prepare for the attack. According to one scholar of the opera, who has detected the principles of Official Nationality in it, the implicit message is that "one peasant life is expendable—it is the tsar who must be saved to ensure Russia's future."[7] The political bias of the opera is quite explicit, as in the final refrains: "Glory, glory to our Russian tsar." Moreover, the political nature of *A Life for the Tsar* was highlighted during the 1905 Revolution, when its performance provoked a certain degree of hostility among sections of the audience who found its theme repugnant in the context of the struggle for reform (see Chapter 6). But the fact that *A Life for the Tsar* was the only work of the twelve most popular opera productions at the Mariinsky to have such a direct patriotic and political theme underlined the extent to which the other eleven were essentially apolitical. To be sure, the other operas include certain scenes that openly glorify the Russian monarchy. For example, toward the end of act two of *The Queen of Spades*, which is set in St. Petersburg at the end of the eighteenth century, the Empress Catherine II briefly appears at a masked ball, providing the cue for a moment of collective genuflexion on the stage and a rousing choral tribute to the tsarina (this scene is not in Pushkin's original story). Yet such moments are rare and in no way constitute the essential points or defining elements of the operas.

The content of the Mariinsky opera repertoire was quite stable during the period under consideration, with only two notable developments occurring: the introduction and growing popularity of Wagner's operas, and the less emphatic but important attention paid to Rimsky-Korsakov's operas. Until 1899, Wagner's music was known to Russians via concert performances, while the Italians dominated the opera stage. In the 1890s, the Directorate was encouraged to produce Wagner's operas, but Vsevolozhsky was not enamored of the composer's style. Volkonsky, however, was more predisposed toward Wagner, and the first Russian production of *Tristan und Isolde* was mounted in April 1899. Following that success, during the subsequent few years *Der Ring des Nibelungen* was introduced to the repertoire, to the great appreciation of Mariinsky audiences. The Empress Alexandra was particularly fond of Wagner which, according to one scholar, possibly explains why his operas were performed more in St. Petersburg than in Moscow.[8] *Die Walküre, Lohengrin, Tannhäuser, Tristan und Isolde, Siegfried*, and *Götterdämmerung* all remained in the Mariinsky repertoire until the First World War.

Wagner's popularity at the Mariinsky contrasted with the attention accorded new Russian operas. With the exception of Glinka's compositions, there were no notable Russian operas prior to the second half of the nineteenth century. From the 1860s on, however, a distinctive and vibrant Russian national school of music emerged, led by Milii Balakirev, Alexander Borodin, Tsezar' Kiui (César Cui), Alexander Dargomyzhsky, and Modest Mussorgsky. Perhaps the most prominent representatives of the burgeoning musical creativity were Tchaikovsky and Rimsky-Korsakov. The Russian national school in music rooted itself in traditional Russian folk melodies, and the new Russian operas drew upon Russian legends and historical themes. It has been argued that this musical creativity was part of the general growth of Russian nationalism in the late imperial period.[9] Yet the new Russian national opera was not conspicuous at the Mariinsky. Of course, Tchaikovsky's *Eugene Onegin* and *The Queen of Spades* dominated the repertoire, but they were not considered operas in the Russian national style, having more in common stylistically with Mozart and Verdi. Glinka's two popular operas remained prominent within the repertoire, but they were traditional and established favorites. None of the new operas were able to displace the established favorites. Mussorgsky's *Boris Godunov*, arguably the archetypal Russian national opera, was rarely performed at the Mariinsky. Between the 1900-01 and 1909-10 seasons, it was staged only nine times, all during the 1904-05 season.

Under Telyakovsky, the Directorate's only persistent endeavor to accommodate the new national school related to the operas of Rimsky-Korsakov, which were derived from classic Russian folk tales, a key inspiration for the new national school. *Sadko* had been in the repertoire for some years and remained under the last Director. Telyakovsky introduced *The Maid of Pskov* (in the repertoire during the 1903-04 season), *The Snow Maiden* (in the repertoire from the 1905-06 season), *The Legend of the Invisible City of Kitezh and the Maiden Fevronia* (in the repertoire from the 1906-07 season), and *A Night in May* (in the repertoire from the 1910-11 season).[10] Yet, although the premieres of these operas were "events" in themselves, they did not match the popularity of Wagner in the repertoire. Thus, the overall impression is of a repertoire that paid little more than lip service to the new Russian national operas; patrons and/or the Directorate continued to prefer Western operatic works. One critic even remarked that, under Telyakovsky, the Mariinsky had been turned into a German theater.[11] Although this point was something of an exaggeration (and it was made after the First World War had commenced), it is nevertheless instructive. To some extent, the Western operatic repertoire of the Mariinsky reinforced the impression of a theater associated with the Westernized elite. This national dimension of the repertoire stood out in sharp relief during the First World War, and Wagner was quickly abandoned by the Mariinsky Theater (see Chapter 7).

Ballet at the Mariinsky

Russian ballet during the second half of the nineteenth century was less popular than opera and was regarded as an outlandish and marginal art form. Writing of the 1870s and 1880s, Benois recalled that patrons of the ballet were looked upon as "somewhat eccentric and slightly depraved." He continued: "Society in those days was still full of moral prejudices and ballet was considered just a shade questionable. We must remember that this was the epoch of dresses to the ground and even long trains, whereas in the ballet very scantily-dressed young ladies appeared in skirts not reaching to their knees."[12] It was also believed that ballet was beginning to stagnate after the successes of the romantic era. One of the foremost balletomanes and ballet critics of the late imperial era, Valerian Svetlov, considered that the late nineteenth and early twentieth centuries comprised "a period of severest decline for the ballet."[13] That judgement seems harsh, even incorrect in retrospect. In fact, during the period under consideration, Russian ballet experienced a major renaissance. This renaissance was heralded by the appearance of the first histories of ballet in Russia and the first book of Russian ballet criticism. In 1882 Konstantin Skalkovskii had published *Dances and the Ballet*, but the first major work and substantial history was Alexander Pleshcheev's *Our Ballet*, first

View of the Mariinsky from Officer Street. Author's Collection

published in St. Petersburg in 1896 and reappearing in a second edition in
1899. The first book of critical remarks on Russian ballet, Svetlov's *Terpsi-
chord*, appeared in 1906.[14] Although Pleshcheev resisted Svetlov's idea that
ballet was in decline anyway, there is no doubting the fact that, in the years
after the appearance of *Our Ballet*, its profile was certainly raised. Although
the number of critics and patrons remained small, interest in the ballet spread.
At the same time, the Imperial Theater *Yearbooks* began to feature more critical material on ballet. The profiles of individual dancers, particularly female
dancers until Nijinsky came along, became more prominent, and newspapers
carried increasingly large numbers of ballet reviews. Ballet soon became a focal
interest for members of the *World of Art* group, who believed it was one of
the most appropriate formats for the pursuit of their "art for art's sake" ideal.
In the process, ballet became part of the contemporary theater debate and
inspired artistic reforms and innovations.

One individual in particular personified and realized reforms in the Russian ballet, Mikhail Fokin (1880–1942). Fokin was almost alone in seeking
reform at the Mariinsky. His teacher, Petipa, was a proponent of classical ballet, as was the influential Nicholas Legat, a partisan of tradition and classicism. In fact, the majority of the ballet troupe was artistically conservative:
Fokin once issued his colleagues with a questionnaire to determine whether
they favored ballet reforms; the replies were negative, and he considered aban-
doning ballet altogether for painting.[15] Fokin was determined to advance from
the classical ballet that had predominated under Petipa. Beaumont effectively
summed up Fokin's criticism of ballet under Petipa:

No ballet was composed as the result of collaboration between librettist, composer, *maître de ballet*, and decorative artist. Everyone worked independently, shut up, as it were, in his own office, until music, dances, costumes, and scenery were complete, when the whole was assembled with results that sometimes were far from satisfactory.[16]

In classical ballet, purity of dance and perfection of technique mattered, not plot or scenic authenticity. Fokin wanted to render ballet performances more authentic in the sense of coordinating the creative efforts of all artists involved in the production, of harmonizing all the balletic components. Unlike classical ballet of the nineteenth century, the music should correspond to the mood of the dance and vice-versa; it should not be incidental. Where possible, traditional dress should be used. In a sense, Fokin wanted to transform ballet in the manner that Stanislavsky had helped transform drama, from exaggerated and unconvincing theatricality to realistic, natural performances.

Fokin's reformist ideas were first set out in a plan submitted to the Directorate in 1904 for a production of *Daphnis et Chloé* (rejected at the time, but eventually created in 1912). Telyakovsky was lukewarm about the idea, and not until 1907 did Fokin make a breakthrough when he staged two new works he had choreographed, *Chopiniana*[17] and *Eunice*. These two short pieces were performed in aid of a children's charity, and brought the attention of Fokin to the erstwhile *World of Art* artist Alexander Benois, who suggested they collaborate on a new ballet, *Le Pavillon d'Armide*. When this was performed for the imperial ballet school examination with great success, it was granted a performance at the Mariinsky in the autumn of 1907. Fokin then worked with *World of Art* on *Egyptian Nights* and a new version of *Chopiniana*. These were performed, along with *Eunice*, at the Mariinsky in 1909. In 1911 Fokin created *Petrushka* with Stravinsky, a dazzling new production that was made complete by the performance of Nijinsky. *Petrushka* was premiered by the Ballets Russes in Paris in the summer of 1911, some months after Nijinsky had been dismissed from the Imperial Theaters (see Chapter 2). In all these new ballets, Fokin applied the reformist principles he had advocated for several years, and the manner in which the protagonists of *World of Art* were gradually co-opted by the Imperial Theaters demonstrated that the Directorate was not entirely averse to artistic innovation.[18] Thus Svetlov concluded in 1909: "It is impossible not to see that ballet is situated at a transitional stage from old forms to new."[19]

It was inevitable that the Mariinsky would be closely associated with any ballet reform; there were no private ballet troupes to challenge the supremacy of the imperial ballet, and only the Imperial Theater had the resources, in particular the artists trained at the Imperial Theater School, for experimentation. Yet the Mariinsky ballet repertoire, contrary to what the heightened profile of the reformers might suggest, was very much a traditional one. Although the innovations of Fokin marked an important stage in the historical evolution of Russian ballet, it was the traditional ballets of Petipa which dominated.

Between 1900 and 1911, the total number of ballets produced at the Mariinsky was fifty-one and the average number of times a ballet was performed was fourteen. The twelve most popular ballets of the period 1900 to 1911 were those performed twenty times or more. When they are removed from the equation, the average number of performances for a ballet drops to nine, making the popular ballets responsible for boosting the average number of performances by five. The twelve, in descending order of popularity, were *The Hump-Backed Horse* (forty-nine performances), *The Sleeping Beauty* (forty-one performances), *Swan Lake* (thirty-four performances), *La Bayadère* (thirty-two performances), *Paquita* (thirty-two performances), *Raymonda* (thirty-two performances), *The Awakening of Flora* (thirty-one performances), *Don Quixote* (twenty-nine performances), *The Nutcracker* (twenty-seven performances), *Le Corsaire* (twenty-four performances), *La Fille Mal Gardée* (twenty-three performances), and *Giselle* (twenty performances).

All of these ballets are *ballets d'action*. That is to say, they all have a story to tell through the medium of dance. Yet, as with the popular operas at the Mariinsky, the stories are based on universal themes rather than topics peculiar to late imperial Russia. Similarly, most of them are concerned with romance in an "aristocratic" milieu, with the occasional evil sorcerer or magical object added for good measure.

In *The Hump-Backed Horse*, which was based on a Russian fairy tale, a Khan entrusts his hump-backed horse to Ivanushka, to whom the horse presents a whip capable of making wishes come true. The horse uses the magical powers of the whip to bring to life a Tsar-maiden for the Khan, but she insists that the Khan immerse himself in boiling water in order to retrieve his youth. Ivanushka tests the boiling water and survives, but the Khan dies when he immerses himself in the water, whereupon Ivanushka and the Tsar-maiden marry. In *La Bayadère*, Nikia and Solor are in love with one another but Solor is betrothed to Gamzatti. Jealous of Nikia, Gamzatti murders her by concealing a poisonous snake in a basket of flowers which she sends to her. In *Paquita*, the eponymous character is a Spanish Gypsy who falls in love with a French officer, Lucien, who is betrothed to Seraphina. Later, when it is discovered that Paquita is of noble birth, she and Lucien are able to announce their mutual love. The story of *Raymonda* is that of a struggle between Jean de Brienne, Raymonda's betrothed, and a saracen knight for the heart of the eponymous heroine. *Le Corsaire* tells the story of the slave girl Medora and the pirate Conrad who fall in love and, after many tribulations, are shipwrecked together. In *Giselle*, the eponymous character is a peasant girl who is in love with a Count, but she does not know his true aristocratic identity. The love is mutual, but, as usual, the Count is betrothed to someone else. Hilarion, whose love for Giselle is not returned, vindictively reveals the truth about the Count and Giselle kills herself. *Don Quixote* is essentially a story of the romance of Basil and Kitri (Quiteria).

As far as Tchaikovsky's famous ballets are concerned, Svetlov observed that their "subject-matter is insignificant. It is invariably a fairy tale without dramatic incident."[20] *The Sleeping Beauty* and *Swan Lake* are conventional love stories, while *The Nutcracker* is practically bereft of plot, its principal attraction lying in its various well-known dance sequences.

At the Mariinsky ballet, dance overwhelmed plot. As Nijinsky's wife recalls: "The ballets of Petipa were on a spectacular scale, but whatever story they embodied was merely a transparent pretext for a consecutive series of dances calculated to display the greatest technique."[21] This was one of Fokin's complaints—he lamented of *Les Sylphides* that "this ballet contains no plot whatsoever."[22] Insofar as the popular ballets had plots they tended to be tales of love, thwarted or otherwise. Yet their principal attraction lay in their importance as vehicles for the popular dancers. Svetlov remarked that "in no other theater in the world is there such close intercourse of the public with the artists as in our ballet."[23] It was the *ballerinas* who attract the balletomanes, not the prospect of an engaging story. The chief delight for the audience was the ballerina, who was usually portraying a part in a love story, but principally was looking to the audience, with a "pleading gaze," for approval.[24] The focus of the critics was generally the female dancer, who was often given a grade according to the quality of her performance.[25] The balletomanes delighted in determining the relative success or failure of a particular dancer according to their responses. One observer described the front rows at the Mariinsky ballet as a sort of *birzha* (stock exchange) for dancers.[26]

It was also the visual splendour of a production, not the plot, which attracted ballet patrons. Fedorov went so far as to write in 1897 that "our contemporary ballet is not a temple of choreographic art, but an exhibition of luxurious costumes, costly properties, and painted scenery."[27] Time stood still in the ballet and plot was irrelevant. As Svetlov observed of some of Pavlova's dances, "they had neither period nor nationality but were eternal like the laws of life, only more beautiful and more truthful than life, being a synthesis which captured an aromatic quintessence from life."[28]

These themes recur in the ballet reviews. To emphasize the point, it is apposite to reproduce in full a typical review, this of *Swan Lake* by "A. P." in 1914:

> On Wednesday, O. O. Preobrazhenskaya, who recently appeared in "The Hump-Backed Horse," danced once more in the ballet "Swan Lake." These are her ballets, in which we have all seen the ballerina and all know with what experience she is able here to make use of her choreographic talent. Preobrazhenskaya's chief strength is the technical virtuosity of execution. The public always appreciated, and appreciates, her noble [*blagorodnyi*] dances which remind us of Petipa's era.

The Spanish Dance and the Mazurka were performed with outstanding success. In the former, Fedorova 3, Smirnova, Orlov and Romanov, substituting for the ill Monakhov, stormed [*bushevali*]. The temperament of the dancing was broken up by nerve, and the public responded to this. Kshesinskii, whose return to the troupe it is impossible not to rejoice in, enlivened the Mazurka: apart from the fact that he belongs to an artistic family that sustains the glory of our ballet, he is an amazing performer of character dances and roles demanding dramatic expressiveness. He gave tone to the Mazurka and absorbed all the dancers with it. There is not enough of Kshesinskii in the ballet troupe.

With Preobrazhenskaya danced Semenov, a young person, richly gifted, unusually light and decorous. He was probably timid supporting the ballerina, but when alone he is very good. His effort and tension are not noticeable, his movements light and simple.

From among the soloists of the troupe, Gerdt continues to improve. Her dances are correct, smooth, lacking inspiration, but stylish in the meaning of classicism. Gerdt's gestures are more extensive and free than before. Poliakova is a conscientious soloist, performing a *pas de trois* with Gerdt, but she is heavier than the latter and it would be good if both of them found a more suitable partner. I do not want to disparage Poliakova's merit, but I point out only that the character of her choreographic talent differs sharply from that of the young Gerdt.[29]

The Mariinsky ballet repertoire in itself conveyed little about the institutional identity of the St. Petersburg Imperial Theaters and their relationship to the Russian court. Yet two aspects of the Mariinsky ballet nevertheless enhanced the image of privileged *pridvornyi* institutions. First, as already mentioned, only the Imperial Theaters enjoyed the resources and facilities to produce professional ballet in St. Petersburg at that time. Second, as a cultural phenomenon, ballet was accessible mainly to the elite patrons of the Mariinsky, chiefly by subscription. Thus by default there occurred a practical coincidence of balletic culture and state power.

In conclusion, the Mariinsky repertoire cannot be understood directly in terms of the court status of the Imperial Theaters. It did not identify the Mariinsky specifically as a court theater. The repertoire was "apolitical"; its significance was cultural and artistic, rather than overtly political. Whereas the Alexandrinsky repertoire arguably formulated a partial image of a middle-class cultural institution rooted in indigenous social types and conditions (in particular the merchantry), the Mariinsky repertoire defied such a manner of classification.

At the same time, as noted in Chapter 3, the Mariinsky had a more exclusive clientele than the Alexandrinsky or any other theater in St. Petersburg. And therein lies a possible dilemma: Were the elite sophisticated connoisseurs of exemplary operatic and balletic art; or was the art prestigious because the elite patronized it? This question is impossible to answer. Opera and especially ballet are apolitical, but they catered to the elite audience.

Thus, it might be suggested that this was art for the powerful. However, the real litmus test for the institutional identity of the St. Petersburg Imperial Theaters in the early years of the twentieth century was the revolutionary crisis that confronted the tsarist state, to which we now turn.

Chapter 6

The 1905 Revolution and Its Aftermath

Late one evening in the winter of 1908, having given another successful performance to a captivated audience, Fyodor Chaliapin ascended the staircase to the vast attic of the Mariinsky Theater. There he changed into his costume for the role of Holofernes in Serov's opera *Judith*. The attic was used as the workshop of the Imperial Theater set designer and painter Alexander Golovin, and Chaliapin had agreed to pose for him throughout the night as Holofernes. During a break in the proceedings Chaliapin began sketching caricatures, a particular hobby of his. One of the caricatures was of Nicholas II and was the subject of much hilarity. Amidst the laughter, one of the small group present commented: "One despot mocks another!" In other words, Chaliapin as Holofernes was ridiculing the tsar.[1] Although such a fleeting episode has little significant meaning in itself, it points to a wider question that must be addressed: how oppositional were the St. Petersburg Imperial Theaters, particularly during the periods of reform and revolution? Did one recorded instance of prominent and renowned Imperial Theater artists laughing at Nicholas the "despot" in the rafters of the Mariinsky Theater signify that these court institutions were more likely to associate themselves with the radical intelligentsia than with their tsarist paymasters when the latent conflict between state and society erupted in revolution?

Events and developments of the late tsarist period compelled Russians to directly confront political issues, particularly during the revolutionary flashpoints of 1905 and 1917, when it seemed that the vast majority of Russian society was politicized. During those crises, it might be expected that the "Emperor's Theaters" would remain loyal to the government. After all, as Nicholas Legat had remarked, Imperial Theater artists were the tsar's "servants." Yet in times of political crisis, traditional hierarchies and loyalties are challenged and often appear to disintegrate, at least temporarily. As we will

Portrait by A. E. Iakovlev of the Imperial Theater set designer and artist Alexander Golovin in his Mariinsky attic workshop. *Vospominaniia* (Moscow-Leningrad, 1965)

see, the institutional identity of the St. Petersburg Imperial Theaters during the 1905 Revolution fluctuated and the appearance of aloof loyalty was undermined by varieties of subversion.

More broadly, during the course of the Revolution, the artists appeared to identify more strongly than ever before with an increasingly restless civil society that was pitted against the autocracy, thereby rendering the Imperial Theaters' identity as loyal court institutions more equivocal. Until 1905, the Imperial Theaters' connection with, and contribution to, civil society was largely limited to the activities of the Russian Theater Society (*Russkoe teatralnoe obshchestvo*). The RTS was founded in St. Petersburg in 1883 by Maria Savina as a philanthropic voluntary organization to assist needy artists from any of the new Russian theaters, not just the Imperial Theaters. Its leading members included the Alexandrinsky artists Vladimir Davydov and Nicholas Sazonov, as well as D. V. Grigorovich, Chairman of the St. Petersburg Section of the Theater-Literary Committee. In 1894 it redefined its aim as the general development of theater affairs in Russia, and began to organize various congresses of theater people, including the 1897 and 1901 Congresses of Stage Workers. The patron of the 1897 Congress was Grand Duke Sergei Alexandrovich and its Organizing Commission was dominated by prominent individuals from the Alexandrinsky, not least Savina. The Congress, which took place in Moscow, attracted over 1,000 delegates, the majority of whom were not associated in any way with the Imperial Theaters. This remarkable gathering of Russian theater people from all over the country discussed a variety of issues, including working conditions, rights, and pay. The Congress cannot be discussed more fully here, but the key point to be emphasized is that, in taking the initiative to organize the RTS and convene general congresses of Russian theater workers, the artists of the Imperial Theaters (in particular the Alexandrinsky) were already joining in and contributing to civil society, helping to blur the formal distinction and separation between court and society, and helping to lay the basis for a more prominent and radical alliance with civil society in 1905.[2]

The 1905 Revolution

In 1905 rising popular discontent and liberal opposition created a crisis of authority for the tsarist government. Many of the popular grievances were long-standing, but a variety of factors, not least the disasters of the Russo-Japanese War, brought them to a head. The crisis began in January with Bloody Sunday: Unarmed Petersburgers, peacefully demonstrating for better working conditions and political reforms, were gunned down by the tsar's soldiers. It reached its high point in October, when a general strike forced the government to concede a limited measure of political reform. Tsarism survived, but in retrospect the events of 1905 merely foreshadowed the fatal crisis of authority in 1917.[3]

In 1905 two main categories of subversion challenged the St. Petersburg Imperial Theaters' image of loyalty to the tsarist state: demonstrations in the auditoria and radical activities by some of the artists. By illustrating how the government endeavored to cope with such subversion, evidence will be provided to suggest that it recognized the Imperial Theaters had an important symbolic value, that it did not regard them simply as superfluous havens of entertainment.

First, anti-government demonstrations in the auditoria. The St. Petersburg Imperial Theaters were prominent public buildings located in the center of the city. To be sure, they did not possess the strategic importance of the telegraph agency or the various bridges, but they were significant because they were public arenas and were viewed as such by opponents of tsarism, who evidently considered the Imperial Theaters an appropriate platform for protest (as we will see). The explanation for this perception is two-fold. First, by striking at an exclusive state institution the radicals were attacking what they considered to be essentially an established reserve of tsarist support. The hearts and minds of generally conservative audiences were a better target than, for example, the universities, which were already in ferment. Second, *ad hoc* demonstrations in ostensibly sacrosanct buildings were safer than parading through the streets, especially after Bloody Sunday. In addition to these considerations, there always remained the possibility of spontaneous, unplanned demonstrations in the auditoria, particularly during moments of high drama both on stage and in the streets.

The government's chief means of coping with demonstrations in the theaters was the regular police. Four days after Bloody Sunday N. K. Von Bohl, Manager of the Moscow Office of Imperial Theaters, wrote to Telyakovsky about the strikes that were breaking out across Moscow. He assured the Director that theater performances had not yet been interrupted and that he intended to ensure this remained the case. "At the moment, the police defence of the theaters has, at my request, been significantly strengthened," he informed Telyakovsky.[4] Even more important was the secret police, the Okhrana. Its activity in the Imperial Theater auditoria merits consideration because it indicates, first, the government's awareness of the potential for unrest in the theater and, second, its determination to quell such subversion in a state institution. The Okhrana first became involved in the Imperial Theaters soon after it was set up early in the 1880s.[5] George Kennan (1845–1924) noted that the Russian police "exercise supervision over all theatrical performances, concerts, tableaux, [and] theater programmes...."[6] A. T. Vasilev, the last chief of the Police Department before the February Revolution in 1917, admitted that the External Agency of the Okhrana monitored "suspicious characters in the streets, theaters, hotels, railway stations, and similar places of public resort."[7]

A certain number of seats in the St. Petersburg Imperial Theater auditoria were reserved each season for agents of the secret police. In April 1905 the number of places to be reserved was set by Mosolov. This should not suggest that the Okhrana was posted to the theaters by the Ministry of the Imperial Court, rather than the Ministry of Internal Affairs. It may well have been the case that the Ministry of Internal Affairs requested seats for the agents, as they did later in 1905, and that Mosolov was merely implementing a dictate, or request, received from elsewhere. At any rate, according to Mosolov's instructions, eleven seats at the Mariinsky Theater were to be reserved for Okhrana agents. At the Alexandrinsky there would be thirteen, at the Mikhailovsky seven.[8] Yet Mosolov did not state why seats were to be reserved for the secret police. The key to explaining the presence of the Okhrana in such an ostensibly innocuous place as a theater lies in Vasilev's reference to the theater as a place of "public resort." Three feasible explanations can be posited. First, because one of the chief tasks of the secret police was to monitor the activities of suspicious characters, provision had to made in case suspects decided to go to the theater. The agent could then follow his suspect and, although he might not be seated next to him, he would be able to observe whom he conversed with and so forth. Most of the seats reserved for the Okhrana were located in the upper reaches of the theater where radicals were more likely to be, that is, in the cheaper, non-subscription seats frequented by students, some workers, and members of the intelligentsia. The likelihood of this explanation for reserving seats for the Okhrana is further supported by the fact that during the 1905-06 theater season in St. Petersburg only three secret agents worked in each Imperial Theater, even though more places had been reserved in case they were needed.[9] Second, according to one historian, one of the main functions of the security police was to monitor public opinion.[10] The theater, as a public resort, was an obvious place to do this. Conversation was more than likely to occur among members of the audience, particularly before a performance, during the intervals, and at the end of a performance. With hundreds of people milling around in the relatively enclosed spaces of the Imperial Theater corridors and foyers, an Okhrana agent intent on assessing the content and tone of conversations would be quite inconspicuous. A possible third explanation for reserving seats for agents of the Okhrana is related to the threat of anti-government demonstrations in the auditoria. One attempt at such a demonstration was in fact pre-empted by the security police. In early February 1905 Telyakovsky was informed by the Director of the Police Department, Lopukhin, that his agents had uncovered a plan by a circle of radicals to disrupt the February 15 performance of Sophocles's *Antigone* at the Alexandrinsky. Lopukhin warned that "the leaders of the above-named circle intend to use the content of this play for the organization of an anti-government demonstration." Certain lines uttered by the character King Kreon, such as "[i]n my land, I alone reign," and "the land belongs to he who reigns over it by right," were to be accompanied by cries of "Down with the autocracy!" Lopukhin's letter did not explicitly request the cancellation of *Antigone*, but the play was not performed at all on the Imperial stage during 1905.[11] The threat of a planned demonstration had alerted the government to the possibility of a scandal. Yet, unless the secret police pre-empted such events, it was very difficult for them to prevent anti-government demonstrations in the auditoria.

Police activity in the Imperial Theaters was not a new phenomenon in 1905, but there does seem to have been a strengthening of this presence throughout 1905 and after. In September 1905, at the request of the town governor, an additional seat in each St. Petersburg Imperial Theater was reserved for Okhrana agents.[12] One year later, in September 1906, he secured three places in each St. Petersburg Imperial Theater for the Investigation Police (*Sysknaia politsiia*).[13] The cause of this augmentation might have been Lopukhin's information about a possible demonstration but there is no direct evidence to support this. There was, however, a general recognition that attending the theater might be dangerous, especially for prominent figures of the ruling elite. In December 1907, seats were reserved in the Alexandrinsky and Mariinsky for Grand Duke Nicholas Nikolaevich's personal bodyguard, D. P. Rusanov, who was responsible for the Grand Duke's security.[14] On August 30, 1911, two days before Prime Minister Stolypin was fatally wounded in a Kiev theater, one O. Vendorf, in a "top secret" letter to Mosolov, spoke of the necessity of strengthening security measures in theaters; Vendorf had witnessed an assassination attempt in the Vologda town theater on the life of a prison inspector.[15] Such evidence indicates that the government recognized the potential dangers posed by attendance at the Imperial Theaters, especially as they were frequented, more than private theaters, by notables and government officials, and even by members of the tsarist court.

The revolution made its first impact on the St. Petersburg Imperial Theaters on the night of January 9, 1905, the evening of Bloody Sunday. The fact that the Imperial Theaters opened that night was considered deeply insensitive by some. In a sense it represented for many the indifference of the court; certainly it was a sign of its determination to proceed as though nothing important had occurred. All tickets for the Mariinsky performance had been sold but the theater was by no means full. The Alexandrinsky was full for a performance of Ostrovsky's *A Passionate Heart*. After the first act, Gnedich was approached by the writers Dmitry Merezhkovsky, Zinaida Gippius and Dmitry Filosofov, representing their Religious Philosophical Society. They requested him to stop the performance, but Gnedich replied that he did not have the authority to do that. During the second act of the performance, someone in the auditorium yelled: "It will be broken up, enough! Not on such a day!" "Bring down the curtain! Lights!" shouted others from the auditorium. Telyakovsky decided it was impossible for the performance to continue and money was refunded to patrons. Both the Mariinsky and Alexandrinsky closed for three days, reopening on January 13.[16]

The government came to recognize that the most efficient way to avoid hostile demonstrations in the auditoria was to ban ostensibly provocative material. The experience of Rimsky-Korsakov was a case in point. In February 1905 the composer publicly added his signature to a letter published in *Our Days* (*Nashi dni*) by, among others, Rakhmaninov and Chaliapin. The letter demanded artistic freedom and general radical reform in Russia.[17] In March 1905, having allied himself with the reform movement, Rimsky-Korsakov complained about the lack of democracy at the Conservatory, where he was a professor, and he was promptly dismissed from his post for speaking out. Conservatory students responded by staging a performance of Rimsky-Korsakov's opera *Kashchei the Immortal* at Vera Komissarzhevskaya's theater to show their support for the composer. The performance turned into a political demonstration that was curtailed by the police.[18] Consequently, on March 31, 1905, the St. Petersburg governor-general, Trepov, dispatched the following communication to Telyakovsky:

> In consequence of the growing discontent in several strata of society with regard to the dismissal of N. A. Rimsky-Korsakov from the staff of professors of the St. Petersburg Conservatory, any public performance of his musical works may give cause for undesirable demonstrations. In view of this, I have the honour of requesting Your Excellency not to permit for some time the public performance of Rimsky-Korsakov's work.[19]

Thus, to avoid a potential public demonstration in favor of a supporter of the reform movement, the government had deemed it necessary to withdraw Rimsky-Korsakov's works from performance.

Similarly, when the 1905-06 opera season commenced with *A Life for the Tsar*, such lines as "I lay down my life for the tsar and for Rus" were accompanied by booing from the auditorium, a reflection of the growing unpopularity of Nicholas II. To avoid further confrontation, it was considered wise not to perform this opera again until February 1906. Even then, the performances in St. Petersburg and Moscow were attended by strong police contingents.[20] *Antigone*, as noted above, was banned during 1905. Even when it was revived at the beginning of 1906, there were signs that it was still unsuitable—when Kreon uttered the line "a free land cannot belong to one person," there was, recalls the Alexandrinsky actor Nicholas Khodotov, who played Kreon, an "outburst of enthusiasm among the audience."[21] Again, to avoid a scandal the government had banned what had become, in the context of 1905, a provocative production. This was an unusual form of censorship. It was neither preliminary censorship, whereby the Chief Administration for Press Affairs considered a work before it was performed in public and had the power to prohibit its public performance, nor punitive censorship, whereby the government banned a work that had already been made public, but transgressed official boundaries of acceptability. Yet it certainly constituted censorship, or control, of what was performed in the Imperial Theaters, the intention being to prevent a repetition of the type of disruptions noted above.

In this respect the St. Petersburg Imperial Theaters were not exceptional. For example, Vera Kommissarzhevskaya's Drama Theater was compelled to close for an evening in January 1905 because the scheduled play, Gorky's *Summerfolk*, had been banned by the government in view of the growing unrest.[22] In fact, the practice of removing certain productions from the repertoire to ensure "security or order" in the theater occurred throughout Russia at this time.[23] The point here is that, even as state-controlled institutions, the St. Petersburg Imperial Theaters were not immune from the wider social unrest or its consequences.

Tension in St. Petersburg was at its highest in October 1905, the zenith of the 1905 revolution. It was not always possible to avoid a scandal. Telyakovsky recorded two particular incidents which occurred on October 18, the day after the proclamation of the October Manifesto. At the Alexandrinsky the small audience, watching Ostrovsky's *Not Always Shrovetide for a Cat*, demanded the national anthem at the end of the third act, an expression of loyalty to the government, a symbolic manifestation of unflinching, or restored, faith in its legitimacy. The anthem was played three times.* When the fourth act began, someone who disagreed with the sentiments behind the renditions of the anthem yelled "Down with the autocracy!" At that precise moment on stage, tea was being drunk. The actress Shmitova-Kozlovskaia spilled the tea all over her lap and went into hysterics. A commotion erupted in the auditorium, causing the actors to cease performing. Telyakovsky was urged to close the curtain, but after a few minutes calm returned and the play proceeded.[24]

Events at the Mariinsky were rather more dramatic. To mark the proclamation of the October Manifesto, the audience had requested three renditions of the national anthem before the performance of *Lohengrin* began. Again, this indicated that much of the audience was satisfied with the tsar's concession, although whether patrons agreed with the sentiment of the October Manifesto, or simply regarded it as a sign that the tsar had regained the political initiative, and would thereby vanquish the popular unrest, is not clear. At any rate, the mood in the auditorium that evening was one of loyalty. According to Telyakovsky, during the second act of the performance

---

*Whenever the anthem was played it was performed three times, a triple repetition that had sacramental origins in the Trinity. This practice occurred elsewhere at court. Nicholas I introduced at his coronation ceremony in 1826 the practice of making a triple bow to those gathered at the coronation (see R. S. Wortman, Scenarios of Power: Myth and Ceremony in Russian Monarchy, volume I (Princeton, 1995), p. 280), although this might be explained by the shape of the room. Bows often occur in threes—an actor bows to the left, right, and middle.

Vuich, Manager of the St. Petersburg Office, was summoned to the office of the Police Master in the theater to meet two representatives from the Conservatory. They had been instructed by radical associates to seek the cessation of the performance and the closure of the theater. The Conservatory, particularly its student body, at that time was generally hostile to the Imperial Theaters and had spoken about the need to "democratize" them even before the proclamation of the October Manifesto. At a meeting on October 9, the following resolution had been passed by the students:

> Taking into consideration that the Imperial Theaters are supported by the people's money and must serve the aims of art and the wide stratum of the population, we consider necessary the abolition of the bureaucratic regime of the Imperial Theaters' administration, the abolition of subscriptions, which are all but passed on by inheritance and can be used only by the capitalist bourgeoisie, and a reduction of the cost of attending [the Imperial Theaters] to a minimum; besides this, finding French performances in the Mikhailovsky Theater inappropriate to the tasks of art, we insist on their cessation.

The resolution concluded with the demand that Conservatory students be permitted to attend Imperial Theater dress rehearsals, which were essentially the first public performances of a production and were quite prestigious.[25] Now, nine days later on October 18, the students were taking action. Vuich informed them that only the Minister, that is, Fredericks, was authorized to close the theater. Consequently, the representatives of the Conservatory resorted to other measures. After the second act, someone, somewhere, shouted "Down with the autocracy!" The cry was sufficient to cause an uproar. Fearing a violent demonstration, people suddenly bolted for the exits, jumping over chairs as they went. The officers in the audience responded to the disruption by drawing their sabres. Then, according to Telyakovsky's account, people in the boxes spotted bombs and grenades in the stalls. Everyone, including the orchestra, panicked. Fighting broke out simultaneously. Golovin claims that chairs from the boxes were thrown into the stalls.[26] According to Telyakovsky, the auditorium divided into two factions, one of the "left" and one of the "right." One newspaper report claimed that the fight was between the supporters of the October Manifesto, who had "burst in" on the performance, and the audience.[27] Meanwhile, exit from one of the Mariinsky stairways was impeded by a huge, inebriated, red-haired merchant who had his sleeves rolled up and was brandishing a chair, yelling: "Right, you revolutionaries, come to me, I'll reduce you to splinters!... So, now that full freedom is granted everywhere, you really think it's permitted to cause a scandal in an Imperial Theater, do you? You really are ungrateful swine!"[28] When the police arrived the merchant accused them of being ungrateful for his assistance against hooligans. He was then escorted from the theater. The "not more than twenty-five people" left in the auditorium demanded three further renditions of the national anthem and then the theater closed.[29]

Similar scandals occurred at the Moscow Imperial Theaters. On November 26, Chaliapin was performing at the Bolshoi. At the end of one of his numbers, the audience called for an encore. Some shouted for the "revolutionary" folk song *The Little Cudgel* (*Dubinushka*) and Chaliapin duly obliged. It was futile for Von Bohl to order the curtain closed because Chaliapin was standing at the very forefront of the stage, and the curtain would fall behind him rather than in front of him, so the song was performed in its entirety. The patrons of the Bolshoi gallery were overjoyed with this rendition, but those in the boxes retired to the foyer. Others left the theater in indignation. In the eyes of the ruling elite, Chaliapin's rendition of *The Little Cudgel* amounted to profanity. The empress Alexandra argued that the singer should be dismissed in order to set an example to others, but Telyakovsky simply wanted to impose a fine. Chaliapin, he believed, was too famous to be dealt with harshly and his dismissal would provide the revolutionaries with a useful martyr. Besides, he would only sing *The Little Cudgel* elsewhere.[30] These events in the Alexandrinsky, Mariinsky and Bolshoi Theaters demonstrated the impossibility of effectively guarding against spontaneous "subversion." They indicated that the struggle between tsarism and the revolutionary movement manifested itself not only at the barricades or in the factories and villages, but in the Imperial Theater auditoria. This meant that the court theaters were not simply isolated havens of entertainment, but targets for the radicals, perhaps not important targets in the context of the totality of the revolution, yet nevertheless significant because they were court institutions which were seen to be under attack. Yet at the height of the 1905 revolution there was little the government could do to avoid such occurrences, short of closing the theaters temporarily, which it was not prepared to do (see below).

While the above mentioned events indicated that the St. Petersburg Imperial Theaters were not immune from public acts of political protest and that contingents of their audiences were politically radical, the ostensible loyalty of the court theaters most notably was undermined during the 1905 Revolution by the activities of some of the artists. Here it should be mentioned that among the artists there were Okhrana agents, although there is little extant information about them. Telyakovsky informs us that there were two agents present on the stage of the Alexandrinsky to ensure the maintenance of political loyalty. The artists knew which of their colleagues acted as agents. One preferred dramatic art to police surveillance. He was frequently drunk and often ridiculed.[31] But the presence of the Okhrana and the relatively apolitical attitude of most of the artists was no guarantee that the artists would maintain their traditional countenance of loyalty during the revolution. There were two interrelated aspects to the "rebellion": a desire to cancel performances when conditions outside the theaters were tense, resulting in a strike by some members of the ballet troupe; and demands for autonomy from the Directorate.

The first indication of trouble occurred on October 13, 1905, when the artists declared that they did not want to perform due to the tense situation in the city. Telyakovsky communicated this sentiment to Fredericks and suggested that the Imperial Theaters temporarily be closed, yet Fredericks believed that such a closure would have a dispiriting effect on the population of the city. In Telyakovsky's opinion, the presence of military forces on the streets and the arrival of fresh contingents had already created such an effect and closing the Imperial Theaters would make no difference. It would be better, argued Telyakovsky, for the government to close the Imperial Theaters rather than have them closed forcibly by a public scandal. Nevertheless, the Minister of the Imperial Court instructed the Director to ensure the normal functioning of the theaters and to speak with governor-general Trepov about strengthening the police presence in them.[32]

On October 14, a stranger appeared at the Alexandrinsky and distributed pamphlets calling on the artists not to perform. Tension ensued, probably caused by the prospect of a demonstration in the auditorium, and the evening performance was canceled. The opera at the Mariinsky proceeded without disruption. The following day, a group of actors from the Alexandrinsky implored Telyakovsky to secure the temporary closure of the Imperial Theaters. Private theaters had already discontinued performances and the governor-general of Moscow had considered it wise to close the Imperial Maly Theater.[33] Yet Telyakovsky, while sympathetic with the concerns of the artists, was powerless against the combined wills of the Ministers of the Imperial Court and Internal Affairs to keep the court theaters open. Trepov remarked: "If the artists don't want to act, force them." When Telyakovsky suggested that this might not help matters, Trepov instructed him to "take a revolver in your hand, then they will listen!"[34]

Members of the ballet troupe were particularly anxious about performing at this time. Telyakovsky had arranged to meet a delegation of artists from the Mariinsky on Sunday, October 16, but he was summoned to Peterhof, and so Vuich met them instead. The artists insisted that they could not perform in such tense conditions. Vuich attempted to reassure them by stating that Telyakovsky had gone to Peterhof to speak to the Minister about stopping performances. However, Fredericks was with the tsar all day and was unable to meet the Director. When Telyakovsky returned to St. Petersburg, he learned that part of the ballet troupe was on strike. The rebellious artists had prevented others from preparing for the matinee performance of *The Queen of Spades*. Confusion had set in. Vuich had ordered the ballet to appear, but in the end it had not.[35] Imperial Theater artists, in effect, had joined the revolutionary movement.

Telyakovsky telephoned Fredericks to explain that due to the general mood of all artists there could be no performances that evening, but the Minister sent a telegram to the Director ordering that the theaters remain open and that he hoped "the artists of the Imperial Theaters will perform their duty and assist in the calming of the capital."[36] On the afternoon of October 17, Telyakovsky gathered the Police Masters of the St. Petersburg Imperial Theaters and, in accordance with Fredericks's telegram, informed them that the theaters were to remain open. The Mariinsky presented *Eugene Onegin*, and the Alexandrinsky staged Ostrovsky's *The Forest.* Telyakovsky replaced the usual ballet troupe with Imperial school pupils for the dance parts of the opera. During the performance some of the strikers attempted to run across the stage, but this was prevented. On October 23 the ballet performance was canceled after Anna Pavlova, a prominent striker, refused to appear. Contrary to convention, a Sunday opera was presented instead.[37] On November 8-9 the ballet troupe again threatened to strike, but in the end did not.

Members of the public also criticized the Directorate for keeping the Imperial Theaters open when it could not guarantee calm in the auditoria.[38] But Trepov still refused to sanction temporary closure. According to Telyakovsky, the obdurate governor-general believed that keeping the Imperial Theaters open helped to maintain an appearance of calm in the capital ("*dlia naruzhnogo spokoistviia stolitsy*").[39] The St. Petersburg Imperial Theaters were expected to convey an image of normality during the 1905 revolution, however unrealistic that was, given the almost universal opposition to the government.

The most radical collective activity among Imperial Theater artists emanated from a minority of the St. Petersburg ballet troupe. They were motivated in part by the government's refusal to close the Imperial Theaters, hence their strike action, but their activities were invested with demands which were widespread at the time, principally the assertion of autonomy from the Directorate. On October 15 they adopted a resolution stating that, in organizing themselves to secure freedom of association and an improvement in their economic situation, they would not tolerate intimidation from the administration, that is, the Directorate. The statement concluded that, "If there ensues any manner of repression on the part of the administration with regard to our resolutions, we have in mind ways and means to struggle against this arbitrariness."[40] This revolt indicated a growing chasm between the Directorate and some of the artists during the height of the 1905 revolution. Yet events never reached crisis proportions. There were rumors that signatories to the ballet troupe's resolution would be dismissed by the Directorate without any pension rights, and consequently most of the artists signed a declaration of loyalty to it. Twelve did not sign, among them Karsavina and Petipa. Many who signed did so reluctantly. According to Karsavina, Sergei Legat was so ashamed of betraying the rebels that he committed suicide.[41]

The relative feebleness of the ballet troupe revolt is explained by the fact that, in addition to the basic need to safeguard their pensions, most Imperial Theater artists essentially were loyal to the existing order and state which had bestowed so much prestige and adoration upon them. They were, as Karsavina believed, "conservative at heart," "a modest part of the court," echoing Nicholas Legat's comment about Imperial Theater artists as the tsar's "servants."[42] Imperial Theater artists were relatively privileged. They received "a free education and [were] provided for to the end of their lives."[43] Ultimately, few were prepared to jeopardize such privileges.

The autonomy issue lingered in the Alexandrinsky longer than in the Mariinsky. On October 18 the company gathered in the theater. Some expressed loyalty to the tsar now that he had issued the October Manifesto. The majority of the troupe seemed generally loyal; it is true that during the disturbances of that evening's performance one actor was reported to have shouted "Down with the autocracy," but his was a lone voice.[44] Gnedich composed an address to the tsar on behalf of the troupe which elucidated the artists' interpretation of recent events, that is, they now had the possibility to assert their freedom and artistic independence. The pronouncement of the October Manifesto was a "patriotic act." "Now we, the free artists, have been granted the possibility to freely serve the stage and carry the torch of goodness, beauty, and truth, which must be the guiding star in the development of humanity."[45] Many of the "free artists" were keen to assert autonomy from the Directorate and regarded the October Manifesto as a sign that augured well for a greater level of self-administration. They particularly desired a Repertoire Council (*repertuarnyi sovet*) which would be elected from among the members of the troupe and which would have real power. An abortive attempt to establish such a Council had in fact been undertaken on the initiative of the Directorate in 1903,[46] but the seven members of the Council had been appointed by the Directorate and it was only consultative; it fell apart when Savina, one of its appointees, refused to participate because of that.[47] Savina, of course, could afford to refuse to participate, given the power she already enjoyed in the Alexandrinsky. In late 1905, the Directorate decided to grant the "stillborn Repertoire Council" the right to make decisions. It would not simply be consultative. At the same time, the artists of the Alexandrinsky, who were meeting constantly to discuss such affairs, increased their demands. They now considered establishing an elected Council of Artists which would wrest even more authority from the Directorate. This was clear from a discussion paper presented at one of the Alexandrinsky's meetings by Nicholas Arbenin (1863-August 14, 1906), an actor who, having previously worked at the Moscow Maly, had joined the Alexandrinsky in 1895. The following areas, said Arbenin, should be dealt with by an elected Council of Artists:

> 1) the selection and establishment of the repertoire;
> 2) the formulation of an artistic plan for each season, with precise instructions for the participation of each member of the troupe in the projected repertoire, that is, the distribution of roles;

3) the structure of the existing repertoire;

4) a survey of the means to enable all members of the troupe to work, in particular so that the "young forces" get essential practice [there was concern that some artists were being marginalized by the "stars"—M.F.];

5) the invitation and dismissal of artists.[48]

Such tasks corresponded to the chief responsibilities of the Directorate, as outlined in Chapter 2—recruitment and control of artists, selection of the repertoire, and the staging of the repertoire. The artists, it seemed, were intent on wresting from the Directorate its major powers relating to artistic production. But then, from January 1906, the autonomy issue disappeared with a suddenness that suggests its pursuit was inspired chiefly by the all-pervading fashion for rebellion, rather than an innate desire for radical change (though this is not to deny the sincerity of the artist-activists as such). The artists settled down again, and there is no evidence to support Ekaterina Maltseva, who ends her brief discussion of these months by stating of the post–1905 period that "artist discontent increased."[49]

Why was autonomy not achieved in 1905-06? The main reason the Alexandrinsky artists failed to secure autonomy was that they were divided amongst themselves. According to *The Petersburg Gazette* (*Peterburgskaia gazeta*), the chief opponents of autonomy were the elders of the theater, including Savina, Davydov, and Varlamov. With such prominent and intimidating figures coming out against autonomy, it becomes clearer as to why little progress was made, despite endless discussions and proposals. Moreover, the whole company never congregated together at any one time to discuss the matter, suggesting a certain degree of apathy among many of the artists.[50] Viven, who acted at the Alexandrinsky from 1913, claimed that relations between the artists did not really extend beyond the stage. Backstage, it was "each-to-his-own," with no general participation in the life of the theater. There was, he said, a theater troupe, but not a theater collective. Although Viven was speaking of the Alexandrinsky some years after 1905, it is more than likely that his observation applies to 1905-06.[51] The drive for autonomy was closely linked to the revolution, and most artists were against revolution. As Khodotov conceded, for most artists of the Imperial Theaters, "the word 'revolution' was the 'bogey' of sedition and anarchy."[52] Consequently, it is fair to conclude that autonomy was not achieved in the Alexandrinsky, not because of any repression on the part of the Directorate, but because the desire for it among the artists was not strong enough. This in turn suggests that the Alexandrinsky artists, like the ballet troupe, were anxious not to forfeit their privileged positions. The more they organized their own affairs, the less they required the attentions of the court, the source of their prestige.

After the relatively harmless disruptions in the auditoria and the feeble "rebellion" by some of the artists, general order returned to the St. Petersburg Imperial Theaters, and their image as loyal servitors of tsarism was restored.

The ease of this restoration is explained by the loyal and apolitical attitude of the vast majority of the audience and artists. Most evenings at the Imperial Theaters passed without any incident because the audience was there to be entertained, and the artists *wanted* to entertain.

After 1905

The involvement of St. Petersburg Imperial Theater artists in the political movement against tsarism was restricted generally to the spontaneous strikes and demands for autonomy which occurred from October 1905 to January 1906. Thereafter, the St. Petersburg Imperial Theaters returned to a semblance of normality, and the Directorate continued to exercise its authority unimpeded by serious challenges. Yet that is not to suggest there were no aftershocks or that the aspirations of 1905-06 had completely disappeared. For example, after Gnedich's resignation in 1908 and his public letter condemning the Directorate, there was some talk of trying once more to establish an autonomous governing body for the Alexandrinsky, but this came to nothing.[53]

Nor should it be believed that the artists were completely apolitical during the inter-revolutionary years. Many were politically active, even though this was expressly forbidden by the government. In September 1906, the government issued a circular which announced that its employees were not permitted to be involved with any political party. The majority of such parties were committed to opposing the government, and those who received their livelihood from the government were not allowed to oppose it. This circular was applicable to Imperial Theater employees, and it stated that anyone who acted contrary to its instruction would be dismissed from service.[54] The most prominent Imperial Theater artist to whom this circular applied was Sumbatov-Yuzhin of the Moscow Maly, who was a member of the liberal Kadet Party. The interesting point about Sumbatov-Yuzhin in this respect is that, according to a recent biographer, he refused to obey the September 1906 circular and does not appear to have suffered any detrimental consequences. Certainly, he was not dismissed from the theater. In 1909, when he was appointed leader of the Maly, the right-wing press created a fuss over the fact that a Kadet had been appointed to a responsible post, but the Directorate and court turned a blind eye to this, possibly because he was a prince (*kniaz*).[55] It would be inaccurate to conclude from this example, however, that the Directorate had lost any authority over the artists after the events of 1905 or that the government had become less concerned about the political reliability of the artists. Sumbatov-Yuzhin was a highly respected actor and playwright, and that is probably why he was not intimidated by the Directorate (it was noted above that Chaliapin's fame was a factor which allowed him to keep his job after singing *The Little Cudgel* on the Bolshoi stage).

Equally, the Alexandrinsky actor Nicholas Khodotov was politically active. Unusually for an Imperial Theater artist, Khodotov was notorious for his radical sympathies and for storing radical pamphlets and outlawed revolutionaries in his flat.[56] He was not always considered highly by his colleagues, despite being as talented as them, if not more so; possibly the hostility, such as that from Auslender, who spoke of the "hopeless and endless vulgarity of Mr Khodotov,"[57] was a response to his maverick radicalism. In December 1913, he organized a "concert-ball" at the Kalashnikov stock exchange in aid of, and, Khodotov later claimed, at the request of, the local Social Democrats and their paper *Proletarian Truth* (*Proletarskaia Pravda*).[58] Yet Khodotov was exceptional. His activity, while demonstrating that even prominent artists of the court theaters were not incapable of anti-tsarist political activity, was isolated and untypical. No other prominent artists appear to have been involved with revolutionary parties.

Moreover, there is evidence to suggest that the government remained concerned to monitor the political trustworthiness of those it employed. Before the Directorate employed anyone it was required to have him or her vetted by the secret police. In practice, this meant that the Okhrana scanned its records to check whether the potential employee had ever been involved in radical activity.[59] For instance, the Okhrana informed the St. Petersburg Office that a certain Senno Branzburg had been arrested at an unauthorized meeting, and that "a large quantity of proclamations of criminal content and different pamphlets" had been uncovered at his flat (although he nevertheless went on to work in the Directorate's photography department).[60] The actor Alexander Mgebrov claimed that the secret police thwarted his chances of acting at the Alexandrinsky, even though he commanded the support of Meyerhold and the interest of Telyakovsky.[61] Mgebrov had fought at the barricades in 1905. Presumably, to take up arms against tsarism was regarded as a more serious offense than to join a liberal opposition party, as Sumbatov-Yuzhin had done.

* * * *

The flashpoint of the 1905 Revolution thus pointed to an ambiguity of identity for the St. Petersburg Imperial Theaters. As court institutions, they were expected to maintain a semblance of calm loyalty to tsarism. Given the fact that the artists were essentially court employees, and that Imperial Theater audiences consisted predominantly of social and political groups that were essentially conservative allies of tsarism or had much to lose from a revolution (military officials, courtiers, bureaucrats, wealthy merchants, and so forth), this was a natural expectation. The brevity of the artists' revolt and the protestations of loyalty in the auditoria (such as the demands for triple renditions of the national anthem) testified to this. Nevertheless, the St.

Petersburg Imperial Theaters did not entirely avoid the orbit of the radical movement. The artists' flirtation with autonomy and the demonstrations in the auditoria portray cultural institutions that were by no means blindly loyal to the state that they were so closely associated with.

Chapter 7

War, Revolution, and the Provisional Government, 1914–October 1917

The outbreak of the First World War was greeted in Russia by an upsurge of patriotic fervor that appeared to unify a country many historians have argued was on the verge of another revolution. Growing social and political discontent, represented in particular by the strike wave of 1914, receded in the face of the international crisis that threatened the very existence of Russia as an imperial power. By the summer of 1915, however, the patriotic euphoria had given way to widespread dissatisfaction with the conduct of the war, in particular the spectacular defeats suffered by the Russian army at Tannenberg and the Masurian Lakes in the opening stages of the conflict. Military humiliation was compounded by growing domestic problems as the war effort disrupted supplies of food and fuel to the cities. The ostensible impotence of the tsarist government in the face of the growing crises was met by an increasingly proactive civil society, in particular the War Industries Committee and the Zemstvo Union, that effectively appropriated responsibility for the war effort from the government.[1]

At the beginning of the war, the daily paper *The New Times* commented on what it regarded as the renewed importance of Russian theater in 1914 and identified its obvious function in the context of the international crisis in which the country was embroiled:

> Scarcely has the theater had a more exceptional role than at the present moment. In ordinary peacetime, most people go to the theater "to kill the evening." Present events have put to the background both theatrical and personal life. To unite with the interests of the motherland, to aid her defenders—these are the thoughts of everyone. If at the present time people go to the theater, it is to dispel anxious thoughts, to forget about the blood and iron which are now deciding the fates of peoples.[2]

In other words, theater would provide a means of escape from the tribulations of the war. During the first year of the conflict, audiences remained
large and most theaters worked "as never before,"[3] although toward the end
of 1915 there was a decline in theater attendance as a result of increases in
taxes on ticket prices.[4] Yet if the theaters were expected to enable audiences
to forget about reality, they were also expected to use expressions of patriotism to reassure and inspire people about Russia's war prospects. In particular, as public institutions closely connected to state authority, the St.
Petersburg Imperial Theaters—now called the Petrograd Imperial Theaters
in line with the change in the city's name at the beginning of the war—might
be expected to function as megaphones of patriotism. This function was certainly discernible in the patriotic activity of the Imperial Theaters during the
war. Yet the latent ambivalence of their function and identity in late tsarist
Russia was implicit in this activity, most notably in the nature of the patriotism. According to one recent historian of the subject, there are at least two
distinctive forms of patriotism. The first is what might be termed "official
patriotism," that is, patriotism that explicitly supports established state
authority. The other version is "patriotism as social action," expressed most
clearly as support for country or nation. In other words, it was possible to be
patriotic during the war without implying support for the government.[5]
Indeed, many considered it unpatriotic to support a government that was
clearly incapable of protecting the material interests of Russia in an international crisis. As court institutions, the Petrograd Imperial Theaters largely
pursued a line of official patriotism. Yet many of the activities of Imperial
Theater artists served to ally them with the camp of social patriotism and to
identify them implicitly with the wider tasks of civil society.

From the very beginning of the 1914-15 season, efforts were made to
emphasize and expand existing elements of official patriotism in Imperial
Theater performances. When the Mariinsky opera season opened on August 30
with *A Life for the Tsar* in the presence of the ambassadors of Russia's allies,
Telyakovsky described the renditions of the Russian national anthem as "a
grandiose manifestation by the public and the artists."[6] When the ballet season opened the following evening with *The Hump-Backed Horse*, as well as
the customary triple rendition of the Russian national anthem, the anthems
of the Allied countries were performed as a gesture of solidarity. This was
also the case at the Alexandrinsky which, before opening the drama season
with *Krechinsky's Wedding*, staged Alexei Pisemsky's mid-nineteenth-century
Crimean War play, *The Veteran and the Recruit*.[7] Repeated renditions of the
Russian and Allied anthems became a regular feature of performances in the
Imperial Theaters during the war.

However, the repertoire of the Petrograd Imperial Theaters changed
surprisingly little during the war years. There were few new plays, operas, or
ballets, perhaps a result of wartime financial constraints. At the Alexandrinsky,

the only new overtly patriotic drama to be produced was Leonid Andreev's *King, Law and Freedom*, a play about the German invasion of Belgium in 1914. However, this was performed at the Alexandrinsky only fourteen times: four times in December 1914, five times in January 1915, twice in February and March, and then finally once in April 1915. In other words, the play enjoyed only a short period of prominence on the Alexandrinsky stage. One reason might be the poor quality of the drama; it might also be the case that audiences preferred to forget about the war, particularly by 1915, when the nature of Russian patriotism began to change from loyalty to the government to criticism of it. The only other patriotic gesture in the drama repertoire was a revival of Ostrovsky on the Alexandrinsky stage, in particular *A Passionate Heart* which, although generally one of the most popular plays in the repertoire during 1900–17, had not actually been performed since November 1909. One critic attributed the revival of Ostrovsky to the fact that, even though his characters were from the nineteenth century, they were still authentic, contemporary Russian types (*"rodnoe, svoe"*).[8]

At the Mariinsky, there were no new patriotic operas, although *A Life for the Tsar* took on a special significance. Some scenes were even removed from the opera in recognition of the wartime reconciliation between Russia and Poland, such as the arrival of the herald at the ball and the death of Susanin at the hands of the invading Poles.[9] The only new gesture to patriotism was the removal of German works, notably Wagner's operas, from the repertoire until after the war. At the beginning of 1915, a series of ballet dances entitled *The Year 1914* was staged by Sergei Volkonsky, the former Director of Imperial Theaters. It was intended to be a patriotic expression, with the participation of the prominent dancers Karsavina and Preobrazhenskaya, but it was generally regarded as a failure and was quickly dropped from the repertoire.[10] Patrons evidently required the comfort of the traditional repertoire.

If the Petrograd Imperial Theaters did not express official patriotism through the repertoire as such, they did so by staging special performances in aid of Russian war charities or for patriotic inspiration. Imperial Theater artists had often engaged in charity performances for various causes before the war, but during 1914–17 such performances became a prominent feature of their activity. In September 1914, the coloratura soprano Lidiia Lipkovskaia organized a charity evening at the Mariinsky, although she had actually left the Mariinsky for the Theater of Musical Drama the previous year; the proceeds were donated to the charity organized by M. I. Dolina (see below). Like the majority of such special charity events, the program was an amalgamation of dramatic, musical, and balletic scenes performed by members of the Imperial Theater troupes.[11] On October 11, 1914, the spectacle *Triumph of the Powers*, organized by A. A. Suvorina, written by A. V. Bobrishchev-Pushkin, and produced by Meyerhold, took place at the Mariinsky. Part of the program involved the disappearance through a trap door of a caricatured German commander and his HQ followed by the appearance of the victorious Allies; and when the dramatic representatives of the Allies addressed them with patriotic messages, the audience spontaneously broke into cries and applause. Needless to say, the national anthems were played. According to one observer, "The fervor reached extreme bounds when it was time to salute the injured officers, formerly in the theater. They cried 'Ura,' they waved kerchiefs, they wept...." This was followed by the drama *Be Glad, We Are Winning*, followed in turn by a divertissement from the visiting Moscow ballerina, Ekaterina Geltser.[12] The Directorate also arranged an exclusive program at the Mariinsky in aid of the Belgians.[13] And in March 1916, a special performance at the Mariinsky raised money for the Alexandrovsky Committee for Invalids.[14]

One of the most important facts about Petrograd Imperial Theater charity performances during the war is the extent to which individual artists took the initiative in organizing such events outside the Imperial Theaters, in other words to engage in acts of "social patriotism." The most prominent examples of this phenomenon were the "patriotic evenings" organized by the Mariinsky soprano Maria Dolina. Dolina had organized similar events during the Balkan Wars, and their reappearance in 1914 was greeted with great warmth by the population of Petrograd. The first of the Dolina concerts during the First World War was given on August 26, 1914, and they continued as a regular feature, mainly at the Cinizelli Circus, until 1917. The concerts were designed to raise money for various war charities, in particular general help for victims of the war, the soldiers and their families. A typical concert involved renditions of the national anthems, readings of telegrams from the front, and so on, and they were performed by both Imperial and private theater artists.[15]

Dolina's patriotic concerts, although not organized under the auspices of the Imperial Theaters, constituted official concerts in the sense that Dolina was a "Soloist of His Majesty" and her concerts were formally patronized by the tsar. But Dolina was not the only patriot. Other Imperial Theater artists were involved in charitable events organized in other private theaters. The artists either participated in events organized by others, or they organized their own concerts outside the Imperial Theater system. For example, A. A. Suvorina arranged concerts at the Suvorin Theater which included the participation of various Imperial Theater artists, including Meyerhold, who staged a piece entitled *Apotheosis: Memories of the White General*, a dramatization of Skobelev's famous speeches from 1882. General M. D. Skobelev (1843–1882) had become particularly well-known during the Russo-Turkish War of 1877–78 and afterwards as an adventurer in Central Asia. In 1882 he confirmed his status as the hero of the Panslavs when he announced that Germany was the sworn enemy of Russia, both externally and internally.[16] In Meyerhold's production, Skobelev was played by Khodotov.[17] Khodotov himself organized a patriotic concert in the *Narodnyi dom* (The People's House) entitled *In These Days* to raise money for Dolina's charity, and Imperial Theater artist M. A. Vedrinskaya also used the *Narodnyi dom* for two concerts in aid of Belgium.[18] Prominent Imperial Theater artists, such as Savina and Tartakov, participated in a concert at the City Duma's Alexandrovsky Hall to raise funds for war-related causes.[19] The City Duma also organized a reception in aid of warm clothing for frontline soldiers, which included the participation of both Imperial and private theater artists. According to *The New Times*, invitations to the special reception were issued to the diplomatic corps of the Allied countries, to the administration, publicists, artists, composers "and other social activists [*obshchestvennye deiateli*]."[20]

The phrase "social activists" is instructive. This was effectively what many Imperial Theater artists became during the war. Although there are examples of charitable work by Imperial Theater artists prior to 1914, the scale of activity during the period 1914–17 was unprecedented. It was natural that the Petrograd Imperial Theaters, as court institutions, should play a patriotic role during the war. In the end, they were associated with two forms of patriotism: On the one hand, small changes to the repertoire, the endless renditions of the Russian and Allied national anthems, and the formal charity events organized by the Directorate in the Imperial Theaters confirmed that the Imperial Theaters were conduits of official patriotism; on the other hand, the level of personal initiative on the part of many artists and their involvement in charitable events outside the Imperial Theaters pointed to a significant degree of social patriotism among the artists which, according to one scholar, could often be implicitly oppositional. It became particularly pronounced in 1915 when Russia's war effort started to falter; gestures of support for the government became less widespread and social patriotism focused on helping the victims of the war.

If social patriotism was an implicit criticism of the government's war effort, it did not necessarily entail opposition to tsarism in general and was likely pursued on the part of individuals for altruistic reasons. But while the Imperial Theaters as institutions retained the formal forms of official patriotism throughout the war, the involvement of individual artists in social patriotic activities outside the Imperial Theaters, and the consequent blurring of the lines between court theater and other artists, pointed to a temporary merger with the components of civil society.

The February Revolution and the Provisional Government

Ultimately, Russia's participation in the First World War had only served to exacerbate long-standing national problems. In February 1917, tsarism collapsed and was replaced by the dual power of the Provisional Government (essentially a group of liberal Duma politicians) and the Petrograd Soviet (the organ of the revolutionary parties). Meriel Buchanan recalled that "high society" was unaware of impending events in February 1917:

> The social and artistic world of Petrograd was occupied during those days discussing the redecoration and reopening of the Alexander [Alexandrinsky] Theatre, the wonderful performance of "Masquerade" that was to be given, staged with an incredible magnificence that defied all precepts of wartime economy. People paid enormous sums for seats and talked of nothing else but the coming production, seeming to forget in their excitement even the war and the ominous clouds on the horizon.[21]

Yet there were certain forebodings within the Petrograd Imperial Theaters of the impending upheaval. On the eve of the February Revolution, the Directorate was faced with a disruption in an auditorium reminiscent of those of 1905 which so disturbed the image of the Imperial Theaters. This time, the scandal originated not from the auditorium, but from the artists, specifically the Mariinsky chorus. On February 21, 1917, in an event that one observer considered the beginning of the revolution in the theater, the chorus struck over low wages. This had always been an issue with the chorus but in the context of deteriorating material conditions in Petrograd its members decided to take dramatic action. The chorus prepared as usual for the evening performance, Rimsky-Korsakov's *A Night in May*. It appeared on stage—but refused to sing! Initially the audience was patient, and the orchestra played on, but soon unrest bubbled up and cries of "Down with the chorus!" and "Bring down the curtain!" were heard from the auditorium. The artists hesitated and the curtain began to descend, only to rise again before it reached the floor. The performance then proceeded without further incident, but the situation in the Mariinsky remained tense for several days. A majority of artists and workers supported the chorus, and to avoid a repetition of the recent protest the Directorate changed the scheduled performance for the following evening to an opera which could be performed without the chorus. Unfortunately for the Directorate, the *orchestra* then decided to strike and the opera, *Il Barbiere di Siviglia*, was given "unaccompanied" ("*pod surdinu*"). On February 23, the chorus was told it would receive a pay raise, and on February 27 Tartakov, Chief *Régisseur* of the Mariinsky opera troupe, informed Telyakovsky that "the ferment in the chorus had come to an end."[22] But by then the February Revolution had commenced.

The new authorities, chiefly in the guise of the Provisional Government rather than the Soviet, took measures to stamp their authority on the Imperial Theaters. Within days of Nicholas II's renunciation of the throne (March 2), posters appeared outside all three Petrograd Imperial Theaters proclaiming: "The theater has passed to the authority of the Provisional Government. Defend it as national property." Indeed, the theater buildings were being guarded by "military patrols."[23] The process of protection highlighted two interrelated things. First, the theaters were considered important public institutions by the Provisional Government, as they had been under tsarism. Second, the ways in which the theaters were co-opted by the new government, and the discussions surrounding them, shed light on the changing meanings surrounding the Imperial Theaters. In the process, these institutions of the tsarist court, which had represented—and still did represent—the old order's hierarchies and values, rapidly redefined themselves as democratic artistic institutions within "free Russia." Whereas in 1905 the most obvious manifestation of how the official status of the Imperial Theaters was challenged were the radical demonstrations against the tsarist government, in 1917 the challenge came from various manifestations of loyalty to the new, "free Russia," pending the convocation of the Constituent Assembly. What were in 1905 subversive activities—meetings, committees, the drive for autonomy, and so on—became in 1917 protestations of loyalty. The Imperial Theaters, soon to be renamed State Theaters, no longer appeared as bastions of tsarism, but, led by radical members of their organization, asserted themselves as advocates of democratic revolution. This was evident, for example, in the celebrations and miniature festivals which occurred in the Petrograd State Theaters between March and October 1917 (see below). In other words, the former Imperial Theaters rapidly became, in stark contrast to their dominant pre-revolutionary associations with tsarism, emblems for "free Russia."

On March 2, 1917, Mikhail Rodzianko, President of the Duma, signed a decree ordering all officials of the Directorate of Imperial Theaters to carry out the instructions of Nicholas Nikolaevich Lvov, *zemstvo* activist, Kadet member of the Duma, and now commissar of the Provisional Government (not to be confused with Prince G. E. Lvov or V. N. Lvov, who became members of the new government after Rodzianko had been outmaneuvered).[24] On March 3, Lvov issued the following instructions:

> 1. Until subsequent instructions by the supreme governmental power, Vladimir Arkadevich Telyakovsky is to retain the managerial functions of the Directorate of Theaters and Schools, both in Petrograd and Moscow.
> 2. Telyakovsky is granted the right to authorize the Offices to issue banknotes upon urgent requests in the established way.
> 3. All new banknotes from the *Kabinet* of His Majesty are to be received only with my (N. N. Lvov) permission and with my signature.[25]

According to one observer, "Telyakovsky reluctantly agreed [to remain Director], having established the condition that he would remain for no more than a month."[26] At a meeting between Lvov and the Alexandrinsky troupe on March 3, Telyakovsky addressed the artists with "a few words," thanking them for "working with me over the course of many years," and assuring them that he was remaining in his post only temporarily.[27] Telyakovsky recognized that the situation had radically changed, that the function of the old Directorate was all but obsolete in the eyes of the artists. Freedom from tsarism was, for the Imperial Theaters, freedom from the Directorate. According to Bezpalov, Telyakovsky recognized that the artists wanted the Directorate to do two things, namely "to give autonomous troupes money from the exchequer, and to sweep the corridors of the theaters."[28] Telyakovsky had even been "arrested" on March 1 by two artists of the drama troupe, emboldened by an assembled crowd who resented the Director "who lived in a luxurious apartment," but he was quickly released.[29] He remained in his post until early May. The Provisional Government *ukaz* on his removal, which Telyakovsky later attributed to illness, is dated May 6, 1917.[30] Until then, Telyakovsky appears to have played a kind of advisory role during a short transitional period when authority over the state theaters was transferred from one group of individuals to another. For some weeks it was not entirely clear to contemporaries just who had authority in the theaters. Telyakovsky seems to have regarded Lvov as a legitimate successor, allowing him make various decisions without protest; but Lvov regularly consulted Telyakovsky during the transitional phase, and it was Telyakovsky who continued to receive requests of various kinds from people wishing to use the Imperial Theaters for concerts or to have their plays staged.[31]

On March 6, in what was the first official political statement on the new relationship between the Imperial Theaters and the government, Lvov decreed that the Imperial Theaters would now be called State Theaters (*gosudarstvennye teatry*).[32] On March 7, he further decreed that sub-lieutenant Vasilii Fedorovich Bezpalov was appointed commandant of all Petrograd's State Theaters. Bezpalov was a singer with the Mariinsky opera troupe. During the war, when he was not rehearsing at the theater, he was a sub-lieutenant attached to the General Staff Office on Palace Square. All theater staff and office holders were to be subordinate to him, although the following day yet another decree was issued stating that Bezpalov's duties were restricted to ensuring external and internal order "in the buildings."[33] Again, the importance of the theaters as public institutions was recognized by the government. According to his own account, after the February Revolution began, Bezpalov spoke to Telyakovsky about the need to guard the theaters. Bezpalov did this probably because he felt responsible and able to arrange this, due to his position at the General Staff, rather than his position at the Mariinsky. At any rate, Telyakovsky agreed with him, and so Bezpalov went to the Tauride Palace where he spoke to Paul Milyukov who granted official approval that Bezpalov be responsible for safeguarding the State Theaters. He was provided with forty soldiers to guard the three theaters.[34] Early in March, as noted above, Lvov simply confirmed these decisions by offering Bezpalov a provisional appointment to the post of Commandant of the State Theaters with responsibility for their property.[35] This appears to have been Lvov's last act as commissar for the former Imperial Theaters.

Telyakovsky sometime after 1910. The years of administering the Imperial Theaters seem to have aged the Director quite considerably (compare with the photograph on page 29), perhaps a reason why he was not too reluctant to relinquish the post soon after the February Revolution. *Vospominaniia* (Moscow-Leningrad, 1965)

In March 1917, the Ministry of the Imperial Court was replaced by the Department of the Former Ministry of the Imperial Court, headed by Commissar Fyodor Alexandrovich Golovin, the liberal politician and former President of the Second Duma, who appears to have been Lvov's replacement as commissar with responsibility for the State Theaters. His first order, dated March 10, stated that all departments of the former court were to continue working.[36] On April 27, Golovin decreed the appointment of Fyodor Dmitrievich Batiushkov as Chief Representative of the State Theaters for the Commissar of the Provisional Government at the Former Ministry of the Imperial Court. Also appointed at this time was Batiushkov's assistant, Sergei Bertenson.[37] Batiushkov (1857–March 19, 1920), who was Telyakovsky's official replacement, was a Kadet, a former editor (1902–06) of *World of God* (*Mir Bozhii*), and a Professor of the History of Literature at Petrograd University. He was not entirely new to the State Theaters: Before the revolution he had been, from January 1900, Chairman of the Alexandrinsky Theater-

Literary Committee. On May 13, when the government formally established autonomy in the State Theaters (see below), Commissar Golovin decreed that the Directorate of State Theaters and the Petrograd Office be transformed into the Chancellery of the Chief Representative of State Theaters.[38] Thus, by the middle of May 1917, the tsarist Ministry of the Imperial Court and its Directorate of Imperial Theaters had been replaced by the Department of the Former Ministry of the Imperial Court and its office of Chief Representative of the State Theaters. The hierarchy of the state theater administration under the Provisional Government therefore mirrored that which had obtained before the revolution. Only the official titles and the personnel had altered.

Meantime, the artists of the Petrograd State Theaters, according to Bezpalov, talked without rest.[39] The predominant issues were the theater's status in the evolving context of the revolution, and the renewed drive for autonomy. The whole of the Petrograd theater world was abuzz with talk of the possibilities opened up by the demise of the tsarist order, not least the expected abandonment of censorship. Yet it should be noted that the State Theaters tended to remain aloof from other theater organizations which emerged in 1917, such as the Professional Union of Petrograd Stage Workers, which was a union of artists from private theaters.[40] The State Theaters remained privileged institutions after the February Revolution and were still regarded enviously by private theaters. Indeed, Bezpalov described the State Theaters and the private theaters as two hostile camps. While the State Theaters did send a small delegation of artists to a general meeting of Petrograd stage personnel to elect delegates to the Petrograd Soviet on March 7, in general they remained isolated from wider developments in the artistic world. They preferred to set their own agenda, and therefore the history of the State Theaters in 1917 does not necessitate analysis here of organizations not originating within the State Theaters.

Petrograd State Theater artists worked feverishly to ensure their autonomy from the new Russian government, as well as to express their general approbation of recent events, which were viewed as conducive to the successful acquisition and consolidation of organizational autonomy. The artists of the Alexandrinsky were more active politically than those of the Mariinsky. Within days of the collapse of the monarchy, the *régisseur* Evtikhii Karpov was organizing meetings which resulted in the election of an Organizing Committee whose remit was to prepare a draft charter on the internal structure of the Alexandrinsky in anticipation of autonomy from the state. The thirteen artists on the Organizing Committee were to be supplemented by four representatives from the French troupe at the Mikhailovsky, and four representatives from the technical staff of the theaters. At their meeting on March 3, Lvov was well-received by the Alexandrinsky artists as a representative of "free Russia," and the troupe wasted no time in issuing a declaration of support for the Provisional Government, stating that as it was now free from "oppression and arbitrariness," it wanted to "devote its powers and inspiration to the people, towards the consolidation of the good mood of our motherland."[41] The troupe was equally quick to request autonomy from the Provisional Government. The actor Roman Apollonskii approached the Duma about this, but with no immediate results.[42]

At the Mariinsky, there took root a cult of meetings and voting. The whole artistic body split into its constituent parts: the opera troupe, the ballet troupe, the chorus, and the orchestra. The artists were determined to take their affairs into their own hands, to secure autonomy for the theater, and already by March 4 were talking about a commission to discuss autonomy.[43] Lvov, in a speech that was met with "loud applause,"[44] implored the artists of the Mariinsky at a meeting on March 5 to side with "free Russia." The artists responded favorably and the following statement was read by the opera bass-baritone Pavel Andreev on behalf of the whole theater:

> In your person, dear Nicholas Nikolaevich [Lvov], the opera, ballet, chorus, orchestra, workers, and staff of the Mariinsky Theater greet the people's choice. The dawn of a renewed Russia is clearly breaking out upon us, the people of art. We want the approaching flowering of the motherland to carry with it the renovation of our theater, a theater which has been recognized to serve and to reflect the national spirit. Having eliminated the vices of the old regime, we now realize what we did not have, what hindered us. Proceeding from this recognition, and knowing better than others the technical aspect of the most intricate mechanism of the theater, we see a unique way out of the previously existing situation only in the widest autonomy.[45]

The good terms established between the Provisional Government and the former Imperial Theaters augured well for a greater degree of self-administration for the artists. Yet, although the Provisional Government approved autonomy for the State Theaters, like the tsarist and later Soviet governments it was unwilling to relinquish its control of them completely. The desire to retain them as part of an official governmental power structure was still very evident in "free Russia." On April 28, Golovin convened a meeting to finalize the form autonomy would take, which, according to Bezpalov, was suggested by the Alexandrinsky artists and was adapted from the structure of the Comédie Française. This emphasized the comradeship of the artists and workers of the theater—Bezpalov used the word *soseterstvo*, from the French *société*. The "society" controlled the internal artistic and financial affairs of the theater, but there remained a government director to oversee how the state's money was being spent.[46] As from May 13, 1917, when the autonomy statute was published, each of the State Theaters would have an elected committee to take care of the repertoire and artistic business, the so-called Khudrepkom (*khudozhestvenno-repertuarnyi vybornyi komitet*, or Artistic-Repertorial Elective Committee, also sometimes referred to as the

Repkhudkom). Its duties would include some of the chief tasks which had belonged to the Directorate of Imperial Theaters and which Arbenin and the Alexandrinsky artists had endeavored to secure in 1905-06, namely recruitment of artists, selection of the repertoire, and the distribution of roles. But the right of the Khudrepkomy to organize the artistic affairs of the theaters formally remained subject to the approval of the Chief Representative. The statute on autonomy further established (or re-established) the post of Manager of the Troupe (*upravliaiushchii truppoi*), who would be elected by the artists, but subject to the approval of the Chief Representative.[47] The Manager of the Alexandrinsky would be Karpov; the opera troupe would be managed by the well-known organizer of "musical evenings," A. I. Ziloti, the ballet troupe by Boris Romanov.

The theater troupes were surprisingly unified in their purpose, in contrast to the disunity during the rebellious months of the 1905 Revolution. Disagreements and disputes during the early months after the February Revolution were generally trivial. For example, as one newspaper reported, when Golovin convened a meeting to discuss the objectives of drama, he invited the Alexandrinsky to send two delegates, while at the same time extending to Meyerhold a personal invitation. Some artists were offended that Meyerhold did not inform them of this personal invitation while he continued to participate in the election of the other delegates. Meyerhold was not elected but could go to the meeting by virtue of his special invitation. The press reported this as a "conflict in the Alexandrinsky Theater troupe."[48] In fact, there were no serious disputes (political, ideological, or other) and anyone who remained sympathetic to the old order evidently kept the fact hidden.

Nevertheless, despite the ostensible enthusiasm of the artists for running their own affairs, State Theater autonomy during the tenure of the Provisional Government remained fragile, and toward the autumn, as the new season commenced, it began to break down. In September 1917 there were reports that the Alexandrinsky Khudrepkom was not active enough, that the artists were interested only in the distribution of roles, that there was friction between the majority of the artists and Karpov, and that there were no rehearsal plans for plays that were supposed to be premiered in two months' time. According to reports, it was the younger members of the troupe who were causing most of the disruption. In short, discipline was breaking down at the Alexandrinsky.[49] According to Bezpalov, by September 1917, the Alexandrinsky troupe had practically relinquished its autonomous power because it was unable to agree on the new composition of the governing committee. Power consequently had passed to Batiushkov and Karpov. Batiushkov evidently had delusions of grandeur that militated against the consolidation of an effective working autonomy in the theaters. On October 20, in a move designed to outmaneuver his rival Bezpalov, he stipulated that the post of

Commandant—the job of keeping guard ("*nabliudeniia za karaulami*")—was no longer necessary.[50] Batiushkov's position was strengthened by the fact that the artists generally began to lose interest in self-administration by the autumn of 1917.[51] The new season was beginning, and energies were being channelled toward performances, although the October Revolution would once more enliven the issue of the State Theaters' relationship with the Russian government. On the very eve of the October Revolution, there was a last-gasp attempt by the Alexandrinsky Khudrepkom to stave off the appropriation of full power by Batiushkov. The artists announced they would draw up an instruction establishing the Khudrepkom as the authority of the theater. Batiushkov responded that the only law governing the organization of the theaters was the Provisional Statute of May 1917. He even announced that he did not consider the Alexandrinsky autonomous; nor would it be, he claimed, until projected, but unspecified, changes in its structure were made in September 1918. This incensed the artists: "Everyone spoke out. Only questions were raised: Why play at being autonomous, convene general meetings, when all issues had already been decided by higher levels of authority—theater bureaucrats—and when all power [*vlast*] in the Alexandrinsky Theater had passed to E. P. Karpov, who took refuge behind the good name of the Repkhudkom only when it was convenient for him to do so?"[52] The evident malfunctioning of autonomy was probably a combination of personality clashes and the general lack of experience and culture of self-administration. At any rate, before the growing dispute could be resolved, the October Revolution presented the State Theaters with new challenges.

As for the *art* of the Petrograd State Theaters under the Provisional Government, Bezpalov recalled that it was not uppermost in the minds of the artists, taking second place to material needs.[53] The standard repertoire remained practically unchanged (although, as Iurev pointed out, by May 1917, *Masquerade* had been removed from the repertoire because it was considered too "luxurious" for post-tsarist Petrograd[54]) and was to remain substantially the same over the next few years. Yet in another sense there *was* a new kind of repertoire after the February Revolution, best described as the celebration of the new order. The whole symbolism of the theaters was transformed by the collapse of tsarism, as the confusion and uncertainty of the revolutionary days created the need for alternative expressions of identity. On March 12, the State Theaters reopened after a brief period of closure, and all the box-office takings during the first week of performances under the new government were donated to those who fell for the revolution. From then on, the State Theaters were busy with daily meetings and events which actively celebrated the revolution, reinforcing the social, group-integrative function they had had under tsarism.[55] The artists were not hostile to the February Revolution; Petrov recalled that they were glad to cross the name "Imperial" from their passports and to substitute the word "State," as well as to wear red ribbons.[56] Tsarist insignia and symbols associated with the pre-February period in the theaters were now deemed inappropriate. Portraits of the tsars were removed, ushers were no longer to wear tail-coats with double-headed eagles, the tsarist state coat-of-arms on theater programs was replaced by a lyre, the pre-revolutionary *artistic* ensign of the Imperial Theaters, and all the gilded double-headed eagles in the theaters were covered with red cloth. The dark-blue Mariinsky curtain, which was decorated with an imperial double-headed eagle, was replaced by a white lace curtain that had been designed by Golovin for use in the opera *Orphée et Euridice*. The new theatrical authorities meanwhile commissioned Golovin to design a new curtain for the Mariinsky.[57]

On March 12, the revolution was openly celebrated at the Mariinsky. The artists held a requiem at two P.M. and seven P.M. for the victims of the February Revolution. The orchestra performed Nicholas Cherepnin's overture entitled *In Memory of the Fallen Fighters for Freedom*. The audience demanded several renditions of this piece, as they did the *Marseillaise* and other revolutionary songs. The popular Mariinsky tenor Ivan Ershov declaimed, with "great pathos" (Telyakovsky), his revolutionary poem "Freedom" from the Mariinsky stage. *A Night in May* was performed, now regarded as an opera with revolutionary credentials because it was the production which had been affected by the chorus's strike just before the outbreak of the February Revolution. During the intervals, the Chairman of the Petrograd Soviet, Nicholas Chkheidze, delivered speeches. All these elements of the March 12 performance were met with cries of approval: "Ura! Ura!"[58] On the following evening at the Mariinsky, the artists welcomed members of the Provisional Government and the Petrograd Soviet who were present in the theater. Again, cheering broke out, and the *Marseillaise* was sung. According to Bezpalov, this was the "rule" in the theaters during the spring of 1917.

The State Theaters further manifested ideological allegiance to the new regime by organizing what were called festival or gala performances (*torzhestvennye paradnye spektakli*) in honour of the Provisional Government. The first of such galas appear to have been held on Sunday April 9, in both the Alexandrinsky and the Mariinsky, in the presence of members of the Provisional Government and other prominent officials, such as members of the Petrograd diplomatic corps, always keen patrons of the former Imperial Theaters. At the Alexandrinsky, the gala consisted of a performance of *The Government Inspector*, starring the popular actor Vladimir Davydov, and a rendition of *Glory to Free Russia*. At the Mariinsky, a similar gala performance consisted of extracts from the operas *Ruslan and Liudmila* and *Khovanshchina*, along with extracts from the ballet *Chopiniana*, and the Polovtsian Dances from *Prince Igor*. On April 18, the State Theaters joined much of Petrograd and the world in celebrating May Day. They were decorated with red flags, and a wooden tribune that supported artists and workers from the Mariinsky was erected in the square beside the theater between twelve and six P.M. Marchers gathered and there followed a rendition of the *Marseillaise*. That evening, the Mariinsky auditorium was full of workers from around the city, participating in another form of celebration which emerged in those months, the "concert-meeting." Bezpalov recalled that among the orators that evening was the Bolshevik feminist Alexandra Kollontai. The event was extremely successful and similar events occurred in the other State Theaters. The State Theaters, according to Bezpalov, were even used at times by the political parties for meetings. The Alexandrinsky was the preferred venue for the Bolsheviks, the Socialists-Revolutionaries, and the anarchists, as well as for the Petrograd Soviet.[59] Finally, leaders of the Mariinsky even took the initiative in finding a new national anthem for "free Russia." At a meeting attended by prominent artistic luminaries such as Gorky, Meyerhold, Alexander Glazunov, and Pavel Andreev, Chaliapin performed a new song that he had composed and which he proposed as the new anthem. Opinion was divided over the merits of the piece, but the Mariinsky chorus did perform it at events in the theater until the end of March.[60]

The experiences and activities of the former Imperial Theaters and their representatives during these whirlwind months of the Provisional Government raise several questions regarding the theme of the relationship of theatrical culture to state power. First, given the various problems it confronted, why did the Provisional Government insist on retaining the former Imperial Theaters as part of the Russian state structure? Two answers suggest themselves. First of all, the leaders of the Provisional Government had no ready-made program for the governance of Russia and consequently, during the confusion of the February days and their aftermath, when power and authority fluctuated, it was convenient to insist that the state structures and institutions that existed prior to the revolution be retained, although there would be personnel and institutional title changes. As in all revolutions, the rapidity with which events unfolded meant that there was no time to disband the imperial governmental structure and devise a new one; if the new rulers wished to assert their legitimacy, they had to stamp their authority on existing power structures. If one institution that previously constituted part of the state's administrative structure became fully detached from the government, there was a danger that all the government's authority would unravel. Secondly, the Provisional Government appears to have recognized the utility of retaining some control over the old Imperial Theaters; as prominent public buildings they could be used for a variety of purposes, not least public celebration of the revolution, which became one of the chief functions of State Theater art in 1917.

A second question arises: Why did the artists exhibit relatively little resistance to the process of appropriation by the post-February government? Did the swift approbation of the February Revolution by the former Imperial

Theaters signify that the artists had become estranged from the old regime that subsidized them and ensured their prestigious institutional status? After all, many of the artists appeared to be genuinely enthusiastic about the February Revolution, and there is no evidence of resistance to the rapid changes in the theaters' symbolism at the time. Of course, prominent individuals involved with the Imperial Theaters before the revolution, such as Meyerhold and Chaliapin, were hostile to tsarism before 1917, but one still has to account for the artistic troupes which participated in the various celebrations of the revolution during the period of the Provisional Government, yet do not appear to have opposed tsarism before 1917. Did the artists' apparent support for tsarism amount to what has been termed "preference falsification," whereby the outward public signs of support for a government mask private hostility to it?[61] There is little firm evidence to suggest that, by conviction, the artists *collectively* were anti-tsarist before 1917: During the 1905 Revolution, for example, while some artists joined the strike movement for a brief period and demanded autonomy from the Directorate, the majority remained loyal to the court. Nor is there evidence that the artists were motivated by an anti-tsarist mentality *after* 1917. Rather, the State Theaters supported whichever government was in power. The state was the major source of their income and prestige and consequently the government could rely on the theaters to support the continuation of the relationship between the two without particular regard to private conviction.

A third question is: To what extent did the February Revolution constitute a turning point in the history of the St. Petersburg Imperial Theaters? Politically, it inaugurated significant symbolic changes to their institutional identity and granted them an opportunity to experiment with autonomy. In terms of the repertoire, very little changed. Certainly, new productions still required time to be organized and rehearsed; yet the Imperial Theater production system was accustomed to mounting new productions in a short space of time; as was noted in Chapter 2 (note 56), the 1896 production of *The Seagull* at the Alexandrinsky was premiered only nine days after the artists first read the play. In 1917, however, the artists declined to stage any significant new productions, and the only controversy over the repertoire surrounded Alexei Tolstoy's *The Death of Ivan the Terrible*, which premiered at the Alexandrinsky on October 8, 1917. The play had been selected by the Alexandrinsky Khudrepkom to mark the hundredth anniversary of its author's birth, but many of the artists were concerned that critics would construe the performance as monarchist propaganda, thereby confirming suspicions that the former imperial drama troupe was "counter-revolutionary." The production proceeded as planned, but the dispute surrounding it finally led to the demise of the Alexandrinsky Khudrepkom, a development that enabled Batiushkov to further increase his influence over the theater.[62]

Arguably, a more fundamental change in the Imperial Theaters had occurred in the years immediately preceding the February Revolution. During the course of 1915, the Alexandrinsky lost to the grave three of its most prominent and respected elders: Varvara Strelskaia, Konstantin Varlamov, and Maria Savina. Respectively, they had acted at the Alexandrinsky since 1857, 1875, and 1874. In 1916, the Imperial Theaters also lost, after a long illness, the eminent conductor Eduard Napravnik, who had been associated with the Mariinsky since 1863. The older generation of prominent artists had been significantly depleted by their deaths, perhaps making it somewhat easier for the "younger" troupes to support the February Revolution and to pursue autonomy, something which the "elders" had forbidden in 1905.

* * * *

Between 1914 and 1917 the Petrograd Imperial Theaters functioned as loyal institutions of the Russian government. They dutifully pursued a line of official patriotism during the First World War, and after the collapse of the monarchy they quickly adopted the paraphernalia of "democratic Russia" and established a good relationship with the Provisional Government. Yet that was not the complete picture. Although never openly oppositional, the participation of Imperial Theater artists in social patriotic activities during the war, and the strikes in the Mariinsky on the eve of the February Revolution, indicated that the imperial court was losing the confidence of many of the artists. The ease with which the theaters accommodated the February Revolution underlined that growing estrangement.

Yet it would be incorrect to suggest that by February 1917 the Imperial Theaters had completely grown apart from the court and, in a sense, had allied with the cultural intelligentsia, because there never was a major crisis of authority in the theaters to indicate that. Moreover, the immediate alliance between the Provisional Government and the Imperial Theaters can also be explained in terms of the artists' desire to retain subsidies and privileges. In other words, the Imperial Theaters would have remained loyal to whichever government controlled Petrograd, a position that was about to be challenged yet again after the October Revolution.

Chapter 8

Under the Bolsheviks, October 1917–1920

The official reinvention of the Petrograd Imperial Theaters as autonomous State Theaters after the February Revolution ensured that the artists adopted a favorable attitude toward the Provisional Government. As we will see, their response to the October Revolution was altogether different. The Bolsheviks were regarded immediately as a threat to theatrical autonomy, even though it had already become somewhat nominal under the stewardship of Batiushkov. Nevertheless, artists, particularly from the Alexandrinsky, put up fierce resistance to the Bolsheviks between late October 1917 and early January 1918. By the first weeks of 1918, active hostility toward the new government began to be replaced by tentative overtures to cooperation. It became clear that the Bolshevik hierarchy, while encouraging new revolutionary theaters, nevertheless was determined to preserve the old theaters and to treat them with a certain degree of respect. Consequently, despite the animosity of "cultural maximalists" who wanted to abolish the pre-revolutionary theaters, the State Theaters functioned in a more friendly atmosphere than they might have done in the harsh conditions of Civil War Russia, when so many were willing to discard them altogether. Nevertheless, there ensued the gradual, but steady, process of the appropriation of the former Imperial Theaters into the newly emerging Soviet state structure, culminating in 1920 with the imposition of government-controlled individual (*edinolichnyi*) rule in the theaters.

Bolshevik policy toward the former Imperial Theaters highlighted the extent to which those institutions were regarded as components of the state structure, and to which there was a continuing symbiosis between the theaters and the state. In fact, as well as retaining the former Imperial Theaters as State Theaters, the Bolsheviks expanded the number of theaters functioning under the aegis of the government by transforming prominent pre-revolutionary private theaters, such as the Moscow Art Theater and the Kamernyi Theater, into state theaters and eventually nationalizing all theaters in Russia (see below). Yet there was no attempt during the early years of Soviet power to use the old theaters overtly for propaganda purposes; rather, the emphasis was on establishing authority over them. The purpose of this chapter is to explore that process of appropriation in order to emphasize the underlying continuity in the relationship between theatrical culture and state power after the collapse of tsarism in February 1917 and the demise of the Provisional Government in October 1917, and to assess the implications of that continuity.

The Bolshevik Approach to the Tsarist Cultural Heritage

In contrast to the Provisional Government, the Bolsheviks evolved a definite cultural policy. It is important to note, however, that it was formulated in the context of a plurality of views on the tsarist cultural heritage that were current in early Soviet Russia. Two prominent tendencies coexisted. The first advocated the wholesale destruction of all pre-revolutionary "bourgeois" culture (including the Imperial Theaters) and the creation of a new, "proletarian" culture to replace it.[1] For its supporters, proletarian theater entailed both the nurturing of new theatrical forms and the abolition of the old theaters. It was advocated by revolutionary enthusiasts and avant-garde theater activists such as Meyerhold and Platon Kerzhentsev, author of the influential book *The Creative Theater*, which set out much of the radical avant-garde's thinking on theater.[2] Both were members of the Bolshevik Party and worked to create a revolutionary theater using the Bolshevik world view as the immediate inspiration (though much of the long-term inspiration for a new theater was rooted in the avant-garde movement which predated 1917; see Introduction). Meyerhold was the supreme iconoclast. His "October in the Theater" platform argued for the expropriation of the former Imperial Theaters and the use of their resources for revolutionary theater.[3] Many of the revolutionary-theater activists were members of Proletkult, an organization established on the eve of the October Revolution to promote proletarian culture (the term is a contraction of the Russian words for "Proletarian Culture"). Proletkult activists organized theaters for ordinary workers and expatiated at length on the need to adapt the existing repertoire to proletarian needs while sympathetic writers created new, authentically proletarian dramas to replace the "bourgeois" repertoire of the past.[4]

The second prominent tendency supported the retention of all that was considered best in pre-revolutionary culture. This view was espoused by Lenin. As early as 1901, the Bolshevik leader had stated that scientific and artistic treasures must be made "*accessible to all people*, in order to obliterate that alienation from culture of the millions in the villages, which Marx accurately termed the idiotism of village life."[5] Lenin consistently argued that "capitalist culture" should not be abandoned by the revolution, but rather should be assimilated by it. This he regarded as essential for the reordering of society. In January 1919, he asserted that "it is impossible to build socialism without using the remnants of capitalism. It is essential to utilize all that capitalism created against us in the sense of cultural values."[6] In March 1919 he reiterated that "it is necessary to take all the culture that capitalism left, and from it build socialism. It is necessary to take all the science, the technology, all the knowledge, the art. Without it we cannot build communist society...."[7] Again in March 1919 and in February 1920, Lenin made the same point.[8] The program of the Eighth Party Congress in March 1919 developed the theme: "It is essential to open up and make accessible for working people all the treasures of art, created on the foundation of the exploitation of their labor and located until now at the exclusive disposal of the exploiters."[9] Although several of his colleagues, most notably the Proletkult activist Alexander Bogdanov, disagreed with Lenin's views on Russia's cultural heritage, the Bolshevik leader's position amounted to official Communist Party policy. He ultimately ensured that his views prevailed by issuing a resolution on October 8, 1920 which effectively ended the independence of Proletkult from Communist Party control and brought it firmly under the umbrella of the People's Commissariat of Enlightenment.[10] There would be no wholesale rejection of all that was created or discovered before communism. "Values," "knowledge"—these were not items to be discarded, but to be used for the benefit of all people. This was Lenin's definition of proletarian culture; not a newly invented culture, but the appropriation by the proletariat of existing culture. He disagreed with those on the left of the party that the proletariat could not use bourgeois culture because it was "class-alien" to them. What mattered was *who* used the culture. As one writer aptly put it, culture for Lenin was "a neutral entity."[11]

The preservationist sentiment was held by Anatoly Lunacharsky, the Bolshevik revolutionary entrusted to look after Russia's theaters within the newly created People's Commissariat of Enlightenment (or Narkompros, the abbreviated version of the Russian *Narodnyi komissariat prosveshcheniia*). Narkompros emerged in November 1917 and was granted responsibility for the former tsarist Ministries of National Education and the Imperial Court.[12] Lunacharsky was a relatively cultivated man of learning, a writer and dramatist who evinced great respect for the arts. Historians have credited him with the skilful balancing of the competing tendencies which vied for predominance in Bolshevik cultural policy after 1917. He supported the idea of building a new, proletarian theater, but he was equally passionate about preserving the old theaters, specifically the State Theaters, and he constantly endeavored to steer a path between the two tendencies, which he did not regard as

Anatoly Lunacharsky, People's Commissar of Enlightenment after the October
Revolution, and a staunch defender of the
former Imperial Theaters. *On Literature
and Art* (Moscow, 1965)

mutually incompatible. Lunacharsky's advocacy of the State Theaters provoked attacks from the
"theatrical left" who wanted to
transform them into pro-Bolshevik
institutions, but he succeeded in
protecting the former Imperial
Theaters from their designs. Like
Lenin, he had a general respect for
Russia's cultural heritage. Writing
of that heritage in December 1918,
Lunacharsky stated that these are
"pearls which must always be preserved." In January 1919, he warned
any radicals who were reading his
words that the revolutionaries must
not "encroach upon the old cultural
valuables on the pretext of their
bourgeois nature [*burzhuaznost*]."
Again like Lenin, the People's
Commissar of Enlightenment
believed that the old culture should
be used as a foundation for the new.
In 1922, he wrote: "Everyone knows
that I was and am a defender of the
professional theater in its best
expressions. I believe that well-pro-
duced drama and opera performances in the best theaters, created by old Russia, are a hugely important element in the activity of creating a new
theater...."[13]

The concern of Lenin and Lunacharsky to synthesize the two broad
approaches to the pre-revolutionary theater (to retain the old theater, but use
it to construct a new one) shaped official Bolshevik policy toward culture and
the arts during and after the revolution. On the very day that the Bolsheviks
seized Petrograd, October 25, 1917, the Military-Revolutionary Committee,
which organized the takeover of the city under the command of Lev Trot-
sky, appointed two commissars, B. D. Mandelbaum and G. S. Iatmanov, to
protect museums and art collections. Within a few days they had enlisted the
help of Alexander Benois and had established themselves in an office in the
Winter Palace as the Artistic-Historical Commission with responsibility, for
example, for museums and the former imperial residences. The urgency with
which this commission was established is explained by the fact that looting
was widespread in Petrograd at the time, yet it nevertheless demonstrated that

the new government, in keeping with Lenin's preservationist policy, was not prepared to see the treasures of tsarist Russia plundered from under its nose. As well as the preservation of treasures, the Soviet government intended to ensure the normal functioning of cultural institutions, such as the Academy of Arts, the Archeological Commission, and the State Theaters of Petrograd and Moscow.[14]

Autonomy versus State Control

One scholar of the Russian theater has observed that the history of the Soviet theater is the history of the quest for organizational and economic forms.[15] The validity of that statement is demonstrated by the history of the former Petrograd Imperial Theaters in the early years of the Soviet government. During the course of 1918, 1919, and 1920, the State Theaters were gradually subjugated to the direct control of the Soviet state by Narkompros. The process of appropriation was more *ad hoc* than ruthlessly systematic, as the new government experimented with various forms of theatrical administration. The process of subjugation can be divided into three stages, each of which will be elaborated in turn: October 1917 to January 1918; January 1918 to January 1919; and February 1919 to June 1920.

The first period of relations between the old Imperial Theaters and the new Bolshevik government, from October 1917 to January 1918, was the most critical and unstable. On October 27, the Military-Revolutionary Committee (MRC) of Petrograd wrote to the Chief Representative of State Theaters, Batiushkov, notifying him that it had made the following appointments: M. P. Muravev (a former *régisseur*'s assistant at the Suvorin Theater), Commissar of State and private theaters; A. Slobodskoi, Representative of the Commissar of State and private theaters; Bezpalov, Commandant of the Petrograd State Theaters (once again). On the same day, Muravev wrote to the State Theaters informing them of his identity and requesting all staff and artists to remain at their posts, "so as not to disrupt the activity of the theaters." Any evasion of responsibilities would be considered an act of opposition to the new government and would incur "deserved punishment." The theater seats and boxes of members of the former Provisional Government were now to be controlled by the MRC and the Central Petrograd Executive Committee of Soviets of Workers' and Soldiers' Deputies.[16]

The Alexandrinsky troupe responded immediately to this news. On October 28, it issued a statement of defiance against the Bolsheviks:

> The artists of the Russian Drama troupe of the State Petrograd theaters, at a General Meeting on 28 October 1917, having listened to the instruction sent by the self-appointed Commissar of State and private theaters of the Military-Revolutionary Committee and signed by Mikh. Muravev, resolved that:

1. recognizing the power of the Provisional Government in the person of Commissar F. A. Golovin and the Chief Representative F. D. Batiushkov, they cannot take into consideration the instructions of impostors not recognized by the whole of Russia. Therefore, they are returning the instruction to the sender;

2. protesting against the senders of this instruction and the threats set forth in it, they are provisionally stopping performances.[17]

Performances ceased at the Alexandrinsky from October 28. Yet Muravev simply returned the drama troupe's protest, having already informed Batiushkov and Karpov that he was now in charge.[18]

The response from the Mariinsky was equally swift, if less emphatic. Bezpalov observed that the Mariinsky artists were divided into three groups. A small group supported the new government, while another small group opposed it. The largest group did not know how to respond.[19] Four days after the October Revolution, performances at the Mariinsky ceased after the chorus went on strike. It is not clear if this was a renewal of the chorus's wage strike of February, but it certainly enhanced its reputation as the most radical section of the Mariinsky artistic community. The chorus strike continued throughout November and part of December, although performances resumed without it a week after the strike began. However, the October Revolution and the chorus strike inaugurated a period of unpredictability and disruption in the normally tranquil environment of the Mariinsky. Bertenson spoke of "the propaganda that is inflaming our stage hands into mutiny. At no time from now on do we give an order and have any confidence that it will be carried out."[20] For example, at one point during a performance of *Ruslan and Liudmila* at the Mariinsky in November 1917 to mark the opera's seventy-fifth anniversary, the curtain was to be lowered to permit a quick rehearsal of a complicated dance sequence immediately before it was performed. While this was going on one of the lighting crew shouted from above the stage: "Hey! You there! That's enough of this rehearsing! Always repeating the same thing! Let me down!"[21] Although such an incident was not necessarily inspired by the idealism of the October Revolution, it was highly unlikely to have occurred without the general atmosphere of subversion that accompanied it. Yet Bertenson perhaps exaggerated the extent of the problem. Workers of the State Theaters, unlike many of the artists, took a generally ambivalent approach to both the Bolshevik takeover and the strike. In response to Muravev's order of 27 October 27, the Union of Workers of the Petrograd State Theaters resolved on October 31 that:

1. In view of our political immaturity, and not having a clear idea about the revolution that has taken place, we, the workers in the state theaters, cannot officially attach ourselves to any existing political party.

2. And as we are materially dependent upon each working day, we resolve with real duty to fulfill precisely the obligations of our service. And

that is why we cannot bear responsibility for the cessation of performances in the theaters.[22]

The staff of the State Theaters were thus divided in their response to the new authorities. An attempt to organize a more united response came on November 5, 1917 when an effort was made to establish a concerted stand against the Bolsheviks. This was the "General Meeting of State Theater Artists (opera, drama, ballet, orchestra and chorus)," which elected Batiushkov as its chairman. Speakers included Meyerhold, Karpov, Iurev, and, representing the workers of the Mariinsky, a certain Bezobrazov. According to the protocol of the meeting, Batiushkov explained that the theaters had closed in response to Muravev's appointment by the MRC. Batiushkov is quoted as saying that "I refused to recognize M. Muravev as a representative of a legal power, did not allow him to print addresses to the artists in the 'Vestnik Kantseliarii' [successor to the *Zhurnal rasporiazhenii*], but agreed that, to secure the theaters, a guard be posted on the outside." The protocol states that, "[w]ithin a few days, M. Muravev sent a written declaration of his renunciation of his authority." Thus, Muravev appears as a transient figure, never having established any authority over the theaters. The chairman noted that, with the agreement of Golovin, he had considered it possible to restart performances now that calm had returned to Petrograd, but then wondered if this was appropriate, given the disturbances in Moscow.

The General Meeting concluded with an "incident" involving Batiushkov and Bezpalov, who appear to have been rivals for general control of the State Theaters. As noted in the previous chapter, Batiushkov had announced on October 20 that Bezpalov's job of commandant of the State Theaters had become dispensable. Now Batiushkov demanded to know in what capacity Bezpalov wished to speak at the meeting. If it was as commandant of the theaters, then he would not be permitted to speak because he had been reappointed by the "usurpers of power." Besides, now that Muravev had resigned, his instructions were invalidated. Therefore, Bezpalov could not be commandant. Bezpalov argued that he had appointed himself and that he was staying in his post until the convocation of the Constituent Assembly. There ensued a commotion in the hall—laughter, cries, and applause. Bezpalov was prevented from speaking and retired from the hall. He soon returned and declared: "I have reconsidered, I resign the post of commandant." At that, Bezpalov disappeared again. The meeting, in a further act of resistance to the Bolsheviks, resolved to close the State Theaters for three more days.[23]

The new government responded to the theatrical resistance first by appealing to the artists to grant it support. On December 2, Lunacharsky addressed the Khudrepkomy of the Petrograd State Theaters, calculating that their resistance was grounded on a fear of state bureaucratic control:

> The Workers' and Peasants' Government highly values the significance of the theater and, of course, is sympathetic to the needs of the State Theaters.... I anticipate that the Office and all the bureaucratic personnel of the theater administration, as mere governmental organs with nothing in common with these theaters, which are cultural institutions, will one of these days be completely disbanded.[24]

Lunacharsky invited the artists to enter into relations with Narkompros, but they remained unenthusiastic and suspicious of his intentions. The Alexandrinsky troupe reiterated that it was an apolitical autonomous organ and that a "change of government cannot serve as an occasion for changing the autonomous constitution [of the theater]."[25]

Lunacharsky consequently abandoned his conciliatory approach and attempted to exploit latent divisions between the theater artists and workers. He argued that cooperation was necessary between the government and the State Theaters in order to overcome "sharp disagreements among the toilers of the state stage," which was disrupting the life of the theater, and he threatened Batiushkov with dismissal from his post if he did not agree to an audience with the Narkom. Batiushkov pointedly refused to submit to this threat and declined to meet Lunacharsky. After all, the attempt to replace him with Muravev had failed, so why should Lunarcharsky's threats be taken more seriously? Batiushkov argued that there were no "sharp disagreements" within the troupes. "On the contrary," he asserted, "the artists and the majority of workers in the State Theaters are activated by a feeling of complete solidarity in defence of the independence of art from political parties and in recognition of the autonomous administration of the artistic collectives." Batiushkov denounced the new government as counter-revolutionary for using "force and arbitrariness," actions which, he said, ran counter to the spirit of the February Revolution.[26]

Consequently, on December 12, the Soviet government issued a decree dismissing the Chief Representative of the State Theaters, who had been appointed in April by Lvov.[27] Lunacharsky informed Batiushkov that he was being dismissed in view of his "boycott of the new power." Lunacharsky was not impressed by Batiushkov's claim to be defending artistic autonomy from political interference. Was not Batiushkov's appointment by the Provisional Government as its Chief Representative in the State Theaters "political interference"? Was that a "defence of autonomy"? "Whose Chief Representative are you? Kerensky's government? But that does not exist. Of the new government? But you do not recognize it." According to Lunacharsky, Batiushkov was not defending the theaters from politics because, in his defence of "liberal ideas against the basic principles of democratic and socialist revolution," he was, *ipso facto*, involving the theaters in politics and defining them politically.[28]

On the same day, December 12, Lunacharsky addressed the artists and workers of the Petrograd State Theaters and began by informing them that the new government did not demand that they take any oaths of loyalty to it. "The shameful times when you were like servants at the tsar's court have gone forever. You are free citizens, free artists, and no one will encroach upon that freedom." Yet, at the same time, he was keen to stress that now there was a new ruler in the country, namely the laboring masses. "The laboring masses cannot support the State Theaters if it is not certain that they exist, not for the amusement of the land-owners, but for the satisfaction of the great cultural needs of the laboring population."[29] The implication of this speech clearly was that the former Imperial Theaters would have to serve the interests of the Soviet government.

Additionally, on December 12, 1917, Lunacharsky issued an instruction on the provisional administrative structure of the State Theaters of Petrograd. The existing bureaucratic structure was abolished and its functions transferred to a projected Theater Soviet (*Teatralnyi sovet*) consisting of two representatives each from the artists of the drama troupe, opera soloists, the orchestra, the chorus and the ballet, one representative each from the Chorus Masters, the conductors, the *régisseurs* and the scenery artists, and six representatives from the technical personnel. All relations with the government were to be conducted by the newly proposed Theater Soviet. Crucially for the development of cordial ties between the government and the theaters, Lunacharsky's instruction guaranteed the continuation of state subsidies, the level of which would be decided by the Narkom in agreement with the Theater Soviet.[30] Batiushkov, based in the offices of the old Directorate in Theater Street, tried to resist Narkompros encroachments for a little longer, challenging Lunacharsky to arrest him. The Alexandrinsky actor and *régisseur* Anatoly Dolinov took the initiative, with Batiushkov, to transfer Alexandrinsky performances temporarily to the Akvarium, a former *café-chantant* on the other side of the city, a move which partially split the troupe for a short time.[31] The fact that some of the troupe followed Batiushkov to the Akvarium indicated that he still had allies in his struggle with Narkompros. At the end of the month, however, Narkompros informed him that one L. D. Metsner had been delegated to take over from him all the business of State Theater administration. From then on Batiushkov was absent from the scene.[32] Early in the New Year, the Bolsheviks finally entered the offices of the old Directorate. The writer Smirnova-Sazonova, who was well-acquainted with theater affairs because her daughter, L. N. Shuvalova, was an actress at the Alexandrinsky, wrote on January 2, 1918: "The Office of State Theaters has been dispersed and occupied by Red Guards. Batiushkov and all Office bureaucrats have been ordered to clear government flats."[33]

Now that Lunacharsky had won this battle he was content for the State Theaters to function as autonomous institutions. A notice in *Izvestiia*, January 6, 1918, confirmed that administrative power over the State Theaters was now in the hands of a Theater Soviet consisting of representatives from all groups in the theaters. The notice further announced the creation in each of the State Theaters of a new Khudrepkom which would be responsible to the Theater Soviet. The Theater Soviet, however, in one of those bemusing bureaucratic quirks of the period, did not actually start to function as an extant body until later in the year, by which time its purpose had been rendered futile by the creation of a new State Theater Subdepartment in Narkompros (see below). The notice further stated that, "[s]uch close contact between the individual theaters and the organ of leadership (the Soviet), destroying any bureaucratic red tape [*kantseliarskaia volokita*], will create a natural unity of action, such as is necessary for the development of the artistic life of autonomous theaters."[34] This had the effect of pacifying enough artists to allow the situation to calm down and to permit normal relations between Lunacharsky and the State Theaters to commence. Lunacharsky thus had established contacts between the Bolsheviks and the tsarist theater heritage.

The second distinct phase of relations between the State Theaters and Soviet power occurred from January 1918 to January 1919. This phase saw the continuation of State Theater autonomy, but signaled the growing involvement of the government in theater affairs. In January 1918, Lunacharsky informed representatives of the Alexandrinsky that he supported autonomy for the theaters.[35] For the time being, self-administration was a reality, and during 1918 the Alexandrinsky and Mariinsky functioned autonomously.* Autonomy was formalized on March 11, 1918 by a Charter of Autonomous State Theaters (*Ustav avtonomnykh gosudarstvennykh teatrov*), which had been agreed upon at a meeting between representatives of the State Theaters and the government. The Charter established a Council of State Theaters (*Sovet gosudarstvennykh teatrov*) to regulate relations between the state and autonomous troupes, although it appears to have become defunct as the focus for theater-state relations shifted to the Narkompros Department of State Theaters (see below). The Alexandrinsky actor G. G. Ge even remarked that "Lunacharsky, in the sense of autonomy, gave us more than we wanted."[36] Smirnova-Sazonova likewise remarked in her diary that Lunacharsky had given the Alexandrinsky artists "more than they asked for: the fullest autonomy...."[37] While such remarks possibly indicated a pleasant surprise and gratitude that full autonomy was granted, it is equally plausible that performers

---

*The Mikhailovsky Theater officially ended its existence on March 6, 1918, when the Maly Opera Theater opened on its premises. However, the Maly Opera was not known as such until some years later, and the former home of the French drama troupe continued to be known as the State Mikhailovsky Theater. On January 1, 1920, it was renamed the State Academic Theater of Comic Opera; from August 1, 1921 it was known as the Maly Petrograd State Academic Theater; from October 20, 1926 as the Leningrad State Academic Maly Opera Theater. It is not clear what became of the French troupe, but many of the artists probably returned to France. For the early history of the Maly Opera, see Leningradskii gosudarstvennyi ordena Lenina akademicheskii Malyi opernyi teatr (Leningrad, 1961).

betrayed apprehension about it, that they did not want too much autonomy. As in 1905, the artists appeared reluctant to distance themselves too far from the state, presumably because of the resources, privileges, and prestige which previously had accompanied the connection between the two. Such benefits were particularly important given the general privation and widespread shortages of basic items that accompanied the Civil War. The 1918-19 and 1919-20 seasons were particularly harsh, as food and fuel shortages began to bite. When Gnedich complained in January 1919 that the Alexandrinsky artists lacked conviction and discipline in their work, Ge responded with an open letter (February 1919) in which he reminded Gnedich of the realities of contemporary life: "Weary, hungry, cold, freezing at home, freezing on stage in a torrent of icy air in a poorly heated theater, we are trying to keep our spirits up and play in eight performances a week."[38] During the 1919-20 season, fuel shortages meant that performances were often given in temperatures "close to zero." This was particularly bad for the ballet troupe because it performed in attire that afforded little protection from the cold. The quality of performances suffered further because the absence of electric lighting in daytime precluded rehearsals.[39] Provincial tours, particularly to the south where it was warmer in the winter, became popular with the artists as a way of escaping difficulties in Petrograd. An English actress who toured with the Alexandrinsky troupe in the summer of 1918 claimed that Vologda was a preferred destination for touring artists because the food supply situation was better in that area.[40] Such conditions provided a compelling reason for the artistic troupes to maintain close relations with the state. Privileges and preferential treatment could never be guaranteed, but the closer the formal connection to the authorities, the more likely the continuation of subsidies and general support, more necessary than ever.

Yet the artists need not have worried that the state was going to abandon them. The former St. Petersburg Imperial Theaters remained State Theaters, and consequently, parallel to the survival of a functioning autonomy, the government continued to develop its own organs of State Theater administration. On February 18, 1918, a Narkompros Subdepartment of State Theaters was created; in June 1918 it was renamed the Narkompros Department of State Theaters. This organ was headed by Ivan Ekskuzovich, who was known as the Superintendent (*zaveduiushchii*) of State Theaters. Zolotnitskii states that one of the main tasks of this organ was "the activization of social self-administration in the State Theaters [and] the participation of the elected representatives of actors' collectives in the construction of a Soviet theater."[41] Yet, at the same time, the text of the notice announcing the creation of the Subdepartment and the post of Superintendent established that, because the artistic side of theater affairs was closely connected to the financial side, the state would retain for itself the right of control over artistic affairs, "since only the highly artistic organization of the latter can justify the huge expenses which the state incurs in relation to the State Theaters."[42] Throughout the remainder of 1918, the government continued to make other administrative changes in Russian theaters, but these did not affect the State Theaters directly, whose administrative segregation in the Department of State Theaters was part of Lunacharsky's general program of shielding them from some of the more destructive designs of the radicals. For instance, in June, the Theater Department of Narkompros (*Teatralnyi otdel*, or TEO) was established on a formal basis (it had existed in embryo since January 1918), but the State Theaters did not come under its remit, much to the annoyance of the "cultural maximalists" who wanted to "expropriate" the former Imperial Theaters and who were prominent in TEO, such as Olga Kameneva, the head of its Moscow section, who argued that the State Theaters should be brought within its jurisdiction.[43]

Lunacharsky was provided with an opportunity to defend his policy on the State Theaters to the officials of TEO in December 1918, when the latter convened a two-day conference to discuss theater affairs. Lunacharsky, opening the first session of the meeting, argued that the State Theaters could not simply be handed over to the proletariat, as the "left" demanded. Rather, the State Theaters should be opened to the proletariat. "The proletariat, of course, will find its own paths, but meantime it should be given that educational value [*tsennost*] which the classic repertoire of all nations possesses...." Moreover, "[t]he defence of the exemplary theaters is essential. Let the State Theaters renovate their repertoire themselves without unnecessary haste...." The long-term task was to preserve the State Theaters by "democratizing" and subsidizing them.[44] On the second day of the conference, D. Kh. Pashkovskii, Alexandrinsky actor and one of the first artists to advocate support for the Bolsheviks, spoke about the drama theater. He noted that the Alexandrinsky troupe had cooperated with TEO from its inception, but that they "differed somewhat with it in ideological terms." Relations were, however, strengthened when Ekskuzovich was put in charge, and were now quite friendly with TEO, even though in practice this was not vitally important because State Theater autonomy was guaranteed by the existence of the separate Department of State Theaters.[45] However, the fact that Pashkovskii alluded to TEO at all was indicative of the administrative uncertainty that characterized the early years of Soviet power.

The third clear stage in the early relations between the Soviet state and the former Imperial Theaters lasted from February 1919 to June 1920. In February 1919, Narkompros once again altered the administrative structure of the State Theaters and strengthened the links between government and theaters by establishing directories (*direktorii*) in each of the State Theaters. The initial Narkompros documents relating to this development envisaged that the Alexandrinsky *direktoriia* would consist of three members, two of whom would be elected from within the theater (one representative each from the artistic and service-technical personnel). The Mariinsky *direktoriia* would consist of five members, three of whom would be elected from within the theater (one representative each from the opera, ballet, and service-technical personnel). In practice, however, the Alexandrinsky *direktoriia* comprised five members and the Mariinsky's eight. I have been unable to establish how many representatives under the revised membership figures came from within the theaters, but the important point is that, in the case of the Alexandrinsky at least one member of the *direktoriia* was a Narkompros official, and in the case of the Mariinsky at least two of them were.

The official task of the *direktorii* was to plan the repertoire and ensure that the artistic standards of the theaters were maintained. All plans and arrangements had to be approved by the Narkompros Department of State Theaters.[46] The *direktorii* replaced the Khudrepkomy, which had organized the internal artistic affairs of the State Theaters since January 1918. The significant aspect of this reorganization was that not all members of the *direktorii* were elected from within the theaters; some were appointed from, and by, Narkompros. The government appeared to be encroaching upon the autonomy of the theaters. Meantime, the principal event in the Russian theater world in 1919 was the promulgation of the Sovnarkom decree of August 26 on the nationalization of Russian theater property. The chief consequence of this decree was that all theater property passed into the hands of the Soviet state. Yet this did not affect the State Theaters because, as government theaters, they were already "nationalized." In other words, the state had never relinquished its ownership of the former "Emperor's Theaters." The nationalization decree additionally created Tsentroteatr, a new central administrative organ, controlled personally by Lunacharsky, which oversaw the activities of both the TEO and the Department of State Theaters.[47]

In a further move that again highlighted the importance of the State Theaters to the Soviet government, Lunacharsky decreed on December 7 a simple but significant change. From that day on, the State Theaters were to be called State Academic Associated Theaters (*Gosudarstvennye akademicheskie assotsiirovannye teatry*), later just State Academic Theaters, often referred to as *Akis*. For the Petrograd State Theaters, the decree came into effect from January 1, 1920.[48] (On the same date, the *direktorii* were renamed *direktsii*.) The term "academic" had been used in reference to the Imperial Theaters before 1917, although not widely. In 1900, Pogozhev had referred to the Imperial Theaters as an "academy" (see page 40). One theater critic wrote of the Alexandrinsky as the "guard of academic habits,"[49] while another wrote that the purpose of the Alexandrinsky was to be an "Academic Theater."[50] What did "academic" mean in this context? The word appears to have entered the Russian language, via French, from the Italian *accademia*, meaning academy or school, but with implications of excellence. In 1922, an Alexandrinsky "declaration" shed some light on the sense in which the word was used at the time. Derzhavin quotes from it: "Usually, the term 'academical' is granted unto every institution, where achievements in Art or Science, experimentally verified and firmly ascertained are allowed to settle in. Only that which was generally acknowledged, had the honour to become a principle and a method propagated by the Academy."[51] The term therefore signified the value which the Soviets attached to the former Imperial Theaters as exemplars of the tsarist cultural heritage.

The extent to which autonomy was a reality for the State Academic Theaters came into doubt in April 1920. It was then that the *direktsii* were abolished and replaced by government-controlled, individual (*edinolichnyi*) administration of the theaters (April 15, 1920). This development does not appear to have troubled the artists, or at least its implications were not immediately evident. For example, at a meeting of the Mariinsky *direktsiia*, the members were more concerned with the question of whether part of the ballet troupe should be defined as a "cadre of mime artists" (item one of the protocol) than by the move to *edinolichnyi* rule (item six of the protocol).[52] Yet in retrospect, this change in the administration of the State Theaters can be regarded as a turning point in the history of Soviet theater administration because, from then on, the State Theaters were controlled exclusively and directly by Narkompros. Finally, on June 11, 1920, Lunacharsky signed the "Statute on the autonomous State Academic Theaters of Petrograd." According to the terms of this statute, the Petrograd *Akis* were now subordinate to the jurisdiction of a general five-member *pravlenie* (governing board). Its members were Ekskuzovich (Chairman), Chaliapin, Karpov, the conductor E. A. Kuper, and the conductor and chorus master G. I. Iakobson. Chaliapin was given responsibility for the general artistic affairs of the theaters. The statute re-established the post of Manager (*upravliaiushchii*) for individual theater troupes, and Karpov became Manager of the Alexandrinsky drama, Kuper of the Mariinsky opera and ballet, and Iakobson of the Comic Opera at the former Mikhailovsky.[53] However, the presence of prominent artists on the *pravlenie*, while indicative of the troupes' general willingness to cooperate with Narkompros, should not obscure the extent to which the government, in the person of Ekskuzovich, now supervised the work of the theaters. Two points should be emphasized with regard to this development. First, it is clear that Narkompros remained determined to co-opt the former St. Petersburg Imperial Theaters into the Soviet state structure. Second, although the word "autonomy" was used in the statute, its meaning clearly had changed. According to clause four of the statute, the State Theater *pravlenie* was to be autonomous from local Petrograd education departments which wanted to use the arts. Autonomy, therefore, signified protection against interference from organizations other than the appropriate organs of Narkompros, or from hostile elements such as the radical "cultural maximalists" in TEO. It no longer signified administrative and artistic freedom in relation to the state, as it had done in 1905 and 1917-18, but active preservation by the state of the old Imperial Theaters, under close control. Standing back from the confusing array of administrative changes that had occurred since 1917, that is the one stark fact.

Why had autonomy, in the sense that the artists had understood it in 1905 and 1917-18, been eclipsed? The official Soviet line was that the government had to bring wayward "bourgeois specialists" under control, after having granted them a provisional opportunity to ingratiate themselves with Soviet power.[54] The explanation more common in Western historiography is that the growth of the new state and its impulse to totalitarian control were incompatible with autonomy.[55] Thorpe has tempered this view with a third explanation:

> The movement away from democratic self-management to appointive administration was in no way a simple manifestation of a party-state imperative to ideological control; quite the contrary, for both Lunacharsky and the upper strata of the artistic personnel of the state theaters these reforms were intended to strengthen the academic theaters' ability to resist those who would have imposed such controls.[56]

All these explanations have some validity, although none is entirely satisfactory on its own. The Communist Party could not employ too much force against the artistic intelligentsia because it had acknowledged the necessity of using its "bourgeois expertise." There were authoritarian tendencies in Bolshevism, but arguably Russian political culture was innately authoritarian and the impulse to control was not unique to the Bolsheviks. After all, the State Theaters had been controlled Russian governments before the October Revolution. Moreover, while it was certainly the case that Lunacharsky wanted to protect the State Theaters from radicals on the "theatrical left," protection need not have entailed the end of autonomy in the earlier sense of the word. To a great extent, the government had already guaranteed the integrity of the theaters against radical attacks by setting up a separate Department of State Theaters.

Even if autonomy had conformed to the ideal (the state provides subsidies but leaves the artists to run the theaters on their own without any interference), the question that still remains to be answered is why did the Bolsheviks show any interest in the theaters in the first place, particularly in the middle of a brutal civil war that gave them more pressing matters to worry about? It is not too difficult to conceive why the artists wanted to maintain some connection with the state, but why were the Bolsheviks determined to stamp their authority on the theaters? A possible explanation—although the evidence is circumstantial and the assessment must remain tentative—is that, if the Bolsheviks wished to govern Russia in the midst of a civil war, it was convenient to appropriate established state institutions for their own use. Like the Provisional Government, the Bolsheviks' policy toward the State Theaters indicated a general desire to avoid losing control of the existing governmental apparatus and to assimilate the trappings of pre-revolutionary state authority in the cultural sphere. Thus they could align their administration with symbols of tradition and continuity, again as the Provisional Government had sought to do before them.

It might be objected that the Bolsheviks were anti-tsarist. How, then, can it be argued that they were prepared to befriend tsarist institutions? The answer to that objection is that the Imperial/State Theaters were, like culture for Lenin, a "neutral entity." They could be used—and were used—by the three different regimes that struggled for state power during the Russian Revolution, namely the tsarist regime, the Provisional Government, and the Bolshevik regime. The artists were accustomed enough to their proximity to the government to enable new regimes gradually to assimilate the State Theaters, or at least to pin their labels on them. This was the underlying significance of the convergence of the State Theaters and the new Soviet state between 1918 and 1920. In the language of the period (contained in pronouncements and decrees such as those mentioned earlier in this chapter), the former Imperial Theaters were, in a sense, "invented" as traditions. In choosing preservation, in line with much of the leadership's conservative cultural instincts, the Bolsheviks emphasized continuity of the Russian cultural heritage.

Continuity and Change after 1917

It might be suggested that the process of the gradual assimilation of the former St. Petersburg Imperial Theaters into the new Soviet state structure was part of a Bolshevik agenda to radically transform the character of those institutions and, in particular, to politicize their repertoire for propaganda purposes. Yet, as we have seen, the official policy toward the State Theaters was preservation, not transformation, and there was no serious attempt to force a new repertoire upon them until later in the 1920s. Derzhavin even referred to the "creative prostration" of the Alexandrinsky during the 1918-20 period.[57]

Although eleven of the twenty-four most popular plays produced at the Alexandrinsky between 1900 and 1917 were not performed during the 1917 to 1920 period—Ostrovsky's *Enough Stupidity in Every Wise Man* and *A Passionate Heart*, Gnedich's *The Assembly*, Ryshkov's *Philistines* and *The Passers-By*, Shchepkina-Kupernik's *The Wings*, Sumbatov-Yuzhin's *The Old School*, Tikhonov's *The Great Secret*, Guinon's *Décadence*, Meyer-Förster's *Alt Heidelberg*, and Zuderman's *Johannisfeuer*—they were not replaced by radically different types of drama. During the 1917-18, 1918-19, and 1919-20 seasons, one hundred different plays were produced by the Alexandrinsky troupe. By far the most popular were Gnedich's *Slaves* (fifty-five performances) and *The Decembrist* (thirty-four performances), Eugene Scribe's *Le Verre d'Eau* (thirty-seven performances), Ibsen's *Fruen fra havet* (*The Lady From the Sea*) (thirty-two performances), Gogol's *The Government Inspector* (thirty performances), and Ostrovsky's *The Lady Without a Dowry* (thirty performances).[58] Only three of the most popular pre–1917 Mariinsky operas were not performed during the immediate post–October Revolution seasons—*A Life for the Tsar* (for obvious reasons), *Les Huguenots*, and *Tannhäuser*. The most popular operas during those years were *Il Barbiere di Siviglia* (thirty-seven performances), *Prince Igor* (twenty-seven performances), *Boris Godunov* (twenty-six performances), *Eugene Onegin* (twenty-three performances), *The Queen of Spades* (twenty-three performances), *Ruslan and Liudmila* (twenty-three performances), *The Demon* (twenty performances), and *La Bohème* (twenty performances). Of the pre-1917 Mariinsky ballet repertoire, only one of the twelve most popular productions was absent during the 1917-20 seasons, *The Awakening of Flora*. (*La Bayadère* was performed only once during those years.) The most popular ballets in the aftermath of the Bolshevik Revolution were *The Sleeping Beauty* (twenty performances), *Le Corsaire* (seventeen performances), *Raymonda* (seventeen performances), *Esmeralda* (seventeen performances), *The Hump-Backed Horse* (sixteen performances), and *Swan Lake* (sixteen performances).

In other words, the repertoire did not undergo a fundamental transformation during the three years after the October Revolution. This was despite the fact that the former Imperial Theaters were accustomed to mounting new productions in relatively short spans of time, and they would have been quite capable of significantly overhauling their repertoire between 1917 and 1920 had they so desired. To be sure, it would take time for a new, explicitly pro-Bolshevik dramaturgy to emerge, but there was still a corpus of "radical" plays from the late tsarist period that had not been performed at the Imperial Theaters and could now be turned to. An obvious example would be the works of Gorky, yet *The Petty Bourgeois* was performed only four times (once in April 1917, three times during the 1917-18 season); *The Lower Depths* was finally premiered at the Alexandrinsky in October 1919 and had a run of nineteen performances during the season, but it was still not one of the most dominant plays in the repertoire of those years.

Nevertheless, it is possible to detect a slight shift within the existing repertoire to an emphasis on plays that arguably constituted implicit criticisms of the old order. The dominance in the Alexandrinsky repertoire of Gnedich's *Slaves* and *The Decembrist* (perhaps not unconnected with the fact that Gnedich himself returned to the theater affairs in the 1918-19 season as a member of the Repertoire Section of the Petrograd Branch of TEO, and in the 1919-20 season as a *régisseur* at the Alexandrinsky) indicated a tendency, not to proselytize the revolution, but at least to stage themes that were implicitly critical of the old order. In the case of *Slaves*, this was serfdom; in the case of *The Decembrist* (a play banned by the censor before 1917), an abortive coup against the monarchy. Of course, context was of crucial importance. *Slaves* was a popular play at the Alexandrinsky prior to 1917, but there is no evidence that it was viewed primarily by audiences then as a denunciation of tsarism. After 1917, however, the play assumed a new significance because in the context of a new regime that denounced tsarism, it could be viewed as a criticism of the old regime and a justification for its demise.

The most marked and significant change in the State Theaters which accompanied the events of 1917 and the years of Civil War occurred in the auditoria. The artists were now performing for a new, more "popular" audience, the *narod*, as Iurev called it.[59] The change in the composition of the audience was evident soon after the fall of the monarchy. Meriel Buchanan, eloquent as ever, recalled an evening at the Mariinsky in aid of widows and orphans of the revolution in April 1917:

> For the first time that night the real, devastating change which had been made by the Revolution came home to me in its full force. Here was indeed the same blue and white Opera House, here were the same glass chandeliers, the same blue velvet curtains. But the Imperial Arms and the big golden eagles which had surmounted the boxes had been torn down, leaving gaping holes which had not been filled up, the men who showed people to their places had cast off their gold-braided Court uniforms and wore plain grey jackets which made them look indescribably shabby and dingy, soldiers in mud-stained khaki lolled everywhere, smoking evil-smelling cigarettes, spitting all over the place and eating the inevitable sunflower seeds out of paper bags. A few *nouveaux riches*, who had known how to profit from the Revolution, lolled in the boxes, over-dressed, over-scented, over-jewelled; the stalls were filled with long-haired men and short-haired women whose high woollen blouses and unwashed appearance showed that the doctrine of liberty was one that preached a contempt for beauty.[60]

The English writer H. G. Wells visited Petrograd and Moscow in October 1920 and attended theater performances in both cities. His observations supported the view that it was the auditoria that were changed most by the revolution in the theaters in the early years of Soviet power:

> When one faced the stage, it was as if nothing had changed in Russia; but when the curtain fell and one turned to the audience one realised the revolution. There were now no brilliant uniforms, no evening dress in boxes and stalls. The audience was an undifferentiated mass of people, the same sort of people everywhere, attentive, good-humoured, well behaved and shabby…. [O]ne's place in the house is determined by ballot. And for the most part there is no paying to enter the theatre. For one performance the tickets go, let us say, to the professional unions, for another to the Red Army and their families, for another to the school children, and so on. A certain selling of tickets goes on, but it is not in the present scheme of things.[61]

The official Bolshevik policy of opening up the tsarist cultural heritage to the "proletariat" was proving successful during the Civil War years. This was ensured by the Narkompros practice of encouraging theaters to issue tickets to various institutions where proletarians were found in large numbers. For example, from January 1918 Ekskuzovich began to organize inexpensive weekly performances (including performances for schoolchildren, trainee proletarians) which were attended in increasing numbers to the point where auditoria were full. "The proletariat," observed Ekskuzovich, "gives ovations." The opera troupe was performing once a week at the sailors' club at Kronstadt. Sailors were able to attend such performances because, now that much of the bourgeoisie had abandoned Petrograd, prices had come down.[62] During the 1918-19 season, the Petrograd State Theaters gave seventy-five "Special Performances." The following season, the Mariinsky alone gave more than eighty, including thirty-three for the Soviet of Trades Unions, twenty-seven for the Red Army, fifteen for Narkompros, four for the Baltic Fleet, and two for the Metalworkers Union.[63]

* * * *

Bolshevik policy toward the former St. Petersburg Imperial Theaters was shaped by a desire to co-opt them as part of the Soviet state structure. It was also predicated on a general respect for the Russian cultural heritage. Consequently, while Lunacharsky and Narkompros diligently pursued the confidence of the old theaters while steadily tightening their administrative grip over them, this process was not accompanied by measures to transform the State Theaters into propagandistic mouthpieces for Soviet power. The Bolsheviks encouraged the theaters to enter into cordial relations with them. But there is evidence that the former Imperial Theaters themselves were content to remain closely connected to the state, despite some resistance from the troupes to Bolshevik rule in the late months of 1917 (a resistance that was perhaps exaggerated by Batiushkov's determined efforts to hang on to his position). Many State Theater artists supported the new government, or at least were happy to cooperate with it. No doubt this had much to do with the trust that Lunacharsky inspired, in addition to the resources that the state offered, notwithstanding wartime privations.

The process of assimilation of the former St. Petersburg Imperial Theaters by the Bolsheviks thus pointed to a continuing symbiosis of theatrical culture and state power after the collapse of tsarism and the Provisional Government. While the city of Petrograd radically changed in so many ways, the State Theaters, notwithstanding certain symbolic changes after the February Revolution and regular administrative modifications under the Bolsheviks, experienced a surprising degree of institutional continuity. As Wells sagely observed: "For a time, the stablest thing in Russian culture was the theatre."[64]

Conclusions

In 1900 Vladimir Pogozhev reviewed the status of the Imperial Theaters in the context of a transformed Russian theatrical world and concluded that, while the "Emperor's Theaters" were required to represent the splendor of the tsar's court, they also had to function collectively as an "academy," as exemplary model theaters. This assessment was echoed in 1907 by the Alexandrinsky *régisseur* Gnedich, who wrote in the *Yearbook of the Imperial Theaters* that the task of the government theaters was "to create that fundamental aesthetic repertoire which could be an eternal school."[1] Indeed, the chief aspiration of the artists was to produce outstanding dramatic, operatic, and balletic entertainment for audiences. Of course, this was also the chief aspiration of the artists of other theaters in St. Petersburg.

What made the Imperial Theaters unique was their court status—the fact that, before 1917, they were subsidized and administered by a department of the Ministry of the Imperial Court. This book has examined the institutional history and identity of the St. Petersburg Imperial Theaters from that perspective in order to assess how important the *pridvornyi* factor was during a period of formidable change and deep uncertainty in both the theatrical and political worlds of tsarist Russia. By their very institutional definition, the St. Petersburg Imperial Theaters were constituent parts of both worlds, the theatrical and the political. This "dual status" provided the starting point for the investigation undertaken by this study and prompted the three main questions which were set out in the Preface and which we must now consider.

The first broad question was: Did the Russian state seek to utilize the St. Petersburg Imperial Theaters, and was artistic freedom compromised by court supervision? The answer to the first part of that question is a qualified yes. It is clear from the Pogozhev commission that the Imperial Theaters were regarded as adornments of the court; they were used by the government to mark special occasions and to honor visiting foreign dignitaries; and during the 1905 Revolution, it was clear that governing circles—in particular

Fredericks and Trepov—believed the Imperial Theaters should set an example of loyalty by ignoring the strike movement and working as normal. Yet there was little sense in which the court sought to manipulate the Imperial Theaters or compel them to serve politics in a direct manner. This is evident from the history of the relationship between the Directorate of Imperial Theaters and the artists. While the Directorate had considerable authority in most areas of the artistic life of the theaters, there is little evidence that it used its powers to ensure an overtly "political" repertoire; by and large, Telyakovsky and his "huge phalanx" of bureaucrats allowed the artists to pursue their creative impulses unimpeded, and the extent to which the Directorate interfered in the process of artistic creativity has always been exaggerated (although that is not to deny an active presence on its part). Of course, there was no artistic freedom for the theater troupes in the sense that the repertoire was censored by the Chief Administration for Press Affairs and the Directorate enjoyed ultimate authority over all aspects of artistic life: recruitment of artists, selection of the repertoire, and staging of the repertoire. Yet the issue of artistic freedom rarely surfaced. Many of the prominent artists, in fact, enjoyed considerable authority within the Imperial Theaters themselves and felt quite free to pursue their artistic interests without fear of sanction.

The second broad question was: How far was court association an important factor in the status and reputation of the Imperial Theaters in the cultural life of St. Petersburg? Although the presence in the auditoria of St. Petersburg's elites served to closely associate the Imperial Theaters with the centers of power in the Russian Empire, suggesting a direct connection between culture and power, there is no evidence that the principal attraction of the St. Petersburg Imperial Theaters for theatergoers was their court status. Nor did the repertoire serve to identify the Imperial Theaters as court institutions—there was little that was specifically *pridvornyi* about most of the popular works that were performed, although many plays at the Alexandrinsky, such as *Alt Heidelberg* and *The Assembly*, certainly revolved around courts or their princes, as did many of the operas and ballets produced at the Mariinsky. On the other hand, it can be argued that much of what rendered the Imperial Theaters prominent institutions and attracted patrons would have been impossible without state subsidies, such as the opulent auditoria and the grand productions, particularly of ballet.

The third broad question was: How were the St. Petersburg Imperial Theaters affected by the pressures of war and revolution, and did they remain loyal to the state that subsidized them in its times of crisis? It is clear that war and revolution had an impact on the Imperial Theaters that served to render their status ambivalent. During 1905, when the pressures of the Russo-Japanese War contributed directly to the revolutionary upsurge that resulted in the proclamation of the October Manifesto, many Imperial Theater artists became caught up in the radical movement and, in particular, demanded organizational autonomy from the tsarist autocracy, specifically from the Directorate. Furthermore, during the First World War artists participated in acts of "social patriotism" as well as "official patriotism," and ultimately welcomed the February Revolution with a rapidity that appeared to indicate an underlying hostility to tsarism that had been germinating for some time. That is to say, it was not always evident that the court could rely entirely on the loyalty of the King's Players.

Yet despite recurrent signs that the court was incapable of supervising the activities of its employees, the St. Petersburg Imperial Theaters generally remained loyal to the government that subsidized them. This was not, however, a conscious choice to support a particular type of political system, as was amply demonstrated during the three years after the collapse of the Romanov monarchy. The history of the St. Petersburg Imperial Theaters under the Provisional Government, and then—despite initial hostility—under the Bolsheviks, suggests that the theaters were prepared to work happily under any regime: What was important was their status as institutions associated with and subsidized by the state, an imperative that transcended the political identity of government.

Yet the relationship between theater and state was symbiotic. The artists demonstrated their desire to remain wedded to the state by the feebleness of their autonomy revolt in 1905 and by quickly adapting to the new governments in 1917, even if this was only for the sake of subsidies. Similarly Russian governments of the period also demonstrated their desire to retain the Imperial Theaters as part of the Russian state structure. State patronage of exemplary art was considered a useful component of the paraphernalia of state power. Of course, the Russian Revolution constituted a direct challenge to state power which, in a sense, became dysfunctional during the late imperial and early Soviet periods of Russian history, its operation restricted as a consequence of the increasingly widespread disobedience and fragmentation of Russian society. The St. Petersburg Imperial Theaters were not isolated from that process and, indeed, their official status altered to suit the color of individual governments. But their essential status as state theaters remained unaltered according to the wishes of both artists and politicians.

Ultimately, then, to what extent did court status shape the identity of the St. Petersburg Imperial Theaters as cultural institutions? The simple fact of court administration set them apart and implied a range of privileges not found in other theaters in the imperial capital. In particular, state subsidies distinguished them from other theaters in St. Petersburg in terms of overall resources and potential creative opportunities. Court status also meant that the Imperial Theaters might be used by the government for special occasions, and during times of revolutionary crisis, such as 1905, it was clear that the Imperial Theaters' unique status had implications for their expected behavior. Other aspects of the institutional history of the St. Petersburg Imperial Theaters less obviously left traces of their court status. For instance, the repertoire was not *pridvornyi* as such, although there were certainly some signs of court influence, for example over the decision to ban Gorky's *The Lower Depths* from the imperial stage. Furthermore, the St. Petersburg Imperial Theater audience, while essentially elitist, was not composed exclusively of courtiers and government officials, but rather reflected a wider cross-section of Petersburg society. Nevertheless, the Imperial Theaters remained a kind of club for the elite and this tended to reinforce the image of theaters associated with the loci of power in tsarist Russia.

Study of the St. Petersburg Imperial Theaters as cultural institutions from the various perspectives pursued by this book therefore reveals an identity and function that was shaped in many ways by *pridvornyi* status, as might be expected. Yet their institutional identity was much wider than the narrow confines of the Directorate and its administration might suggest. The St. Petersburg Imperial Theaters were not simply court theaters; they were cultural institutions whose significance transcended—or at least was set apart from—their court status. There was even a certain ambivalence about their institutional identity; content to remain part of the state system, they were nevertheless often attracted to movements that challenged it. In that sense, the history of the St. Petersburg Imperial Theaters in the era of the Russian Revolution offers an additional perspective on the ways in which tsarist authority was gradually being undermined and destabilised.

Ultimately the relationship between theatrical culture and state power was symbiotic, which raises a final query: Were the origins of Stalinist cultural policy firmly embedded in the nature of the pre-revolutionary relationship between culture and power? The institutional history of the St. Petersburg Imperial Theaters would appear to suggest an affirmative answer to that query, but its exploration belongs to another study.

Appendix of Titles

Throughout the book the titles of Russian plays, operas, and ballets have been rendered into English, and the titles of non–Russian works have been given in their original. The following lists are designed to assist anyone wishing to identify the original Russian titles. Titles on the left are those used in the text, titles on the right are the Russian renderings. Two exceptions to the Russian-into-English rule are *La Bayadère* and *Le Pavillon d'Armide*, both of which are original Russian ballets but are known to Western audiences by their French rather than English titles.

Russian Works

Apotheosis: Memories of the White General	Apofeoz: Pamiati belogo-generala
The Assembly	Assambleia
The Awakening of Flora	Probuzhdenie Flory
La Bayadère	Baiaderka
Be Glad, We Are Winning	Raduites', my pobezhdaem
Boris Godunov	Boris Godunov
Breakfast with the Marshal of Nobility	Zavtrak u predvoditelia
The Cherry Orchard	Vishnevyi sad
Children of the Sun	Deti solntsa
Chopiniana	Shopeniana
The Death of Ivan the Terrible	Smert' Ivana Groznogo
The Death of Tarelkin	Smert' Tarelkina
The Decembrist	Dekabrist
The Demon	Demon
Dubrovskii	Dubrovskii

177

Egyptian Nights	Egipetskie nochi
The Election to the Realm of	Izbranie na tsarstvo Mikhaila
Tsar Mikhail Fedorovich Romanov	Fedorovicha Romanova
Enough Stupidity in Every Wise Man	Na vsiakogo mudretsa
	dovol'no prostoty
Eugene Onegin	Evgenii Onegin
Eunice	Evnika
The Fire Bird	Zhar-ptitsa
The Forest	Les
The Fruits of Enlightenment	Plody prosveshcheniia
The Gambler	Igrok
Glory to Free Russia	Slava Svobodnoi Rossii
God Save the Tsar	Bozhe tsaria khrani
The Golden Cockerel	Zolotoi petushok
The Government Inspector	Revizor
The Great Secret	Velikaia taina
The Heart Is Not a Stone	Serdtse ne kamen'
The Hump-Backed Horse	Konëk-gorbunok
The Lady Without a Dowry	Bespridannitsa
In Memory of the Fallen Fighters	Pamiati pavshikh bortsov
for Freedom	za svobodu
In These Days	V eti dni
Judith	Iudif'
Kashchei the Immortal	Kashchei bessmertnyi
Khovanshchina	Khovanshchina
King, Law and Freedom	Korol', zakon i svoboda
Koz'ma Zakhar'ich Minin-Sukhoruk	Koz'ma Zakhar'ich
	Minin Sukhoruk
Krechinsky's Wedding	Svadba Krechinskogo
The Legend of the Invisible City of	Skazanie o nevidimom
Kitezh and the Maiden Fevronia	grade Kitezhe i deve
	Fevronii
A Life for the Tsar	Zhizn' za tsaria
The Little Cudgel	Dubinushka
The Living Corpse	Zhivoi trup
The Lower Depths	Na dne
The Maid of Pskov	Pskovitianka
Masquerade	Maskarad
The Minor	Nedorosl'

A Month in the Country	Mesiats v derevne
Mystery-Bouffe	Misteriia-Buff
A Night in May	Maiskaia noch'
The Nightingale	Solovei
Not Always Shrovetide for a Cat	Ne vse kotu maslenitsa
The Nutcracker	Shchelkunchik
The Old School	Staryi zakal
The Passers-By	Prokhozhie
A Passionate Heart	Goriachee serdtse
Le Pavillon d'Armide	Pavil'on Armidy
Petrushka	Petrushka
The Petty Bourgeois	Meshchane
The Pharaoh's Daughter	Doch' Faraona
Philistines	Obyvateli
The Power of Darkness	Vlast' t'my
Prince Igor	Kniaz' Igor'
The Queen of Spades	Pikovaia dama
Raymonda	Raimonda
Rogneda	Rogneda
Ruslan and Liudmila	Ruslan i Liudmila
Sadko	Sadko
The Seagull	Chaika
Slaves	Kholopy
The Sleeping Beauty	Spiashchaia krasavitsa
The Snow Maiden	Snegurochka
Storming of the Winter Palace	Vziatie zimnego dvortsa
Summerfolk	Dachniki
Swan Lake	Lebedinoe ozero
Les Sylphides	Sil'fidy
Triumph of the Powers	Torzhestvo derzhav
Tsar Fyodor Ioannovich	Tsar Fëdor Ioannovich
The Veteran and the Recruit	Veteran i novobranets
The Wings	Kulisy
Woe from Wit	Gore ot uma
The Year 1914	1914 god
Yolande	Iolanta
Zabava Putiatishna	Zabava Putiatishna

Non-Russian Works

Aida	Aida
Alt Heidelberg	Staryi Geidelberg
Antigone	Antigona
Il Barbiere di Siviglia	Sevil'skii tsiriul'nik
La Bohème	Bogema
Carmen	Karmen
Le Corsaire	Korsar
Daphnis et Chloé	Dafnis i Khloia
Décadence	Zhanina
Don Juan	Don Zhuan
Don Quixote	Don Kikhot
Esmeralda	Esmeral'da
Faust	Faust
La Fille Mal Gardée	Tshchetnaia predostor-ozhnost'
Der Freischütz	Vol'nyi strelok
Fruen fra havet	Doch' moria
Gengangere	Privedeniia
Giselle	Zhizel'
Götterdämmerung	Gibel' bogov
Les Huguenots	Gugenoty
Joannisfeuer	Ogni Ivanovoi nochi
Julius Caesar	Iulii Tsezar'
Lohengrin	Loengrin
The Merchant of Venice	Venetsianskii kupets (or Sheilok)
Le Nozze di Figaro	Bezumnyi den'
Orphée et Euridice	Orfei i Evridika
Paquita	Pakhita
Der Ring des Nibelungen	Kol'tso Nibelunga
Romeo and Juliet	Romeo i Dzhul'etta
Siegfried	Zigfrid
Sylvia	Sil'viia
La Sylphide	Sil'fida
Tannhäuser	Tangeizer
Tristan und Isolde	Tristan i Izol'da
Le Verre d'Eau	Stakan vody
Die Walküre	Val'kiriia

Bibliographical Note

For detailed information on the sources used for this study, the reader is asked to consult the notes. Here I simply wish to indicate sources which have been most useful, as well as to suggest some suitable starting points for further reading.

An indispensable general reference tool for all aspects of the subject is the excellent *Teatral'naia entsiklopediia* (five volumes, plus supplement with index: Moscow, 1961–67), while a veritable treasure trove of information on the personalities and repertoire of the Imperial Theaters in particular is the *Ezhegodnik imperatorskikh teatrov* (St. Petersburg, 1892–1915). The extensive range of archival sources is very usefully surveyed in I. F. Petrovskaia (ed.), *Materialy k istorii russkogo teatra v gosudarstvennykh arkhivakh SSSR: Obzor dokumentov* (Moscow, 1966).

A major source on the administration and its activities to 1917 is the archive of the Directorate of Imperial Theaters, located in St. Petersburg at the *Rossiiskii gosudarstvennyi istoricheskii arkhiv* (fond 497). Equally important are the published and unpublished materials relating to Teliakovskii. His fifty-volume diary, covering the period from 1898 to 1917, is located in Moscow at the *Tsentral'nyi gosudarstvennyi teatral'nyi muzei imeni A. A. Bakhrushina* (fond 280). Some fragments of the diary from 1899 to 1905 have been published in the journal *Soglasie* (January, 1992, pp. 85–105), and the whole diary for the duration of his tenure as Manager of the Moscow Office has been published as *Dnevniki Direktora Imperatorskikh teatrov, 1898–1901* (Moscow 1998). Telyakovsky's diary formed the basis for the informative and fairly balanced memoirs which he wrote in the early 1920s: *Vospominaniia* (Moscow-Leningrad, 1965). An important source on the administration and its thinking is Vladimir Pogozhev, *Proekt zakonopolozhenii ob imperatorskikh teatrakh* (three volumes: St. Petersburg, 1900).

Many aspects of the St. Petersburg Imperial Theaters are illuminated by materials relating to other individual officials and artists. In addition to the collections in *Tsentral'nyi gosudarstvennyi teatral'nyi muzei imeni Bakhrushina*, the manuscript department of the *Gosudarstvennaia Publichnaia Biblioteka imeni M. E. Saltykova-Shchedrina* (St. Petersburg) contains valuable material. A guide to the collection is: V. F. Petrova, *Materialy k istorii teatral'noi kul'tury Rossii XVIII-XX vv.; Annotirovannyi katalog [Gosudarstvennaia ordena trudovogo krasnogo znamenii publichnaia biblioteka im. M.E. Saltykova-Shchedrina]*, 2 vyp. (Leningrad, 1984). Among the most useful published memoirs for the institutional history of the St. Petersburg Imperial Theaters are P. P. Gnedich, *Kniga zhizni: vospominaniia, 1855–1918* (Leningrad, 1929); V. A. Teliakovskii, *Imperatorskie teatry i 1905 god* (Leningrad, 1926), and V. Bezpalov, *Teatry v dni revoliutsii, 1917* (Leningrad, 1927). Telyakovsky's memoir on 1905 also appears in his *Vospominaniia*.

Contemporary journals and newspapers, particularly those which carried regular *khroniki* on theater affairs, provide a wealth of valuable information; they are especially profitable for their reviews of performances. Among those consulted for this study, the most useful were *Birzhevyia vedomosti, Muzykal'nyi mir, Novoe vremia, Rech', Teatr i iskusstvo,* and *Teatral'naia gazeta* (from August 6, 1905, *Muzykal'nyi mir* and *Teatral'naia gazeta,* which were both published by a group called "Teatral'naia Rossiia," appeared as one journal entitled *Teatral'naia gazeta/Muzykal'nyi mir*). There are several others. For a guide to the periodical press that regularly reported on Russian theater affairs, see I. Petrovskaia, *Teatr i zritel' rossiiskikh stolits, 1895–1917* (Leningrad, 1990), pp. 233–248.

For studies of individual Imperial Theaters which concentrate on artistic endeavor, see the relevant sections of: A. D. Alekseev and others (eds.), *Russkaia khudozhestvennaia kul'tura kontsa XIX-nachala XX veka (1895–1907), kniga pervaia: zrelishchnye iskusstva, muzyka,* (Moscow, 1968); A. D. Alekseev and others (eds.), *Russkaia khudozhestvennaia kul'tura kontsa XIX-nachala XX veka (1908–1917), kniga tret'ia: zrelishchnye iskusstva, muzyka* (Moscow, 1977); and *Istoriia russkogo dramaticheskogo teatra, tom 7, 1898–1917* (Moscow, 1987). An extremely informative factual guide to the theater world of St. Petersburg as a whole from the eighteenth century to the October Revolution is: I. Petrovskaia & V. Somina, *Teatral'nyi Peterburg: nachalo XVIII veka—oktiabr' 1917 goda* (St. Petersburg, 1994).

For the 1917–20 period, the collection of primary sources edited by A. Z. Iufit, *Russkii sovetskii teatr, 1917–1921: dokumenty i materialy* (Leningrad, 1968), is the best starting point, while D. Zolotnitskii, *Akademicheskie teatry na putiakh Oktiabria* (Leningrad, 1982) contains interesting material. Informative extracts from the correspondence between Lunacharsky and Batiushkov is to be found in V. D. Zel'dovich, "Pervye meropriiatiia Narkomprosa po upravleniiu teatrami," *Istoricheskii arkhiv* (1959), no. 1, pp. 50–60.

The vast majority of material relating directly to the Imperial Theaters is in Russian, but some relevant works are available in English. Among the memoir material that has been translated into English, Tamara Karsavina's *Theatre Street* (London, 1950) and Alexander Benois's *Reminiscences of the*

Russian Ballet (London, 1941) are particularly worthwhile. The issue of autonomy in the Russian theater world as a whole is treated in P. G. Friel's "Theater and Revolution: the Struggle for Theatrical Autonomy in Soviet Russia (1917–1920)" (unpublished doctoral dissertation, University of North Carolina, Chapel Hill, 1977), while R. G. Thorpe's "The Management of Culture in Revolutionary Russia: The Imperial Theaters and the State, 1897–1928" (unpublished doctoral dissertation, Princeton University, 1990) concentrates on the Moscow State Theaters in the 1920s.

For a brilliant study of Russian theater as a whole during its Golden Age, see Konstantin Rudnitsky, *Russian and Soviet Theatre: Tradition and the Avant-Garde* (London, 1988). For other works, and for the revolutionary period as a whole, see Murray Frame, *The Russian Revolution, 1905–1921: A Bibliographic Guide to Works in English* (Westport, Connecticut, and London, 1995).

Chapter Notes

Preface

1. This is clearly evidenced in recent histories, such as O. Figes, *A People's Tragedy: The Russian Revolution, 1891–1924* (London, 1996) and R. Pipes, *The Russian Revolution, 1899–1919* (London, 1990).

Introduction

1. *Putevoditel' po S.-Peterburgu. Obrazovatel'nyia ekskursii* (St. Petersburg, 1903), p. 248.

2. For an introduction to Petipa and his place in ballet history, see T. Scholl, *From Petipa to Balanchine: Classical Revival and the Modernization of Ballet* (London, 1993); for Diaghilev, see L. Garafola, *Diaghilev's Ballets Russes* (Oxford, 1989) and R. Buckle, *Diaghilev* (New York, 1979).

3. S. V. Taneev, *Iz proshlogo imperatorskikh teatrov* (St. Petersburg, 1885); S. V. Taneev, *Padenie teatra. Materialy dlia istorii imperatorskikh teatrov* (St. Petersburg, 1887); *Arkhiv direktsii imperatorskikh teatrov, 1746–1801 gg.* (St. Petersburg, 1892).

4. *Ezhegodnik imperatorskikh teatrov. Sezon 1890–91 g.g.* (St. Petersburg, 1892), introductory remarks.

5. *Ezhegodnik imperatorskikh teatrov. Sezon 1890–91 g.g.* (St. Petersburg, 1892), introductory remarks.

6. For an interesting overview of the history and format of the *Yearbooks*, see R. J. Wiley, "The Yearbook of the Imperial Theaters," *Dance Research Journal*, IX (1), Fall-Winter 1976–77, pp. 30–36.

7. V. P. Pogozhev, *Proekt zakonopolozhenii ob imperatorskikh teatrov* (St. Petersburg, 1900); N. V. Drizen, *Stopiatidesiatiletie imperatorskikh teatrov* (St. Petersburg, *c.* 1906); *Stoletie organizatsii imperatorskikh moskovskikh teatrov (opyt istoricheskogo obzora)* (St. Petersburg, 1906–08).

8. D. Zolotnitskii, *Akademicheskie teatry na putiakh oktiabria* (Leningrad, 1982); A. A. Ushkarev, "Iz opyta formirovaniia repertuara imperatorskikh teatrov (pervaia chetvert' XIX veka)," in *Teatr mezhdu proshlym i budushchim. Sbornik nauchnykh trudov*, edited by Iu. M. Orlov (Moscow, 1989), pp. 190–202.

9. Recent Western studies relating to Russian theater during this period include, in descending chronological order: C. A. Schuler, *Women in Russian Theatre: the Actress*

in the Silver Age (London and New York, 1996); N. Worrall, *The Moscow Art Theatre* (London and New York, 1996); A. Law and M. Gordon, *Meyerhold, Eisenstein and Biomechanics: Actor Training in Revolutionary Russia* (Jefferson, North Carolina, 1996); E. Braun, *Meyerhold: A Revolution in Theatre*, second edition (London, 1995); S. Golub, *The Recurrence of Fate: Theatre and Memory in Twentieth-Century Russia* (Iowa City, 1994); R. Leach, *Revolutionary Theatre* (London, 1994). For other works, including articles and doctoral dissertations, see M. Frame, *The Russian Revolution, 1905–1921: A Bibliographic Guide to Works in English* (Westport, Connecticut & London, 1995), pp. 262–265.

    10. See in particular E. A. Swift, "Theater for the People: the Politics of Popular Culture in Urban Russia, 1861–1917," unpublished doctoral dissertation, University of California, Berkeley, 1991 and G. Thurston, "The Impact of Russian Popular Theatre, 1886–1915," *Journal of Modern History*, 55 (1983), no. 2, pp. 237–267.

    11. See also R. G. Thorpe, "The Academic Theaters and the Fate of Soviet Artistic Pluralism, 1919–1928," *Slavic Review*, 51 (Fall 1992) no. 3, pp. 389–410.

    12. For some recent examples, see note 9.

    13. A. A. Pleshcheev, *"Pod seniiu kulis"...* (Paris, 1936), p. 148.

    14. For examples, see note 10.

    15. For the history of court spectacles and the development of the Imperial Theaters to the late nineteenth-century, I have relied chiefly on I. Zabelin, *Domashnii byt russkikh tsarits v XVI i XVII st.*, second edition (Moscow, 1872), pp. 397–502; Drizen, *Stopiatidesiatiletie*; I. Petrovskaia and V. Somina, *Teatral'nyi Peterburg: nachalo XVIII veka—oktiabr' 1917 goda* (St. Petersburg, 1994); "Petr Iu.," articles in *Teatr i iskusstvo*, 1913, numbers 7–10; B. Malnick, "The Origin and Early History of the Theatre in Russia," *Slavonic and East European Review*, 19 (1939–40), pp. 203–227.

    16. On the *skomorokhi*, see R. Zguta, *Russian Minstrels: A History of the Skomorokhi* (Oxford, 1978).

    17. Zabelin, *Domashnii byt russkikh tsarits*, p. 441.

    18. J. T. Fuhrmann, *Tsar Alexis: His Reign and His Russia* (Gulf Breeze, 1981), p. 195; P. Longworth, *Alexis, Tsar of all the Russias* (London, 1984), pp. 210–211.

    19. See, for example, R. Zguta, "Peter I's 'Most Drunken Synod of Fools and Jesters,'" *Jahrbücher für Geschichte Osteuropas*, 21 (1973), pp. 18–28.

    20. The decree is reproduced in *Arkhiv direktsii (vypusk I, otdel II)*, p. 54.

    21. M.A.S. Burgess, "The Early Theatre," in *An Introduction to Russian Language and Literature*, edited by R. Auty and D. Obolensky (Cambridge, 1977), p. 237.

    22. See *Teatr i iskusstvo*, 1906, nos. 35 and 36, and Drizen, *Stopiatidesiatiletie*.

    23. Pogozhev, *Stoletie organizatsii*, volume 1, p. 44, note.

    24. Information on the theater buildings is from *Ezhegodnik imperatorskikh teatrov, 1892–1893* (St. Petersburg, 1894), pp. 529–545. For the architectural history of the St. Petersburg Imperial Theaters and others, see M. Z. Taranovskaia, *Arkhitektura teatrov Leningrada (Istoriko-arkhitekturnyi ocherk)* (Leningrad, 1988).

    25. L. Senelick (ed.), *Russian Dramatic Theory from Pushkin to the Symbolists. An Anthology* (Austin, 1981), p. 4.

    26. On civil society and the "middling classes," see E. W. Clowes and others (eds.), *Between Tsar and People: Educated Society and the Quest for Public Identity in Late Imperial Russia* (Princeton, 1991) and H. D. Balzer (ed.), *Russia's Missing Middle Class: the Professions in Russian History* (Armonk, 1996).

    27. H. G. Wells, *Russia in the Shadows* (London, n.d.), p. 24. For my overview of St. Petersburg economy and society I have relied principally upon J. H. Bater, *St. Petersburg: Industrialization and Change* (London, 1976); J. H. Bater, "Between Old and New: St. Petersburg in the Late Imperial Era," in *The City in Late Imperial Russia*, edited by M. F. Hamm (Bloomington, Indiana, 1986), pp. 43–78; D. R. Brower,

"Urban Russia on the Eve of World War One: A Social Profile," *Journal of Social History*, 13 (1980), no. 3, pp. 424–436; G. L. Freeze, "The *Soslovie* (Estate) Paradigm and Russian Social History," *American Historical Review*, 91 (1986), no. 1, pp. 11–36; R. B. McKean, *St. Petersburg Between the Revolutions: Workers and Revolutionaries, June 1907–February 1917* (New Haven and London, 1990).

28. McKean, *St. Petersburg Between the Revolutions*, p. 37.

29. For a discussion of private theaters in late imperial Russia, see E. Ia. Dubnova, "Chastnye teatry Moskvy i Peterburga," in *Russkaia khudozhestvennaia kul'tura kontsa XIX-nachala XX veka (1908–1917), kniga tret'ia: zrelishchnye iskusstva, muzyka*, edited by A. D. Alekseev and others (Moscow, 1977), pp. 148–178. Many wealthy Russian families had private theaters in their houses and on their estates before the 1880s, but they were not open to the public. See, for example, D. Blagovo, *Rasskazy babushki. Iz vospominanii piati pokolenii, zapisannye i sobrannye eë vnukom* (Leningrad, 1989), p. 152.

30. On estrada, see L. McReynolds (ed.), "Russian Nightlife, Fin-de-Siècle," *Russian Studies in History* (1992–93), vol. 31, no. 3, pp. 11–49.

31. On Russian cabaret, see H. B. Segel, *Turn-of-the-Century Cabaret: Paris, Barcelona, Berlin, Munich, Vienna, Cracow, Moscow, St. Petersburg, Zurich* (New York, 1987), chapter six. A recent study of the Crooked Mirror in particular is B. Henry, "Theatrical Parody at the Krivoe zerkalo: Russian 'teatr miniatyur,' 1908–1931," unpublished doctoral dissertation, Oxford University, 1997.

32. See Swift, "Theater for the People"; E. A. Swift, "Fighting the Germs of Disorder: The Censorship of Russian Popular Theater, 1888–1917," *Russian History*, 18 (1991), no. 1, pp. 1–49; G. A. Khaichenko, *Russkii narodnyi teatr kontsa XIX—nachala XX veka* (Moscow, 1975).

33. F.W.J. Hemmings, *Theatre and State in France, 1760–1905* (Cambridge, 1994), p. 194.

34. W. E. Yates, *Theatre in Vienna: A Critical History, 1776–1995* (Cambridge, 1996), pp. 168–169.

35. A. Kugel', "Krizis teatra," *Teatr i iskusstvo*, 1909, no. 31, p. 534.

36. See, for example, Znosko-Borovskii, "Teatr bez literatury (O russkom teatre)," *Apollon*, 1912, no. 7, p. 22.

37. In addition to Braun, *Meyerhold*, see N. Worrall, *Modernism to Realism on the Soviet Stage: Tairov-Vakhtangov-Okhlopkov* (Cambridge, 1989); S. Golub, *Evreinov: The Theatre of Paradox and Transformation* (Ann Arbor, 1984); S. M. Carnicke, *The Theatrical Instinct: Nikolai Evreinov and the Russian Theatre of the Early Twentieth Century* (New York, 1989). For an introduction to Briusov's ideas on theater, see J. B. Woodward, "From Brjusov to Ajkhenvald: Attitudes to the Russian Theatre, 1902–1914," *Canadian Slavonic Papers*, VII (1965), pp. 173–188. For Bely, see G. Kalbouss, "Andrey Bely and the Modernist Movement in Russian Drama," in *Andrey Bely: A Critical Review* (Lexington, Kentucky, 1978), pp. 146–155, and T. Nikolesku, *Andrei Belyi i teatr* (Moscow, 1995).

38. V. Briusov, "Nenuzhnaia pravda," *Sobranie sochinenii*, volume 6 (Moscow, 1975), pp. 62–73. The article was originally published in the journal *Mir iskusstva* (1902, no. 4).

39. *Krizis teatra: sbornik statei*, edited by Iu. Steklov (Moscow, 1908), p. 52.

40. *Krizis teatra*, p. 183.

41. Quoted in L. Kleberg, "Vjaceslav Ivanov and the Idea of Theater," in *Theater and Literature in Russia, 1900–1930*, edited by L. Kleberg & N. Å. Nilsson (Stockholm, 1984), p. 61.

42. K. Rudnitsky, *Russian and Soviet Theatre: Tradition and the Avant-Garde* (London, 1988), pp. 9–10. On Ivanov in general, see J. West, *Russian Symbolism: A*

Study of Vyacheslav Ivanov and the Russian Symbolist Aesthetic (London, 1970). For the Symbolists' ideas about theater, see also B. G. Rosenthal, "Theatre as Church: The Vision of the Mystical Anarchists," *Russian History*, 4, part 2 (1977), pp. 122–141.

43. On the mass festivals, see J. Von Geldern, *Bolshevik Festivals, 1917–1920* (London, 1993); R. Russell, "The Arts and the Russian Civil War," *Journal of European Studies*, 20 (1990), part 3, pp. 219–240; A. Z. Iufit (ed.), *Russkii sovetskii teatr, 1917–1921: dokumenty i materialy* (Leningrad, 1968), pp. 262–276.

44. For an example of the view that the Imperial Theaters were decaying, see *Teatr i iskusstvo*, 1906, no. 35, p. 525.

45. A. Kosorotov, "Krizis teatra," *Teatr i iskusstvo*, 1908, no. 17, pp. 310–313, no. 18, pp. 327–328, no. 19, pp. 340–342, no. 20, pp. 358–361.

46. Rigoletto, "Russkii teatr do i posle Chekhova," *Teatral'naia gazeta*, 1905, no. 27, p. 444.

47. I. Osipov, interview with M. G. Savina, *Teatral'naia gazeta*, 1905, no. 41, p. 1220.

48. Sergei Auslender, "Khronika," *Apollon*, November 1909, pp. 29–30.

49. *"Teatr": kniga o novom teatre. Sbornik statei* (St. Petersburg, 1908), p. 272.

Chapter 1

1. Nicolas Legat, *Ballet Russe [sic]: Memoirs of Nicolas Legat*, translated, with a foreword, by Sir Paul Dukes (London, 1939), p. 33.

2. Pogozhev, *Proekt zakonopolozhenii*, volume 1, p. 249. This *Proekt* is discussed below.

3. V. A. Teliakovskii, *Vospominaniia* (Moscow-Leningrad, 1965), p. 22. Here I have followed the list of Imperial Theater properties provided by Telyakovsky, but have not quoted it verbatim.

4. *Ezhegodnik imperatorskikh teatrov, 1892-93* (St. Petersburg, 1894), pp. 105–108.

5. These figures are based on information published in the *Ezhegodniki imperatorskikh teatrov* between the 1900-01 and 1910-11 seasons inclusive. The *Ezhegodniki* published after 1911 do not contain such information about the theater troupes. However, there is no reason to believe that the available statistics are not representative for the period 1900–20 as a whole. During the 1917-18 season, the Alexandrinsky had forty-one actresses and forty-two actors, and during 1918-19 thirty-eight actresses and forty-one actors (*Gosudarstvennaia publichnaia biblioteka. Otdel rukopisei* (GPB), f.340, nos. 17 & 18). This indicates that the intervening years, 1911–17, did not witness any significant change in troupe numbers. Many Imperial Theater employees were recruited by the army after 1914, but they tended to be technical staff, rather than artists.

6. *Proekt zakonopolozhenii*, volume 1, pp. 253–255. Admittedly, many of the "officials" in the technical section were set designers and might be classed as artists, but the point is that they were part of the administrative structure, not of the theater troupes as such.

7. *Tsentral'nyi gosudarstvennyi teatral'nyi muzei imeni A. A. Bakhrushina*, Moscow (TsGTM), f.58:102—undated paper on drama censorship by I. A. Vsevolozhsky, Director of Imperial Theaters, 1881–99; *Rossiiskii gosudarstvennyi istoricheskii arkhiv*, St. Petersburg (RGIA), f.497, op.10, ed.khr.599—correspondence between Directorate and censor, 1898.

8. RGIA, f.497, op.10, ed.khr.981, l.35—Chief Administration for Press Affairs

to St. Petersburg Office, September 18, 1906; ibid., l.64, 65, 67—Mikhailovsky Theater to St. Petersburg Office, Directorate to Chief Administration for Press Affairs, and Chief Administration for Press Affairs to St. Petersburg Office, December 1906; N. M. Korkunov, *Russkoe gosudarstvennoe pravo*, t. I, seventh edition (St. Petersburg, 1909), p. 507; TsGTM, f.296:201–202—letters from censor to N. A. Chaev, January 1912 and January 1913.

9. RGIA, f.497, op.6, d.4762, l.80–87—manuscript listing officials for whom seats were reserved. Not dated, but most likely from 1912.

10. Teliakovskii, *Vospominaniia*, p. 22.

11. *Teatr i iskusstvo*, 1899, no. 29, p. 498.

12. N. Petrov, *50 i 500* (Moscow, 1960), p. 77.

13. P. P. Gnedich, *Kniga zhizni: vospominaniia, 1855–1918* (Leningrad, 1929), pp. 274–275.

14. "Khronika teatra i iskusstva," *Teatr i iskusstvo*, 1899, no. 3, p. 60.

15. This was for both St. Petersburg and Moscow, although it is noteworthy that the majority of annual expenditure went to the St. Petersburg Imperial Theaters, in 1899–1900 2.3 million rubles as opposed to 1.6 million rubles for Moscow. *Proekt zakonopolozhenii*, volume 1, p. 437.

16. *Proekt zakonopolozhenii*, volume 1, p. 421.

17. RGIA, f.497, op.6, ed.khr.4604, l.7, 8, 12—manuscripts relating to ticket prices.

18. TsGTM, f.280:783—Fredericks to Telyakovsky, December 8, 1905.

19. RGIA, f.497, op.6, d.4780, l.1—*Kabinet* of His Imperial Highness to Directorate, November 30, 1905.

20. "Peterburgskaia khronika," *Teatral'naia gazeta*, 1905, nos. 2–3, p. 40, no. 9, p. 138, no. 14, p. 243.

21. *Teatr i iskusstvo*, 1906, no. 32, p. 477.

22. GPB, f.433, ed.khr.10, l.36—personal ballet diary of D. I. Leshkov.

23. L. Viv'en, "V Aleksandrinskom teatre nakanune revoliutsii," *Zvezda*, 1957, no. 1, p. 180; "Théâtres et Concerts," *Journal de St. Pétersbourg*, September 3, 1906, p. 3.

24. RGIA, op.6, ed.khr.4848, l.1—Telyakovsky to Fredericks, December 21, 1907.

25. RGIA, f.497, op.6, ed.khr.5068, l.111—*Zhurnal rasporiazhenii*, August 14–17, 1914.

26. *Teatr i iskusstvo*, 1915, no. 39, p. 726. For the argument by the last editor of the *Ezhegodniki*, N. V. Drizen, that deficits were not the real reason for its closure, as Telyakovsky claimed, see *Novoe vremia*, October 6 (19), 1915, p. 5. Drizen pointed out that the *Ezhegodniki* had always had deficits, that they were not as bad as they had been at the beginning of the century when Diaghilev was the editor, and that circulation was declining because there were fewer portraits in the *Ezhegodniki* of Imperial Theater artists—who were the chief market for the publication. Drizen stated that despite his attempts to alter the format of the book, few had cooperated with him. Whatever the real reason, the net effect was that the *Ezhegodniki* were losing money.

27. RGIA, f.497, op.18, ed.khr.1208—Mariinsky and Mikhailovsky programs.

28. TsGTM, f.280:11368—Telyakovsky's diary, March 6, 1913; ibid., 11372—Telyakovsky's diary, March 8, 1913; ibid., 11409—Telyakovsky's diary, March 23, 1913. Telyakovsky, *Vospominaniia*, pp. 63–64.

29. Pleshcheev, *"Pod seniiu kulis"...*, p. 175.

30. *Kazënnyi* theaters, such as the three government theaters in Warsaw, were funded by the State Exchequer but were neither administered by the court nor regarded as Imperial Theaters.

31. N. Volkov, "Teatr v epokhu krusheniia monarkhii," *Sto let. Aleksandrinskii teatr—teatr gosdramy* (Leningrad, 1932), p. 306.

32. The military culture of St. Petersburg is a relatively neglected area of study, but see G. Vilinbakhov, "Sankt-Peterburg—voennaia stolitsa," *Nashe nasledie*, 1989, no. 1, pp. 15–22, which forms the basis for the following comments on the city.

33. J. Keep, "The Military Style of the Romanov Rulers," *War and Society*, 1, no. 2 (September 1983), p. 61.

34. Keep, "The Military Style," p. 78.

35. V. A. Nelidov, *Teatral'naia Moskva (Sorok let Moskovskikh teatrov)* (Berlin-Riha, 1931), pp. 100–101.

36. "Novyi direktor Imperatorskikh teatrov i ego vzgliady na iskusstvo," *Teatr i iskusstvo*, 1899, no. 31, pp. 533–534; "Kniaz' Sergei Mikhailovich Volkonskii," *Ezhegodnik imperatorskikh teatrov, 1901–1902 g.* (St. Petersburg, n.d.), pp. 315–317.

37. *Teatr i iskusstvo*, 1899, no. 35, p. 595.

38. For the circumstances of Volkonsky's resignation, see Chapter 2.

39. T. Komisarjevsky [Komissarzhevsky], *Myself and the Theatre* (London, 1929), pp. 20–22.

40. S. A. Zalevskii, "Guards Units in the Russian Armed Forces," *Modern Encyclopedia of Russian and Soviet History*, edited by J. L. Wieczynski (Gulf Breeze, Florida, 1976–).

41. L. Tolstoy, *Resurrection*, translated by L. Maude (London, 1947), pp. 48–49.

42. V. P. Shkafer, *Sorok let na stsene russkoi opery: vospominaniia, 1890–1930 gg.* (Leningrad, 1936), p. 188. The word "phalanx" originally referred to a line of battle in a military confrontation: *Oxford Dictionary of English Etymology* (1966).

43. N. Froud and J. Hanley (eds.), *Chaliapin: An Autobiography as told to Maxim Gorky* (London, 1967), p. 141.

44. Quoted in R. J. Wiley, *Tchaikovsky's Ballets* (Oxford, 1985), p. 164.

45. *Proekt zakonopolozhenii*, volume 1, p. 318.

46. Pleshcheev, "*Pod seniiu kulis*"..., p. 118.

47. Viv'en, "V Aleksandrinskom teatre," p. 180.

48. *Proekt zakonopolozhenii*, volume 1, pp. 180–182.

49. RGIA, f.497, op.6, ed.khr.4799, l.6—Directorate to Palace Commandant, March 17, 1906.

50. P. Krasnov, "Nashi kazënnye teatry," *Muzykal'nyi mir*, no. 7, February 12, 1905.

51. "Khronika," *Teatr i iskusstvo*, 1897, no. 1, p. 7; "Khronika," *Teatral'naia gazeta*, 1905, no. 5, p. 73.

52. *Teatr i iskusstvo*, 1898, no. 50, pp. 916, 926.

53. See repertoire listings, with dates, *Ezhegodnik imperatorskikh teatrov, 1898–1899* (St. Petersburg, n.d.).

54. "Khronika teatra i iskusstva," *Teatr i iskusstvo*, 1899, no. 8, p. 165.

55. V. A. Teliakovskii, *Imperatorskie teatry i 1905 god* (Leningrad, 1926), p. 154.

56. *Ezhegodnik imperatorskikh teatrov, 1896-1897 gg.* (St. Petersburg, 1898), pp. 394–400.

57. *Novoe vremia*, September 20 (October 3) 1916, p. 4.

58. RGIA, f.497, op.6, ed.khr.4890, l.3–"dokladnaia zapiska" by Telyakovsky; D.C. Rawson, *Russian Rightists and the Revolution of 1905* (Cambridge, 1995), pp. 46–55.

59. *Ezhegodnik imperatorskikh teatrov, 1894-95* (St. Petersburg, 1896), p. 386.

60. "Khronika teatra i iskusstva," *Teatr i iskusstvo*, 1897, no. 34, p. 599.

61. "Khronika teatra i iskusstva," *Teatr i iskusstvo*, 1897, no. 2, p. 30.

62. RGIA, f.497, op.6, ed.khr.5032, l.55—St. Petersburg Office to "Committee for the Organization of the Celebration of the Three Hundredth Anniversary of the Reign of the House of the Romanovs," March 11, 1913.

63. RGIA, f.497, op.6, ed.khr.5032, 1.57—Court Chancellery to Directorate, March 29, 1913.
64. RGIA, f.497, op.6, ed.khr.5032, 1.33—St. Petersburg Office to Bestuzhev-Riumin, February 7, 1914.
65. Petrovskaia and Somina, *Teatral'nyi Peterburg,* pp. 198, 304, 252.
66. *Ezhegodnik imperatorskikh teatrov, 1899–1900* (St. Petersburg, 1900), part II.
67. *Proekt zakonopolozhenii,* volume 1, p. 68.
68. *Proekt zakonopolozhenii,* volume 1, p. 50; "Khronika teatra i iskusstva," *Teatr i iskusstvo,* 1899, no. 13, p. 261.
69. *Teatr i iskusstvo,* 1901, no .42, p. 742.
70. *Proekt zakonopolozhenii,* volume 1, pp. 55–66.
71. *Teatr i iskusstvo,* 11 June 1900, no. 24, pp. 433–434.
72. *Proekt zakonopolozhenii,* volume 1, p. 3.
73. *Proekt zakonopolozhenii,* volume 1, pp. 10–12.
74. *Proekt zakonopolozhenii,* volume 1, pp. 17–18.
75. *Proekt zakonopolozhenii,* volume 1, p. 38.
76. *Teatr i iskusstvo,* 1901, no. 30, p. 537.
77. *Proekt zakonopolozhenii,* volume 1, p. 13.
78. *Proekt zakonopolozhenii,* volume 1, pp. 44–45.
79. *Proekt zakonopolozhenii,* volume 1, p. 95.
80. Yates, *Theatre in Vienna,* p. 11.
81. For the struggle for this in Scandinavia, Eastern Europe and, to some extent, Russia, see L. Senelick (ed.), *National Theatre in Northern and Eastern Europe, 1746–1900* (Cambridge, 1991). Senelick suggests that in the Russian case the "hegemonies to be overthrown were those of French and German literary and artistic styles and, more important, the yoke of a bureaucracy infested with Baltic Germans" (p. 14).
82. *Proekt zakonopolozhenii,* volume 1, p. 14.
83. *Proekt zakonopolozhenii,* volume 1, p. 16.
84. *Proekt zakonopolozhenii,* volume 1, pp. 153, 240–241. No such national specifications were made for ballet, though it was expected that at least two new ballet productions would be staged each season. The French troupe was expected to stage at least six new productions of French drama per season (pp. 241–242).
85. *Proekt zakonopolozhenii,* volume 1, p. 28.
86. *Proekt zakonopolozhenii,* volume 1, p. 22.

Chapter 2

1. Hemmings, *Theatre and State in France,* Chapter 1.
2. Volkov, "Teatr v epokhu krusheniia monarkhii," p. 306.
3. V. Bogdanov-Berezovskii, *Leningradskii gosudarstvennyi akademicheskii ordena Lenina teatr opery i baleta imeni S.M. Kirova* (Leningrad-Moscow, 1959), pp. 22–23. The comment about leading artists is a reference to the argument that the Directorate ignored the talents of younger artists in order to indulge the "stars."
4. L. A. Entelis (ed.), *Leningradskii gosudarstvennyi ordena Lenina akademicheskii teatr opery i baleta imeni S.M. Kirova, 1917–1967* (Leningrad, 1967), p. 13.
5. *Teatral'naia entsiklopediia,* volume 3, column 457.
6. N. A. Gorchakov, *The Theater in Soviet Russia,* translated by E. Lehrman (New York, 1957), pp. 14–15.
7. M. Slonim, *Russian Theater: From the Empire to the Soviets* (London, 1963), p. 133.

8. E. W. Clowes, "Social Discourse in the Moscow Art Theater," in *Between Tsar and People*, p. 273.

9. Teliakovskii, *Vospominaniia*, p. 20.

10. TsGTM, f.280:868—Sumbatov-Yuzhin to Telyakovsky, June 14, 1901.

11. TsGTM, f.280:879—Sumbatov-Yuzhin to Telyakovsky, August 30, 1911.

12. Komisarjevsky, *Myself and the Theatre*, pp. 20–22.

13. Froud and Hanley, *Chaliapin*, pp. 136, 141.

14. Froud and Hanley, *Chaliapin*, p. 136.

15. Gnedich, *Kniga zhizni*, p. 278.

16. V. V. Yastrebtsev, *Reminiscences of Rimsky-Korsakov*, edited and translated by F. Jonas (New York, 1985), p. 409.

17. *Teatr i iskusstvo*, 1913, no. 11, p. 241.

18. TsGTM, f.280:11376—Telyakovsky's diary, March 9, 1913.

19. V. Napravnik, *Eduard Frantsevich Napravnik i ego sovremenniki* (Leningrad, 1991), p. 379. Napravnik's son is quoting from the manuscript of his father's memoirs. He quotes a fuller, ostensibly more accurate, version than that in E. F. Napravnik, *Avtobiograficheskie, tvorcheskie materialy, dokumenty, pis'ma* (Leningrad, 1959), pp. 42–43.

20. A. Ia. Golovin, *Vstrechi i vpechatleniia. Pis'ma. Vospominaniia o Golovine* (Leningrad-Moscow, 1960), p. 50.

21. Gnedich, *Kniga zhizni*, p. 277.

22. Napravnik, *Avtobiograficheskie*, p. 42.

23. A. A. Mossolov [Mosolov], *At the Court of the Last Tsar, Being the Memoirs of A. A. Mossolov, Head of the Court Chancellery, 1900–1916*, translated by E. W. Dickes (London, 1935), p. 153.

24. TsGTM, f.35:233—Palitsyn to Telyakovsky, March 22, 1908.

25. TsGTM, f.280:11375—Telyakovsky's diary, March 9, 1913.

26. Telyakovsky, *Vospominaniia*, p. 121; Froud and Hanley, *Chaliapin*, p. 136.

27. *Teatr i iskusstvo*, 1906, no. 22, p. 337 and no. 32, p. 505.

28. Napravnik, *Eduard Frantsevich Napravnik*, p. 427.

29. See K. Rudnitsky, *Meyerhold The Director*, translated by G. Petrov (Ann Arbor, 1981), p. 134.

30. TsGTM, f.411:465—blank Imperial Theater contract.

31. *Teatr i iskusstvo*, 1905, no. 2, p. 29.

32. RGIA, f.497, op. 6, ed.khr.4876, l.7 (reverse side)—*Zhurnal rasporiazhenii*, 27–29 October 1908.

33. RGIA, f.497, op. 6, ed.khr.4876, l.33 (reverse side)—*Zhurnal rasporiazhenii*, 10–13 September 1909.

34. RGIA, f.497, op. 18, ed.khr.1208, l.40 (reverse side)—Mariinsky Theater program, 1902.

35. For example, the first clause of a contract between Rimsky-Korsakov and the Directorate from 1907 states that: "I, Rimsky-Korsakov, transfer [*peredaiu*] to the Directorate of Imperial Theaters the right to present on the stage of the Imperial Theaters in Moscow the opera 'The Legend of the Invisible City of Kitezh and the Maiden Fevronia' in four acts, composed by me." TsGTM, f.227:5—production contract of Rimsky-Korsakov, October 31, 1907.

36. RGIA, f.497, op. 10, no.805, l.1—Telyakovsky to St. Petersburg and Moscow Offices, December 8, 1903.

37. GPB, f.640, op. 1, no.830—Rimsky-Korsakov to Telyakovsky, May 26, 1908.

38. TsGTM, f.317:3321—Telyakovsky to Sumbatov-Yuzhin; "Khronika," *Teatral'naia gazeta*, 1905, no. 20, p. 366.

39. TsGTM, f.280:7946—Telyakovsky's diary, August 4, 1908.

40. *Teatr i iskusstvo*, 1906, no. 36, p. 554.
41. *Teatr i iskusstvo*, 1899, no. 35, p. 594.
42. For the statute of the Theater-Literary Committee, outlining its functions, see *Ezhegodnik imperatorskikh teatrov, 1890–1891 g.g.* (St. Petersburg, 1892), pp. 267–268.
43. GPB, f.106, ed.khr.163, l.6—memoirs of E. P. Karpov.
44. TsGTM, f.280:7967–8—Telyakovsky's diary, August 26, 1908.
45. Gnedich, *Kniga zhizni*, pp. 325–327; "Pis'ma v redaktsiiu," *Teatr i iskusstvo*, 1908, no.48, pp. 841–845.
46. "Khronika," *Teatral'naia gazeta*, 1905, no. 8, p. 121.
47. *Teatr i iskusstvo*, 1908, no. 49, p. 861.
48. Quoted in Gnedich, *Kniga zhizni*, p. 359.
49. TsGTM, f.411:465—blank Imperial Theater contract.
50. "Khronika teatra i iskusstva," *Teatr i iskusstvo*, 1898, no. 21, p. 388.
51. Iur. Beliaev, "Teatr i muzyka," *Novoe vremia*, September 2, 1903, p. 4.
52. "U rampy," *Birzhevyia vedomosti* (vechernii vypusk), February 24, 1917, p. 4.
53. A. Gozenpud, *Russkii opernyi teatr mezhdu dvukh revoliutsii, 1905–1917* (Leningrad, 1975), pp. 16–17.
54. E. Ponomarev, "I. A. Vsevolozhskoi [*sic*] (Ocherk ego khudozhestvennoi deiatel'nosti)," *Ezhegodnik imperatorskikh teatrov, 1899–1900* (St. Petersburg, 1900, pp. 31–32.
55. N. Zograf, *Aleksandr Pavlovich Lenskii* (Moscow, 1955), pp. 309–311; A. P. Lenskii, *Stat'i. Pis'ma. Zapiski* (Moscow-Leningrad, 1935), p. 515; A. Benois, *Reminiscences of the Russian Ballet*, translated by M. Britnieva (London, 1941), p. 202; Golovin, *Vstrechi i vpechatleniia*, p. 50; K. F. Val'ts, *Shest'desiat piat' let v teatre* (Leningrad, 1928), p. 199.
56. Gnedich, *Kniga zhizni*, p. 310; Viv'en, "V Aleksandrinskom teatre," p. 184. To be fair to Varlamov, Alexandrinsky productions were often staged with very little rehearsal time. The 1896 production of *The Seagull*, for example, was premiered only nine days after the troupe first saw the text of the play. Consequently, Varlamov was never alone in relying on prompters ("Russian Nightlife, Fin-de-Siècle," p. 56).
57. Napravnik, *Avtobiograficheskie*, p. 42.
58. V. Teliakovskii, "Na artisticheskom postu. Godovshchina smerti Tartakova," in *Kniga o I.V. Tartakove*, by G. Tartakov (Leningrad, 1987), p. 76.
59. Gnedich, *Kniga zhizni*, p. 303.
60. A. Benois, *Reminiscences of the Russian Ballet* (London, 1941), pp. 210–218; Prince S. Wolkonsky [Volkonsky], *My Reminiscences*, volume II, translated by A. E. Chamot (London, n.d.), pp. 71–75.
61. V. Fokine, translator, *Fokine: Memoirs of a Ballet Master*, edited by A. Chujoy (London, 1961), pp. 90–91.
62. Napravnik, *Eduard Frantsevich Napravnik*, pp. 379–380.
63. Napravnik, *Eduard Frantsevich Napravnik*, p. 429.
64. GPB, f.433, ed.khr.10, l.21—personal ballet diary of D. I. Leshkov. This was in September 1904, when Krupensky was an official of the St. Petersburg office, but not its Manager.
65. TsGTM, f.280:10040—Telyakovsky's diary, January 27, 1911; Romola Nijinsky [Nijinska], *Nijinsky* (New York, 1936), pp. 120–122.
66. V. A. Michurina-Samoilova, *Pol veka na stsene Aleksandrinskogo teatra* (Leningrad, 1935), p. 60.
67. "Khronika teatra i iskusstva," *Teatr i iskusstvo*, 1899, no. 18, p. 340.
68. I. Shneiderman, *Mariia Gavrilovna Savina, 1854–1915* (Leningrad-Moscow, 1956), p. 247.

69. GPB, f.106, ed.khr.158, l.7—memoir of S. K. Boianus.
70. E. Time, *Dorogi iskusstva* (Moscow, 1967), pp. 137–138.
71. B. A. Gorin-Goriainov, *Moi teatral'nyi opyt* (Leningrad, 1939), pp. 55–56.
72. N. N. Khodotov, *Blizkoe-dalekoe* (Moscow-Leningrad, 1932), p. 133.
73. Wolkonsky, *My Reminiscences*, volume I, p. 108.
74. Viv'en, "V Aleksandrinskom teatre," p. 181.
75. Gnedich, *Kniga zhizni*, p. 248.
76. Teliakovskii, *Vospominaniia*, p. 98.
77. Khodotov, *Blizkoe-dalekoe*, p. 120.
78. Gnedich, *Kniga zhizni*, p. 299.
79. R. Aloye Mooser, "La vie musicale," *Journal de St. Pétersbourg*, September 8, 1905, p. 1.
80. Shkafer, *Sorok let*, p. 191.
81. Napravnik, *Eduard Frantsevich Napravnik*, p. 448.
82. Napravnik, *Avtobiograficheskie*, p. 399.
83. Napravnik, *Eduard Frantsevich Napravnik*, p. 379.
84. Napravnik, *Avtobiograficheskie*, pp. 387, 417, 391.
85. Gnedich, *Kniga zhizni*, p. 273.
86. F. Lopukhov, *Shest'desiat let v balete: vospominaniia i zapiski baletmeistera* (Moscow, 1966), p. 106.
87. Romanovsky-Krassinsky [Kshesinskaya], *Dancing in Petersburg: The Memoirs of Kschessinska*, translated by A. Haskell (London, 1960), p. 72.
88. Romanovsky-Krassinsky, *Dancing in Petersburg*, pp. 76–77.
89. Wolkonsky, *My Reminiscences*, volume II, pp. 98–113.
90. "Khronika teatra i iskusstva," *Teatr i iskusstvo*, 1899, no. 41, p. 711.
91. Romanovsky-Krassinsky, *Dancing in Petersburg*, p. 100.
92. Legat, *Ballet Russe* [*sic*], pp. 41–42, 38, 40.

Chapter 3

1. L. McReynolds, *The News Under Russia's Old Regime: The Development of a Mass-Circulation Press* (Princeton, 1991), p. 283. For Russian theater audiences in general, see I. Petrovskaia, *Teatr i zritel' rossiiskikh stolits, 1895-1917* (Leningrad, 1990).
2. Benois, *Reminiscences of the Russian Ballet*, p. 46.
3. RGIA, f.497, op.6, ed.khr.5117, l.14—Telyakovsky to Tartakov, March 28, 1917.
4. S. Hoare, *The Fourth Seal: The End of a Russian Chapter* (London, 1930), p. 83.
5. T. Karsavina, *Theatre Street: The Reminiscences of Tamara Karsavina* (London, 1950), p. 97.
6. P. Krasnov, "Nashi kazënnye teatry," *Muzykal'nyi mir*, no.7, February 12, 1905.
7. Pl. Krasnov, "Pri zakrytykh dveriakh," *Teatral'naia gazeta*, August 20, 1905, no. 34, p. 1049.
8. RGIA, f.497, op.6, ed.khr.5117, l.14—Telyakovsky to Tartakov, March 28, 1917.
9. GPB, f.433, ed.khr.10—personal ballet diary of D. I. Leshkov.
10. *Novoe vremia*, October 20 (November 2), 1915, p. 7.
11. RGIA, f.497, op.6, ed.khr.5117, l.15, reverse side—Telyakovsky to Golovin, March 1917.
12. RGIA, f.497, op.18, ed.khr.358, l.25—from *Journal de Pétrograd*, September 23, 1917.

13. Karsavina, *Theatre Street*, p. 98. See also A. Ros-v, "Ob opere i opernykh vkusakh publiki," *Teatr i iskusstvo*, no. 30, 1897, p. 530.

14. B. A. Al'medingen, *Golovin i Shaliapin: Noch' pod kryshei Mariinskogo teatra* (Leningrad, 1958), p. 4.

15. RGIA, f.497, op.6, ed.khr.4715, l.95—St. Petersburg Office to Chancellery of St. Petersburg gradonachal'nik, November 1903.

16. RGIA, f.497, op.6, ed.khr.4797, l.29—Telyakovsky to O. I. Vendorf, October 12, 1909; ibid., l.32-32 reverse side—St. Petersburg gradonachal'nik to Telyakovsky, December 9, 1910.

17. RGIA, f.497, op.6, ed.khr.4604, l.8—Alexandrinsky ticket prices, October 1900.

18. G. D. Surh, *1905 in St. Petersburg: Labor, Society, and Revolution* (Stanford, 1989), pp. 23–25.

19. "Teatral'nyi dnevnik S. F. Svetlova," *Biriuch petrogradskikh gosudarstvennykh teatrov; sbornik statei*, edited by A. S. Poliakov (Petrograd, June-August, 1919), p. 59.

20. GPB, f.433, ed.khr.10, l.11—personal ballet diary of D. I. Leshkov.

21. RGIA, f.497, op.6, ed.khr.4797, l.1—Telyakovsky to St. Petersburg gradonachal'nik, January 31, 1906.

22. RGIA, f.497, op.6, ed.khr.4797—l.4, Telyakovsky to Chancellery of the Ministry of the Imperial Court, January 25, 1907; l.5, St. Petersburg gradonachal'nik's assistant to Telyakovsky, February 9, 1907; l.7, Chancellery of St. Petersburg gradonachal'nik to Telyakovsky, April 16, 1907.

23. RGIA, f.497, op.6, ed.khr.4797—l.14-15, Chancellery of St. Petersburg gradonachal'nik to Telyakovsky; l.17-18, "Zhurnal soveshchaniia" on *baryshniki*, March 12, 1909; l.25, Telyakovsky to St. Petersburg gradonachal'nik, August 14, 1909.

24. RGIA, f.497, op.6, ed.khr.4797—l.49-50, Dobrovolskii's dokladnaia zapiska on eliminating the *baryshniki*, March 1913; l.54, Telyakovsky to Court Chancellery.

25. M. Paléologue, *An Ambassador's Memoirs, 1914–1917*, translated by F. A. Holt (London, 1973), p. 150.

26. *Ezhegodnik imperatorskikh teatrov, 1896–1897 gg.* (St. Petersburg, 1898), p. 395.

27. Teliakovskii, *Vospominaniia*, p. 77.

28. Hubertus F. Jahn, *Patriotic Culture in Russia During World War I* (Ithaca and London, 1995), p. 29.

29. V. Giliarovskii, *Sochineniia v chetyrekh tomakh. Tom I (Liudi teatra)* (Moscow, 1967), p. 321.

30. Teliakovskii, *Vospominaniia*, p. 78.

31. Karsavina, *Theatre Street*, p. 98.

32. Romanovsky-Krassinsky, *Dancing in Petersburg*, p. 77. Kshesinskaya is here quoting from an illustrated album which was published on the occasion of a benefit performance in February 1900 to mark the tenth anniversary of her career at the Mariinsky. The album provided a description of the performance, as well as the crowd that gathered at the stage door after the event.

33. Slonim, *Russian Theater*, p. 90.

34. Academician Likhachev remembers the elders of his family, who knew the Alexandrinsky before the revolution, referring to it in this way: D. S. Likhachev, *Vospominaniia* (St. Petersburg, 1995), p. 32. My thanks to David Saunders for this reference.

35. Pleshcheev, "*Pod seniiu kulis*"..., p. 148.

36. Petrovskaia and Somina, *Teatral'nyi Peterburg*, pp. 205–206, 304.

37. Senelick, *Russian Dramatic Theory*, p. 19.

38. M. Burgess, "Russian Public Theatre Audiences of the 18th and Early 19th Centuries," *Slavonic and East European Review*, 37 (1951-52), p. 178.

39. V. Avseenko, "Nasha teatral'naia zala," *Teatr i iskusstvo*, no. 6, 1897, p. 114.
40. Pleshcheev, *"Pod seniiu kulis"*..., pp. 91, 150.
41. "Khronika teatra i iskusstva," *Teatr i iskusstvo*, no. 1, 1898, p. 7.
42. M. Buchanan, *The Dissolution of an Empire* (London, 1932), p. 24.
43. Fokine, *Memoirs of a Ballet Master*, p. 140, note; Vilinbakhov, "Sankt-Peterburg—'voennaia stolitsa,'" p. 21.
44. Teliakovskii, *Vospominaniia*, p. 152.
45. I. Duncan, *My Life* (New York, 1927), p. 164.
46. Tolstoy, *Resurrection*, pp. 309–310.
47. *Teatr i iskusstvo*, 1905, no. 29, p. 469.
48. Shkafer, *Sorok let*, p. 197. Shkafer claimed that the Mariinsky ballet audience differed sharply from the Mariinsky opera audience, although he does not elaborate and there is no evidence to confirm that there was any substantial difference.
49. Teliakovskii, *Vospominaniia*, pp. 417–418.
50. Pleshcheev, *"Pod seniiu kulis"*..., p. 100.
51. A. Pleshcheev, *Nash balet (1673–1896). Balet v Rossii do nachala XIX stoletiia i balet v S.-Peterburge do 1896 goda* (St. Petersburg, 1896), p. 109.
52. Teliakovskii, *Vospominaniia*, pp. 415.
53. Teliakovskii, *Vospominaniia*, p. 419 and p. 431.
54. Teliakovskii, *Vospominaniia*, p. 416.
55. Teliakovskii, *Vospominaniia*, p. 429.
56. Buchanan, *Dissolution of an Empire*, p. 36. Elsewhere, Buchanan attributed the tsarina's impatience on that evening to "her cheeks becoming suffused with a deep crimson flush, and her breath coming in short, painful gasps." M. Buchanan, *Diplomacy and Foreign Courts* (London, n.d.), p. 155, though perhaps that was a symptom of her discomfort, rather than its cause.
57. Paléologue, *Ambassador's Memoirs*, pp. 112–113.
58. P. Krasnov, "Nashi kazënnye teatry," *Muzykal'nyi mir*, no. 7, February 12, 1905. New *plays* were far more common than this comment suggests.
59. V. Svetlov, "Pis'ma o balete: 2. O baletnom repertuare," *Teatr i iskusstvo*, 1911, no. 38, p. 703.
60. Fokine, *Memoirs of a Ballet Master*, p. 73.
61. S. Orgel, *The Illusion of Power: Political Theater in the English Renaissance* (London, 1975), p. 11.
62. Teliakovskii, "Deistvitel'no sovremennaia rossiia. Dnevnik. Fragmenty," *Soglasie*, January 1992, pp. 94–95.
63. RGIA, f.497, op.18, ed.khr.1208—Mariinsky and Mikhailovsky programs, which contain requests for women to remove their hats during performances.
64. C. Derjavine [K. Derzhavin], *A Century of the State Dramatic Theatre, 1832–1932* (Leningrad, 1932), p. 21.
65. *Apollon*, October 1909, p. 28.
66. *Russkaia khudozhestvennaia letopis'*, no. 12, September 1911, p. 185.
67. Paléologue, *Ambassador's Memoirs*, p. 634.
68. A. Benua [Benois], *Zhizn' khudozhnika. Vospominaniia*, tom II (New York, 1955), p. 32.
69. Gnedich, *Kniga zhizni*, p. 163.
70. Petrov, *50 i 500*, p. 77.
71. S. L. Grigoriev, *The Diaghilev Ballet, 1909–1929*, translated and edited by V. Bowden (London, 1953), p. 55.
72. A Russian, *Russian Court Memoirs, 1914–1916*, introduction by A. Wood (Cambridge, 1992), pp. 127, 163.

Chapter 4

1. On tsarist censorship, see D. Balmuth, *Censorship in Russia, 1865–1905* (Washington, D.C., 1979); I. P. Foote, "The St Petersburg Censorship Committee, 1828–1905," *Oxford Slavonic Papers (New Series)* 24, 1991, pp. 60–120; B. Rigberg, "The Efficacy of Tsarist Censorship Operations, 1894–1917," *Jahrbücher für Geschichte Osteuropas*, 14 (1966), pp. 327–346; and J. Walkin, "Government Controls Over the Press in Russia, 1905–1914," *Russian Review*, 13, no.3 (July 1954), pp. 203–209.

2. See S. Dreiden, "Teatr 1905–1907 godov i tsarskaia tsenzura," *Teatr*, 1955, no. 12, p. 104.

3. V. A. Tsinkovich, "Narodnyi teatr i dramaticheskaia tsenzura," *Teatral'noe nasledstvo* (Moscow, 1956), p. 377.

4. Tsinkovich, "Narodnyi teatr i dramaticheskaia tsenzura," pp. 375–377.

5. Swift, "Fighting the Germs of Disorder," pp. 17–41; see also Dreiden, "Teatr 1905–1907 godov i tsarskaia tsenzura," pp. 105–109.

6. Tsinkovich, "Narodnyi teatr i dramaticheskaia tsenzura," pp. 379–380, 388, 391.

7. TsGTM, f.280:1266—"Tsenzura i Imperatorskie teatry," undated notes of Telyakovsky.

8. TsGTM, f.280:1266—"Tsenzura i Imperatorskie teatry," undated notes of Telyakovsky.

9. Gozenpud, *Russkii opernyi teatr*, pp. 258–259.

10. J. Benedetti, *Stanislavski* (London and New York, 1988), p. 130. See also J. Benedetti, editor, *The Moscow Art Theatre Letters* (London, 1991), pp. 63, 72, 162, 170, 189–190.

11. N. Gottlieb and R. Chapman (eds.), *Letters to an Actress. The Story of Ivan Turgenev and Marya Gavrilovna Savina* (London, 1973), pp. 26–28.

12. Quoted by Blok in *The Russian Symbolist Theatre: An Anthology of Plays and Critical Texts*, edited by M. Green (Ann Arbor, 1986), p. 36.

13. One observer has even suggested that Stanislavsky's stage directions, as preserved in his copious notebooks, "constitute a literary text almost the equal of Chekhov's". J. Hristic, "Thinking with Chekhov: the Evidence of Stanislavsky's Notebooks," *New Theatre Quarterly*, 11, no. 42 (May 1995), p. 177.

14. Tadeusz Kowzan identified thirteen discrete "signs" in a theater performance: "word, tone, mime, gesture, movement, make-up, hair-style, costume, accessory, decor, lighting, music, and sound effects." Cited by L. Kleberg, *Theatre As Action: Soviet Russian Avant-Garde Aesthetics* (Basingstoke and London, 1993), p. 40.

15. The following calculations are based on the complete repertoire list for the Alexandrinsky, published in *Istoriia russkogo dramaticheskogo teatra, tom 7, 1898–1917* (Moscow, 1987), pp. 447–503.

16. Worrall, *The Moscow Art Theatre*, p. 7.

17. *The Cherry Orchard* was performed twice at the Alexandrinsky, and then fifty-one times at the Mikhailovsky, "a more intimate theater." "Khronika," *Teatral'-naia gazeta*, 1905, no. 34, p. 1055.

18. In 1915, one critic lamented that it had not always been easy to see *The Government Inspector* in recent years because it was chiefly a matinee performance. *Novoe vremia*, October 31 (13 November), 1915, p. 15.

19. Homo novus [Kugel'], "Podorozhnik," *Teatr i iskusstvo*, 1897, no. 5, p. 89.

20. Derjavine, *A Century of the State Dramatic Theatre*, p. 61.

21. Lvoff, "Chronique théâtrale," *Journal de St-Pétersbourg*, September 28, 1906, p. 3.

22. Derjavine, *A Century of the State Dramatic Theatre*, p. 31.
23. N. Dolgov, "Teatr i muzyka," *Birzhevyia vedomosti* (utrennyi vypusk), January 27, 1917, p. 7.
24. Petrov, *50 i 500*, pp. 83–85.
25. N. Dolgov, "Teatr i muzyka," *Birzhevyia vedomosti* (utrennyi vypusk), January 27, 1917, p. 7.
26. Isaiah Berlin, "Introductory Note" to *A Month in the Country*, by Ivan Turgenev (London, 1983), pp. 11, 13.
27. *Teatr i iskusstvo*, 1903, no. 48, pp. 913–916. "Ah, how I love this life, so calm and sweet."
28. Iur. Beliaev, "Teatr i muzyka," *Novoe vremia*, November 20, 1903, p. 4.
29. Berlin, "Introductory Note," pp. 14–15.
30. "Homo Novus," *Teatr i iskusstvo*, 1912, no. 49, pp. 971–974.
31. P. Kondradi, "Teatr i muzyka," *Novoe vremia*, December 8, 1912, p. 5.
32. Iur. Beliaev, "Teatr i muzyka," *Novoe vremia*, February 1, 1901, p. 4.
33. V. A., "Teatr i muzyka," *Rech'*, October 26, 1911, p. 5.
34. "Impr.," *Teatr i iskusstvo*, 1911, no. 44, pp. 828–829.
35. "Teatr i muzyka," *Rech'*, December 24, 1908, p. 5. See also *Novoe vremia*, December 24, 1908, p. 22.
36. J. T. Grein, Preface to *Old Heidelberg. A Play in Five Acts*, by W. Meyer-Förster, translated by C. Pochin (London, c. 1903), pp. iv, vi.
37. Iur. Beliaev, "Teatr i muzyka," *Novoe vremia*, December 5, 1904, pp. 5–6.
38. Homo novus, "Po teatram," *Teatr i iskusstvo*, 1909, no. 43, pp. 744–747.
39. Iur. Beliaev, "Teatr i muzyka," *Novoe vremia*, September 2, 1903, p. 4.
40. Sergei Auslender, "Khronika," *Apollon*, 1909, no. 2, p. 30.
41. Homo novus, *Teatr i iskusstvo*, 1913, no. 4, pp. 93–95.
42. Iu. B., "Teatr i muzyka," *Novoe vremia*, January 25, 1913, p. 6.
43. Derzhavin, *Epokhi Aleksandrinskoi stseny*, p. 167.
44. V. A., "Teatr i muzyka," *Rech'*, September 29, 1911, p. 5.
45. Iur. Beliaev, "Teatr i muzyka," *Novoe vremia*, September 30, 1911, p. 5.
46. "Homo novus," *Teatr i iskusstvo*, 1902, no. 36, pp. 667–668.
47. "Khronika," *Teatr i iskusstvo*, 1907, no. 52, pp. 877–878.
48. L. Vas-ii, "Teatr i muzyka," *Rech'*, December 23, 1907, p. 4.
49. "Khronika," *Teatr i iskusstvo*, 1904, no. 38, pp. 685–686.
50. Iu. Beliaev, "Teatr i muzyka," *Novoe vremia*, November , 1910, p. 5; L. Vas-ii, "Teatr i muzyka," *Rech'*, November 11, 1910, p. 7.
51. Rudnitsky, *Meyerhold The Director*, p. 253.
52. S. D. Balakhaty, *The Seagull Produced by Stanislavsky*, translated by D. Magarshack (London, 1952), p. 20.
53. "Homo Novus," *Teatr i iskusstvo*, 1912, no. 49, pp. 971–974.
54. Iu. M. Iur'ev, *Zapiski*, tom II (Leningrad-Moscow, 1963), p. 8.

Chapter 5

1. "Khronika teatra i iskusstva," *Teatr i iskusstvo*, 1900, no. 4.
2. Pl. Krasnov, "Dve opery," *Teatral'naia gazeta*, 1905, no. 35, p. 1072. My italics.
3. A. Haskell, *Ballet* (1955), p. 62.
4. TsGTM, f.1:5981, l.317—O. Parenka to T. Petrovna, August 31, 1911.
5. "Teatr i muzyka," *Novoe vremia*, December 5, 1904, p. 6.

6. "Mariinskii teatr," *Birzhevyia vedomosti*, September 17 (30), 1917, p. 5.

7. J. Baker, "Glinka's *A Life For the Tsar* and 'Official Nationality,'" *Renaissance and Modern Studies*, 24 (1980), p. 106.

8. R. Bartlett, *Wagner and Russia* (Cambridge, 1995), pp. 59–65, 90.

9. See G. G. Weickhardt, "Music and Society in Russia, 1860s–1890s," *Canadian-American Slavic Studies*, 30, no. 1 (Spring 1996), pp. 45–68.

10. *The Golden Cockerel* was produced on the Moscow, not St. Petersburg Imperial opera stage.

11. *Novoe vremia*, September 7 (20), 1914, p. 6.

12. Benois, *Reminiscences of the Russian Ballet*, p. 47.

13. V. Svetlov, "Mysly o sovremennom balete. Ocherk," *Ezhegodnik imperatorskikh teatrov*, 1909, part 6–7, p. 35.

14. K. A. Skal'kovskii, *Balet. Ego istoriia i mesto v riadu iziashchnykh iskusstv* (St. Petersburg, 1882); Pleshcheev, *Nash balet*; V. Ia. Svetlov, *Terpsikhora* (St. Petersburg, 1906). On Skal'kovskii, Pleshcheev, and a third ballet historian of the period, Sergei Khudekov, see R. J. Wiley, "Three Historians of the Imperial Russian Ballet," *Dance Research Journal*, 13/1 (Fall 1980), pp. 3–16.

15. Fokine, *Memoirs of a Ballet Master*, pp. 52–53.

16. C. W. Beaumont, *Michel Fokine and His Ballets* (London, 1935), p. 19.

17. *Chopiniana* is more widely known in its second, revised version, *Les Sylphides*, not to be confused with Italian choreographer Filippo Taglioni's *La Sylphide* (premiered in Paris, 1832).

18. On Fokin, his collaboration with *Mir iskusstva* and ballet reform in general, see Iu. A. Bakhrushin, *Istoriia russkogo baleta* (Moscow, 1973), pp. 224–238. See also Beaumont, *Michel Fokine and his Ballets*.

19. V. Svetlov, "Mysly o sovremennom balete. Ocherk," *Ezhegodnik imperatorskikh teatrov*, 1909, part 6–7, p. 47.

20. V. Svetlov, *Thamar Karsavina*, translated by H. de Vere & N. Evrenov, edited by C. W. Beaumont (London, 1922), p. 83. Svetlov originally penned this hagiography of the famous dancer in 1917.

21. Nijinsky [Romola Nijinska], *Nijinsky*, pp. 47–48.

22. Fokine, *Memoirs of a Ballet Master*, p. 131.

23. V. Svetlov, "Pis'ma o balete: 2. O baletnom repertuare," *Teatr i iskusstvo*, 1911, no. 38, p. 703.

24. This point is emphasized in Fokine, *Memoirs of a Ballet Master*, p. 48.

25. Fokine, *Memoirs of a Ballet Master*, p. 53.

26. Shkafer, *Sorok let*, p. 197.

27. N. Fedorov, "Pis'ma o balete," *Teatr i iskusstvo*, 1897, no. 8, p. 145.

28. Quoted in O. Kerensky, *Anna Pavlova* (London, 1973), p. 79.

29. *Novoe vremia*, September 19 (October 2) 1914, p. 5.

Chapter 6

1. Al'medingen, *Golovin i Shaliapin*, pp. 40–43.

2. On the Russian Theater Society, see *Teatral'naia entsiklopediia*, volume 1, columns 1038–1040. The proceedings of the 1897 Congress of Stage Workers are published as *Trudy pervogo vserossiiskogo s'ezda stsenicheskikh deiatelei* (St. Petersburg, 1898).

3. For the history of the 1905 Revolution, see A. Ascher, *The Revolution of 1905: Russia in Disarray* (Stanford, 1988).

4. TsGTM, f.280:52—Von Bohl to Telyakovsky, January 13, 1905.

5. RGIA, f.497, op.6, ed.khr.4794, l.7—Directorate to *Kabinet* of His Imperial Highness, June 21, 1906. On the Okhrana in general, see F. S. Zuckerman, *The Tsarist Secret Police in Russian Society, 1880–1917* (London, 1996).

6. G. Kennan, "The Russian Police," *The Century Magazine*, volume XXXVII (New Series, volume XV), 1888-89, pp. 891–892.

7. A. T. Vassilyev [Vasilev], *The Ochrana: The Russian Secret Police* (London, 1930), p. 37.

8. RGIA, f.497, op.6, ed.khr.4762, l.4—list of theater seats reserved for Okhrana. Signed by Mosolov, April 22, 1905.

9. RGIA, f.497, op.6, ed.khr.4794, l.1—St. Petersburg gradonachal'nik (Okhrana section) to St. Petersburg Office, May 1, 1906.

10. D.C.B. Lieven, "The Security Police, Civil Rights, and the Fate of the Russian Empire," in *Civil Rights in Imperial Russia*, edited by O. Crisp & L. Edmondson (Oxford, 1989), pp. 238–239.

11. TsGTM, f.280:935—Lopukhin to Telyakovsky, February 3, 1905. According to Volkov, the decision to postpone *Antigone* was taken by Fredericks. See Volkov, "Teatr v epokhu krusheniia monarkhii," p. 320.

12. RGIA, f.497, op.6, ed.khr.4762—l.7, St. Petersburg gradonachal'nik (Dediulin) to Telyakovsky, September 2, 1905; l.8, Telyakovsky to the Minister of the Imperial Court, September 24, 1905; l.9, Ministry of the Imperial Court to Telyakovsky, October 6, 1905.

13. RGIA, f.497, op.6, ed.khr.4762—l.13, St. Petersburg gradonachal'nik to Telyakovsky, September 2, 1906; l.15, Ministry of the Imperial Court approval, September 11, 1906.

14. RGIA, f.497, op.6, ed.khr.4762, l.32—D. P. Val'tsov to Telyakovsky, December 8, 1907.

15. RGIA, f.497, op.6, ed.khr.4762, l.159-160—Vendorf to Mosolov, August 30, 1911.

16. Gnedich, *Kniga zhizni*, pp. 306–307; *Teatr i iskusstvo*, 1905, no. 3, p. 42.

17. Yastrebtsev, *Reminiscences*, pp. 352–353.

18. Yastrebtsev, *Reminiscences*, pp. 355–358.

19. TsGTM, f.280:1266—"Tsenzura i Imperatorskie teatry," undated notes by Telyakovsky.

20. Teliakovskii, *Imperatorskie teatry*, p. 73. According to the repertoire lists in *Ezhegodnik imperatorskikh teatrov, 1905-1906 gg.* (St. Petersburg, n.d.), a matinee performance of *A Life for the Tsar* was given at the Mariinsky on October 2, 1905, and at the Bolshoi on October 5 and 8, and then not until February, as Telyakovsky states.

21. Khodotov, *Blizkoe-dalekoe*, p. 235.

22. "Peterburgskaia khronika," *Teatral'naia gazeta*, January 22, 1905, no. 4, p. 56.

23. *Teatr i iskusstvo*, 1905, no. 4, p. 49.

24. Teliakovskii, *Imperatorskie teatry*, p. 50; Gnedich, *Kniga zhizni*, p. 312.

25. "Khronika," *Teatral'naia gazeta*, October 22, 1905, no. 42–43, p. 1252.

26. Golovin, *Vstrechi i vpechatleniia*, p. 79.

27. "Khronika," *Teatral'naia gazeta*, October 22, 1905, no. 42–43, p. 1251.

28. Teliakovskii, *Imperatorskie teatry*, p. 49.

29. Teliakovskii, *Imperatorskie teatry*, pp. 47–49.

30. Teliakovskii, *Imperatorskie teatry*, pp. 98–100. Telyakovsky reproduces a letter from Von Bohl that describes what happened in the Bolshoi on November 26, 1905.

31. Teliakovskii, *Imperatorskie teatry*, p. 26.

32. Teliakovskii, *Imperatorskie teatry*, p. 24.

33. The Malyi was closed October 14–27. *Istoriia russkogo dramaticheskogo teatra*, p. 314.

34. Teliakovskii, *Imperatorskie teatry*, p. 33.
35. TsGTM, f.280:1230—Telyakovsky's draft report to the Minister of the Imperial Court on the events in the ballet troupe, October 1905.
36. Teliakovskii, *Imperatorskie teatry*, p. 42.
37. Teliakovskii, *Imperatorskie teatry*, p. 59.
38. Teliakovskii, *Imperatorskie teatry*, p. 51.
39. Teliakovskii, *Imperatorskie teatry*, p. 52.
40. Teliakovskii, *Imperatorskie teatry*, pp. 38–39.
41. Karsavina, *Theatre Street*, pp. 125–126; Lopukhov, *Shest'desiat let v balete*, pp. 123–124.
42. Karsavina, *Theatre Street*, p. 122.
43. Karsavina, *Theatre Street*, p. 128.
44. "Khronika," *Teatral'naia gazeta*, October 29, 1905, no. 44–45, p. 1270.
45. Quoted by Gnedich, *Kniga zhizni*, p. 313.
46. Arbenin (see below) incorrectly dates the genesis of the Council to early 1904. In fact, it was in place in the autumn of 1903. "Teatr i muzyka," *Novoe vremia*, October 3, 1903, p. 4.
47. N. F. Arbenin, "Ob avtonomii imperatorskikh teatrov (okonchanie)," *Teatr i iskusstvo*, 1905, no. 2, p. 26.
48. N. F. Arbenin, "Ob avtonomii imperatorskikh teatrov (okonchanie)," *Teatr i iskusstvo*, 1905, no. 2, p. 26.
49. E. G. Mal'tseva, "Akterskoe samoupravlenie v Rossii," in *Teatr mezhdu proshlym i budushchim. Sbornik nauchnykh trudov*, edited by Iu. M. Orlov (Moscow, 1989), p. 171.
50. Teliakovskii, *Imperatorskie teatry*, pp. 103–108.
51. Viv'en, "V Aleksandrinskom teatre," p. 185.
52. Khodotov, *Blizkoe-dalekoe*, p. 250.
53. *Teatr i iskusstvo*, 1908, no. 47, p. 821.
54. RGIA f.497, op.6, ed.khr.4810—*Zhurnal rasporiazhenii*, October 9–11, 1906.
55. Iu. Aikhenval'd, *Aleksandr Ivanovich Sumbatov-Iuzhin* (Moscow, 1987), pp. 254–255.
56. N. A. Tiraspol'skaia, *Iz proshlogo russkoi stseny* (Moscow, 1950), pp. 133–134; Khodotov, *Blizkoe-dalekoe*, pp. 231–232.
57. S. A., "Peterburgskie teatry," *Apollon*, 1909, no. 3, p. 36.
58. S. Dreiden, *Muzyka-revoliutsii* [*sic*] (Moscow, 1981), pp. 362–367.
59. RGIA, f.497, op.6, ed.khr.4821—correspondence between Okhrana and St. Petersburg Office, January 1907–March 1908.
60. RGIA, f.497, op.6, ed.khr.4821, l.18—Okhrana to St. Petersburg Office, January 30, 1907.
61. A. A. Mgebrov, *Zhizn' v teatre* (Leningrad, 1929), p. 150.

Chapter 7

1. On Russian patriotism during the war, see Jahn, *Patriotic Culture*. On the role of the War Industries Committee, see L. H. Siegelbaum, *The Politics of Industrial Mobilization in Russia, 1914–17* (London and Basingstoke, 1983). On the Russian war effort in general, see N. Stone, *The Eastern Front, 1914–17* (London, 1978).
2. *Novoe vremia*, 3 (16) September, 1914, p. 5.
3. Vl. S., "Petrogradskie teatry," *Apollon*, 1915, nos. 4–5, p. 109.
4. Jahn, *Patriotic Culture*, p. 135.

5. Jahn, *Patriotic Culture*, pp. 2, 9.

6. TsGTM, f.280:12246—Telyakovsky's diary, August 30, 1914.

7. *Novoe vremia*, September 1 (14), 1914, p. 5, and September 17 (30), 1914, p. 6. The Alexandrinsky season opened two weeks later than usual because some maintenance work was being undertaken.

8. *Novoe vremia*, October 1 (14), 1914, p. 5.

9. *Novoe vremia*, September 10 (23), 1914, p. 5.

10. Bakhrushin, *Istoriia russkogo baleta*, p. 249.

11. *Novoe vremia*, September 22 (October 5), 1914, p. 4.

12. *Novoe vremia*, October 13 (26), 1914, p. 5.

13. *Novoe vremia*, November 8 (21), 1914, p. 14.

14. *Novoe vremia*, March 26 (April 8), 1916, p. 14. Concerts in aid of this Committee had been performed by Imperial Theater artists before 1914.

15. *Novoe vremia*, August 25 (September 7), 1914, p. 5 and August 26 (September 8), 1914, p. 6.

16. Internal German "foes," according to the Panslavs, included N. K. Giers, Assistant Foreign Minister under A. M. Gorchakov and Foreign Minister from 1882 to 1895, who was descended from Swedish and German families, and whose pro-German diplomatic orientation incurred the wrath of the Panslavs.

17. *Novoe vremia*, August 29 (September 11), 1914, p. 6. On the Skobelev cult in Russia, see Hans Rogger, "The Skobelev Phenomenon: the Hero and His Worship," *Oxford Slavonic Papers (New Series)*, 9 (1976), pp. 46–78.

18. *Novoe vremia*, September 4 (17), 1914, p. 5 and November 17 (30), 1914, p. 5.

19. *Novoe vremia*, October 11 (24), 1914, p. 15.

20. *Novoe vremia*, November 1 (14), 1914, p. 15.

21. Buchanan, *Diplomacy and Foreign Courts*, p. 199.

22. V. Bezpalov, *Teatry v dni revoliutsii, 1917* (Leningrad, 1927), pp. 10–12; TsGTM, f.280:13734—Telyakovsky's diary, February 27, 1917.

23. "U rampy," *Birzhevyia vedomosti* (vechernii vypusk), March 6, 1917, p. 5.

24. RGIA, f.497, op.6, ed.khr.5117, l.1—Vremennyi Komitet Gosudarstvennoi dumy, *prikaz* no. 140, March 2, 1917. Signed by M. Rodzianko.

25. RGIA, f.497, op.6, ed.khr.5117, l.3—Akt, March 3, 1917. Signed by N. N. Lvov.

26. Bezpalov, *Teatry*, p. 27.

27. TsGTM, f.280:13744-5—Telyakovsky's diary, March 3, 1917.

28. Bezpalov, *Teatry*, p. 37. Bezpalov's own words.

29. "U rampy," *Birzhevyia vedomosti* (vechernii vypusk), March 6, 1917, p. 5; TsGTM, f.280:13739—Telyakovsky's diary, March 1, 1917.

30. RGIA, f.497, op.6, ed.khr.5124, l.6—Telyakovsky to Prince S. V. Gagarin, May 5, 1917; Bezpalov, *Teatry*, pp. 30–31, footnote.

31. TsGTM, f.280:13745—Telyakovsky's diary, March 3, 1917; ibid., 13755—Telyakovsky's diary, March 8, 1917; ibid., 13814—Telyakovsky's diary, March 30, 1917; ibid., 13823—Telyakovsky's diary, April 4, 1917 (in this case, it was none other than Nicholas Lvov himself, some weeks after he had left the state theater administration [see below], who asked Telyakovsky if it would be possible to get his play staged).

32. RGIA, f.497, op.6, ed.khr.5117, l.4—*prikaz* of Lvov, March 6, 1917. The *prikaz* was not made public until the following day. TsGTM, f.280:13752—Telyakovsky's diary, March 7, 1917.

33. RGIA, f.497, op.6, ed.khr.5117, l.3, 5—*prikazy* of Lvov, March 7 & 8, 1917.

34. Bezpalov, *Teatry*, p. 25.

35. Bezpalov, *Teatry*, p. 27.
36. RGIA, f.497, op.6, ed.khr.5117, l.9—*prikaz* /*ukaz* of Golovin, March 10, 1917.
37. RGIA, f.497, op.6, ed.khr.5117, l.20—*prikaz* of Golovin, April 27, 1917.
38. RGIA, f.497, op.6, ed.khr.5117, l.21—Batiushkov to Commissar of Former Ministry of the Imperial Court, May 18, 1917.
39. Bezpalov, *Teatry*, p. 31.
40. Bezpalov, *Teatry*, p. 33.
41. TsGTM, f.280:13744-5—Telyakovsky's diary, March 3, 1917; "U rampy," *Birzhevyia vedomosti* (vechernii vypusk), March 7, 1917, p. 4.
42. Bezpalov, *Teatry*, p. 34.
43. TsGTM, f.280:13747—Telyakovsky's diary, March 4, 1917.
44. TsGTM, f.280:13748—Telyakovsky's diary, March 5, 1917.
45. GPB, f.1056, ed.khr.521—"Pis'mo artistov Mariinskogo teatra Nikolaiu Nikolaevichu L'vovu ob avtonomii teatra," March 5, 1917; "U rampy," *Birzhevyia vedomosti* (vechernii vypusk), March 7, 1917, p. 4. According to Mal'tseva, who cites the last sentence of this declaration in her article ("Akterskoe samoupravlenie," p. 171—see note 49 in Chapter 6), it was published in the periodical *Teatral'naia gazeta* on March 12, 1917. Mal'tseva's article gives the impression that these words are the journal's, whereas the archive source clearly shows that the declaration came from the Mariinsky Theater.
46. H. Lecomte, *Napoléon et le monde dramatique* (Paris, 1912), referred to by E. Kuznetsov in Bezpalov, *Teatry*, note on p. 35.
47. Golovin's *prikaz* on State Theater autonomy of May 13, 1917 is reproduced in *Vestnik vremennago pravitel'stva*, May 16 (29), 1917, p. 2.
48. "Iskusstvo v dni Revoliutsii," *Birzhevyia vedomosti* (utrennyi vypusk), April 7, 1917, p. 6.
49. "Iskusstvo v dni revoliutsii," *Birzhevye vedomosti* (utrennyi vypusk), September 17, 1917, p. 5.
50. RGIA, f.497, op.6, ed.khr.5117, l.25—glavnoupolnomochennyi to Commissar of Former Ministry of the Imperial Court, October 20, 1917.
51. Bezpalov, *Teatry*, pp. 78–79, 81.
52. "Iskusstvo v dni revoliutsii," *Birzhevye vedomosti*, October 22, 1917, p. 5.
53. Bezpalov, *Teatry*, p. 38.
54. Iur'ev, *Zapiski*, tom II, p. 239.
55. Bezpalov, *Teatry*, p. 39.
56. Petrov, *50 i 500*, p. 152.
57. TsGTM, f.280:13752—Telyakovsky's diary, March 7, 1917; "U rampy," *Birzhevyia vedomosti* (vechernii vypusk), March 28, 1917, p. 4.
58. TsGTM, F.280:13768-9—Telyakovsky's diary, March 12, 1917; Bezpalov, *Teatry*, pp. 39–40.
59. Bezpalov, *Teatry*, pp. 50–54.
60. Bezpalov, *Teatry*, pp. 42–44.
61. T. Kuran, "Why Revolutions Are Better Understood Than Predicted: The Essential Role of Preference Falsification," in *Debating Revolutions*, edited by N. R. Keddie (New York and London, 1995), pp. 27–35.
62. V. E. Rafalovich, editor, *Istoriia sovetskogo teatra. Tom pervyi. Petrogradskie teatry na poroge oktiabria i v epokhu voennogo kommunizma, 1917–1921* (Leningrad, 1933), p. 38; Time, *Dorogi iskusstva*, p. 186.

Chapter 8

1. See, for example, L. Mally, *Culture of the Future: The Proletkult Movement in Revolutionary Russia* (Oxford, 1990), and B. Thomson, *Lot's Wife and the Venus of Milo: Conflicting Attitudes to the Cultural Heritage in Modern Russia* (Cambridge, 1978).
2. P. Kerzhentsev, *Tvorcheskii teatr: puti sotsialisticheskogo teatra*, second edition (1918). A third edition was published in 1920.
3. See Rudnitsky, *Meyerhold The Director*, chapter six, "Theatrical October."
4. See Mally, *Culture of the Future*, and S. Fitzpatrick, *The Commissariat of Enlightenment: Soviet Organization of Education and the Arts under Lunacharsky, October 1917–1921* (Cambridge, 1970), chapter five.
5. Cited in Iu. N. Zhukov, *Stanovlenie i deiatel'nost' sovetskikh organov okhrany pamiatnikov istorii i kul'tury, 1917–1920gg.* (Moscow, 1989), p. 56.
6. V. I. Lenin, *V. I. Lenin o kul'ture* (Moscow, 1985), p. 178.
7. Lenin, *V. I. Lenin o kul'ture*, p. 179.
8. Lenin, *V. I. Lenin o kul'ture*, pp. 179–180.
9. "Iz programmy rossiiskoi kommunisticheskoi partii (bolshevikov)," March 18–23, 1919, in *Russkii sovetskii teatr, 1917–1921: dokumenty i materialy*, edited by A. Z. Iufit (Leningrad, 1968), p. 22. Hereafter cited as *Sovetskii teatr*.
10. The resolution is in V. I. Lenin, *Collected Works*, volume 31 (Moscow, 1966), pp. 316–317. This was followed by a Central Committee "Letter on the Proletkults," published in *Pravda* on December 1, 1920, which reiterated and reinforced Lenin's resolution.
11. C. Claudin-Urondo, *Lenin and the Cultural Revolution*, translated by B. Pearce (Hassocks, Sussex, 1977), p. 27.
12. On the formation and activity of Narkompros see M. B. Keirim-Markus, *Gosudarstvennoe rukovodstvo kul'turoi: stroitel'stvo Narkomprosa (noiabr' 1917-seredina 1918 gg.)* (Moscow, 1980) and Fitzpatrick, *Commissariat of Enlightenment*.
13. A. V. Lunacharskii, *Sobranie sochinenii, t. III: dorevoliutsionnyi teatr: sovetskii teatr: stat'i, doklady, rechi, retsenzii (1904–1933)* (Moscow, 1964), pp. 41, 46, 93.
14. Zhukov, *Stanovlenie i deiatel'nost'*, pp. 60–63.
15. N. Zikevskaia, "Organizatsiia teatral'nogo dela v SSSR: Istoricheskii ocherk," *Teatr*, 1969, no. 7, p. 35.
16. RGIA, f.497, op.6, ed.khr.5129, l.1—Military-Revolutionary Committee to Chief Representative of State Theaters, October 27, 1917; ibid., l.2—Murav'ev to State Theaters, October 27, 1917.
17. RGIA, f.497, op.6, ed.khr.5129, l.3—drama troupe statement, October 29, 1917.
18. RGIA, f.497, op.6, ed.khr.5129, l.4—Murav'ev to drama troupe, October 29 (30?), 1917.
19. Bezpalov, *Teatry*, pp. 89–90.
20. Sergei Bertensson [Bertenson], "Fokine: A Memory," *American Slavonic and East European Review*, 12 (1953), no. 3, p. 378.
21. Bertensson, "Fokine," p. 379.
22. RGIA, f.497, op.6, ed.khr.5129, l.8—protocol of the Soiuz Rabochikh i Sluzhashchikh Petrogradskikh Gosudarstvennykh teatrov, early November 1917.
23. RGIA, f.497, op.6, ed.khr.5129, l.5—protocol of the Obshchee Sobranie artistov Gosudarstvennykh teatrov, November 5, 1917.
24. "Obrashchenie narodnogo komissara po prosveshcheniiu A. V. Lunacharskogo k khudozhestvenno-repertuarnym komitetam petrogradskikh gosudarstvennykh teatrov ob uregulirovanii vzaimootnoshenii etikh teatrov s Narkomprosom," December 2, 1917, *Sovetskii teatr*, pp. 36–37.

25. GPB, f.340, ed.khr.16. This is from a *proekt* which is undated, but which is contained within a batch of materials relating to a general meeting of the Alexandrinsky troupe on December 4, 1917. Given the context of Lunacharsky's appeal to the artists, it is not unreasonable to date the *proekt* to that time.

26. V. D. Zel'dovich, "Pervye meropriiatiia Narkomprosa po upravleniiu teatrami," *Istoricheskii arkhiv* (1959), no. 1, p. 53.

27. "Rasporiazhenie soveta narodnykh komissarov ob uvol'nenii glavnoupol-nomochennogo vremennogo pravitel'stva po gosudarstvennym teatram F. D. Batiushkova i zaveduiushchego zagotovochnoi chast'iu S.L. Bertensona," December 12, 1917, *Sovetskii teatr*, p. 24.

28. Zel'dovich, "Pervye meropriiatiia," pp. 54–55.

29. "Obrashchenie narodnogo komissara po prosveshcheniiu A.V. Lunacharskogo k artistam i rabotnikam gosudarstvennykh teatrov Petrograda o neobkhodimosti ustanovleniia kontakta rabotnikov gosudarstvennykh teatrov s novoi vlast'iu," December 12, 1917, *Sovetskii teatr*, p. 37.

30. Zel'dovich, "Pervye meropriiatiia," pp. 56–57.

31. The breakaway troupe was based at the Akvarium from December 28, 1917 to January 21, 1918.

32. Zel'dovich, "Pervye meropriiatiia," p. 60.

33. "Iz dnevnika S. I. Smirnovoi-Sazonovoi," *Sovetskii teatr*, p. 228.

34. "Izveshchenie narodnogo komissara po prosveshcheniiu A.V. Lunacharskogo ko vsem artistam i rabotnikam gosudarstvennykh teatrov o perekhode vsei vlasti po upravleniiu gosudarstvennymi teatrami v vedenie organov samoupravleniia," not earlier than January 2, 1918 (published in *Izvestiia*, January 6, 1918), *Sovetskii teatr*, p. 37.

35. G. I. Il'ina, *Kul'turnoe stroitel'stvo v Petrograde: Oktiabria 1917–1920 gg.* (Leningrad, 1982), p. 77.

36. Zolotnitskii, *Akademicheskie teatry*, p. 37.

37. "Iz dnevnika S.I. Smirnovoi-Sazonovoi," *Sovetskii teatr*, p. 229.

38. *Sovetskii teatr*, p. 243, note 37.

39. *Biriuch petrogradskikh gosudarstvennykh teatrov; sbornik statei*, edited by A. S. Poliakov (Petrograd, June-August, 1919), p. 370; see also pp. 172–176. (This collection of articles and general information on the State Theaters during the Civil War is dated 1919, but judging from the contents it must have appeared no earlier than mid–1920.)

40. S. Arbenina (Baroness Meyendorff), *Through Terror to Freedom: The Dramatic Story of an English-Woman's Life and Adventures in Russia Before, During & After the Revolution* (London, n.d.), p. 128.

41. Zolotnitskii, *Akademicheskie teatry*, p. 11.

42. "Iz izveshcheniia narodnogo komissara po prosveshcheniiu A. V. Lunacharskogo i zaveduiushchego podotdelom gosudarstvennykh teatrov Narkomprosa I. V. Ekskuzovicha o pravakh zaveduiushchego podotdelom gosudarstvennykh teatrov Narkomprosa," not earlier than February 18, 1918, *Sovetskii teatr*, p. 38.

43. Fitzpatrick, *Commissariat of Enlightenment*, pp. 139–140.

44. "Iz protokola zasedanii osobogo soveshchaniia po teatral'nomu voprosu," December 10, 12, 1918, *Sovetskii teatr*, p. 48.

45. "Iz protokola zasedanii osobogo soveshchaniia po teatral'nomu voprosu," December 10, 12, 1918, *Sovetskii teatr*, p. 51.

46. "Postanovlenie Narkomprosa o reorganizatsii upravleniia gosudarstvennymi teatrami i uchrezhdenii v teatrakh direktorii," not later than February 1919, *Sovetskii teatr*, pp. 58 and 80, note 191.

47. For an account of the nationalization issue, see A. Iufit, *Revoliutsiia i teatr* (Leningrad, 1977), chapter three. See also Fitzpatrick, *Commissariat of Enlightenment*, pp. 144–145.

48. "Vypiska iz otnosheniia narodnogo komissara po prosveshcheniiu A. V. Lunacharskogo k zaveduiushchemu gosudarstvennymi teatrami I. V. Ekskuzovichu o pereimenovanii gosudarstvennykh teatrov i Moskovskogo khudozhestvennogo teatra i o prisvoenii im zvaniia 'akademicheskikh,'" December 7, 1919, *Sovetskii teatr*, p. 65.

49. L. Vas-ii, "Teatr i muzyka," *Rech'*, November 11, 1910, p. 7.

50. Vl. S., "Petrogradskie teatry," *Apollon*, 1914, no. 8, p. 68.

51. Derjavine, *A Century of the State Dramatic Theatre*, p. 92.

52. "Iz protokola No. 102 zasedaniia direktsii gosudarstvennogo akademicheskogo teatra opery i baleta po voprosu o perekhode teatra k edinolichnoi sisteme upravleniia," April 14, 1920, *Sovetskii teatr*, p. 202.

53. "Polozhenie ob avtonomnykh gosudarstvennykh akademicheskikh teatrakh Petrograda," June 11, 1920, *Sovetskii teatr*, p. 66.

54. See, for instance, S. Fedyukin, *The Great October Revolution and the Intelligentsia* (Moscow, 1975), p. 189.

55. This interpretation underpins, for example, R. Pipes, *Russia Under the Bolshevik Regime, 1919–1924* (London, 1994), chapter six.

56. Thorpe, "Management of Culture," p. 202.

57. Derjavine, *A Century of the State Dramatic Theatre*, p. 79.

58. Statistical information on the Petrograd State Theater repertoire is drawn from the relevant repertoire lists in *Sovetskii teatr*.

59. Iur'ev, *Zapiski*, tom II, p. 240.

60. Buchanan, *Dissolution of an Empire*, pp. 201–202.

61. Wells, *Russia in the Shadows*, p. 36.

62. "Iz protokola zasedanii osobogo soveshchaniia po teatral'nomy voprosu," January 10, 12, 1918, *Sovestkii teatr*, p. 49.

63. Entelis, *Leningradskii gosudarstvennyi ordena Lenina akademicheskii teatr*, p. 14.

64. Wells, *Russia in the Shadows*, p. 35.

Conclusions

1. P. P. Gnedich, "O repertuare Aleksandrinskogo teatra v techenie 75 let (1832–1907 g.)," *Ezhegodnik imperatorskikh teatrov*, season 1905–1906 (St. Petersburg, c.1907), p. 47.

Index

estrada 13
etiquette in theaters *see* social function
of auditoria
Eugene Onegin 31, 56, 106, 107–108, 111,
130, 169
Eunice 114
Evreinov, Nicholas 14, 25

Faust 107, 108
February Revolution 2, 3, 67, 86, 140–152
passim 160, 171, 174
Fedorov, N. 116
La Fille Mal Gardée 62, 115
Filosofov, Dmitry 124
The Firebird 45
First World War 3, 25, 79, 111, 136–140,
174
Fokin, Mikhail 46, 50, 59, 77, 80, 116;
and ballet reform 113–114
Fonvizin, Denis 93
The Forest 93, 130
Francis Joseph I (Austrian Emperor) 32,
70
Fredericks, V. B. 20, 24, 28, 33, 49, 54,
88, 127, 129, 130, 173
Freie Volksbühne 12
Der Freischütz 62
Friche, Vladimir 14–15
Friedländer, Max 12
Fruen fra havet (The Lady from the Sea) 169
The Fruits of Enlightenment 93, 100
Futurists 7, 16
Fyodor, tsar 9

Gai, Maria 110
The Gambler 45
Gatchina Theater 21
Ge, G. G. 162, 163
Geltser, Ekaterina 139
Gengangere (Ghosts) 73
Gerdt, E. P. 117
Gerdt, P. A. 63
Giliarovskii, Vladimir 71
Gippius, Zinaida 124
Giselle 59, 62, 115
Glazunov, Alexander 150
Glinka, Mikhail 107, 108, 110, 111
Glory to Free Russia 149
Gluck, C. W. von 59
Gnedich, P. P. 23, 47, 48, 49, 56, 58, 60,
61, 63, 82, 124, 131, 133, 163, 172; bri-
bery scandal and resignation 53–55;
plays in Alexandrinsky repertoire 93,
96, 100–101, 168, 169–170

God Save the King 79
God Save the Tsar 79
Gogol, N. 73, 90, 92, 169
The Golden Cockerel 45, 89
Golitsyn, D. P. 32
Golovin, Alexander 46, 47, 50, 55, 56,
68, 119, 127, 149
Golovin, F. A. 144, 145, 146, 147, 158,
159
Goncharov, Ivan 78
Gorchakov, N. A. 45
Gorin-Gorianinov, B. A. 60
Gorky, Maxim 14, 15, 85, 87–88, 101,
102, 103, 126, 150, 169, 175
Götterdämmerung 111
Gounod, C. F. 107
The Government Inspector 90, 92, 93, 149,
169, 197 (n. 18)
Gozenpud, A. 56
The Great Secret 93, 168
Grein, J. T. 98
Griboedov, Alexander 93
Grigorev, Sergei 82
Grigorovich, D. V. 82, 121
Grimaldi, Henrietta 62
Guinon, Albert 93, 98, 168

Hamilton, Lady 8
Haskell, Arnold 106
The Heart Is Not a Stone 58
Hermitage Theater 21
Hofburgtheater 40
Horse Guards regiment 19, 26, 28, 29, 30
Les Huguenots 107, 108, 169
The Hump-Backed Horse 32, 115, 116, 137,
169
Husar Regiment 76

Iakobson, G. I. 166
Iatmanov, G. S. 156
Ibsen, Henrik 14, 73, 169
Imperial Theaters *see* St. Petersburg
Imperial Theaters; Moscow Imperial
Theaters; "theater crisis"; theater
monopolies
Imperial Yacht Club 76
"Impr." (critic) 97
*In Memory of the Fallen Fighters for Free-
dom* 149
In These Days 140
intelligentsia 3, 10, 15–16, 65, 73, 85, 109,
123
Iurev, Iu. M. 148, 159, 170
Ivanov, Lev 48